SILENT
DEPRESSION

ALSO BY WALLACE C. PETERSON

Our Overloaded Economy

Market Power and the Economy

Transfer Spending, Taxes, and the American Welfare State

SILENT
DEPRESSION

The Fate of the
American
Dream

Wallace C. Peterson

W • W • Norton & Company • New York • London

The text of this book is composed in Goudy Old Style with the display
set in Aachen Bold and Gill Sans.
Composition and manufacturing by the Maple-Vail Book Manufacturing
Group.
Book design by Jack Meserole.

Library of Congress Cataloging-in-Publication Data
Peterson, Wallace C.
    Silent depression : the fate of the American dream / Wallace C.
    Peterson.
        p. cm.
    Includes bibliographical references and index.
        1. United States—Economic conditions—1981–   2. United
States—
    Economic policy—1981–   I. Title.
    HC106.8.P46   1994
    338.973—dc20   93-1295

ISBN 0-393-03586-7

W. W. Norton & Company, Inc., 500 Fifth Avenue, New York, N.Y. 10110
W. W. Norton & Company Ltd., 10 Coptic Street, London WC1A1PU

    2 3 4 5 6 7 8 9 0

TO MY FAMILY

Andrew, Bonnie, Cary, Laura, Lisa, Rebecca, and Shelley

Contents

Preface

If you feel you are making and spending more money than you did ten or twenty years ago but are losing ground, if it appears that your children will do less well than you have done, if your job is less secure than it used to be, you are not alone. Millions of other Americans are equally perplexed. Many millions are angry to find that they have to run faster to stay in the same place.

Well, the truth is that since the early 1970s—since 1973, to be specific—the American economy has not performed well. For reasons that I seek to explain in this book, many of the key numbers by which we measure the health of the economy took a turn for the worse at that time. It is as if a person who had enjoyed years of robust, good health suddenly lost that strength and began to experience a puzzling, debilitating weakness for which there was no apparent explanation. So it has been with the American economy.

For a quarter-century after the end of World War II, Americans enjoyed an economy of sustained growth, low inflation, and good jobs. It was a time of strong economic health. Then came the *silent depression*, two decades of sluggish economic health, a time when, by most of the accepted measuring rods, the economy's performance was subnormal. The word "depression" conjures up scary notions of the Great Depression. It is the appropriate label for our condition because, first, the downturn has continued for such a long period of time—twenty years—and also because from three-fourths to four-fifths of Americans saw the American Dream slipping from their grasp at one time or another during these years. This depression is *silent* because there is none of the sound and fury that come with a major crash such as the one in 1929; much of the public, the press, and people in the government sense that something has indeed gone wrong, but they are unsure of exactly what it is. A major purpose of this book is to explain as clearly as possible exactly what has been happening to the American economy, to Americans and their families, and to the American Dream during these years.

The concerns of this book are not just for our immediate situation. The economic troubles that began in the early 1970s are deeply rooted in laws, policies, attitudes, and practices not easily changed or redirected, having been in place for a long time. In the spring of 1993, the number watchers in Washington reported that the economy was in a recovery—albeit anemic and described as "jobless"—from the slump that began in midsummer 1990. This recovery and the economy's current state of health must be judged against the depression that has silently gripped us for two decades.

The lesson, of course, is that the cure for the silent depression is neither cheap, easy, nor quick. It will require patience and a willingness to shift our focus from the present to the long term. We need to understand that what we must do to end the silent depression will not fit neatly into the normal political cycle of two to four years. The agenda for change proposed in this book—massive investment in public and private physical and human capital, creation of a system of national health insurance that will deliver quality medical care to *all* Americans, and a drastic overhaul of the federal tax system—is one that will occupy our economic and political energies for the rest of this century.

The economic programs involving tax and spending changes presented to the American people and the Congress by the Clinton administration in early 1993 are a step in the right direction, but only a small first step. The economic crisis we now face is in many ways far more complex than what Franklin Roosevelt faced in the early 1930s. Then the ugliness and misery of the Great Depression were clearly evident for all to see. FDR's task was to mobilize the economy as if the nation were on a war footing in order to combat economic collapse and the massive unemployment that accompanied it. The situation we face today is more subtle, one for which the war paradigm is not suitable. Our leaders must persuade us to act now in a variety of ways that will bring disruptive changes and even economic pain to many in the short term so that all Americans and their children will gain over the longer term, so that the American Dream will remain within the grasp of all citizens.

This book is for you and your family, now and in the future. It is about what has transpired in the American economy, and how these developments affect you and your family's present and future economic well-being. The "economy" is not something remote and abstract, existing only in numbers, news headlines, and TV commentary about such matters as the gross domestic product, leading indicators, unemployment rates, wages, inflation, trade deficits, bank closings, and stock prices. The economy affects all of us in one way or another every day of our lives. Like the mind's subconscious, it is always there, influencing our jobs, our incomes, our savings, our retirement, our aspirations for our children, our recreation, our politics—in short, all our hopes and all our dreams. When the economy is doing well, life is better for most of us, and when the economy is doing badly, we all are hurt to some degree, even though our own jobs and income may not be directly threatened.

Acknowledgments

In a book like this, which reflects many years of thinking and writing about the wondrous, ever-changing American economy, I can never list all the people who have contributed generously to my own understanding of how things economic really work. There are some, though, who have been and always will be of special importance to me. Among my colleagues in the economics profession, these include John Kenneth Galbraith, Hyman Minsky, Warren Samuels, Harry Trebing, Marc Tool, George Rejda, Greg Hayden, and Jerry Petr. On the more immediate and practical level of writing the book, I am grateful for the critical reviews and helpful comments by my spouse, Bonnie Watson Peterson, my daughter, Shelley Davis, and my friend Bob Baskins. Joyce Richter was especially helpful in getting successive drafts of the manuscript in shape for the publisher. At W. W. Norton & Company a special thanks is due to the demanding and skilled editing of Drake McFeely, aided by Anne T. Zaroff-Evans and Richard Rivellese. Since we first met many years ago, Donald S. Lamm, president of W. W. Norton & Company, has been a great source of encouragement and support for all my writing. As usual, I accept responsibility for any errors of fact or judgment that remain in this book.

WALLACE C. PETERSON

Lincoln, Nebraska

SILENT
DEPRESSION

CHAPTER 1

·

The Unraveling of
the American
Dream

·

I n the late winter of 1992–93, Americans were told that they could breathe a sigh of relief. The two-year economic slump was finally over, reported economists, number crunchers in Washington, newspaper headlines, and TV commentators. Nevertheless, doubt and worry persisted. As the economy moved upward in 1993, nudged forward by the modest stimulus package urged by President Clinton in January, millions of out-of-work Americans and their families saw little change. Even for the still more millions with jobs, the outlook was bleak: recessionlike conditions of economic decline have been the norm for at least twenty years.

The U.S. economy peaked in 1973. Experts have marked off four separate "recessions" since then, but this cautious term fails to capture the depression that has silently enveloped us. Longer in duration than the Great Depression of the 1930s, arriving without the fanfare of the 1929 stock-market crash, the silent depression affects four out of five American families.

If the situation is this bad, some may ask, why hasn't the economy had another collapse on the scale of 1929–39? Although the potential for a deep depression like that of the 1930s is always present, it has not happened for two basic reasons. First, there are a set of safeguards, mostly put in place during the New Deal in the 1930s, that make a 1930s-style collapse of the nation's financial system highly unlikely. Federal deposit insurance is the best-known example of these safeguards. No depositors lost their money in the current savings-and-loan scandals, though as taxpayers we have to foot the bill. The other major reason we have not had a repeat of the 1930s is the sheer size of the federal government. Federal spending equal to nearly one-fourth the value of production is a floor that keeps economic activity from falling very far in any downturn.[1]

A major consequence of the silent depression is the transformation of the economic system into a "trickle-down" economy. "Trickle-down," the descriptive phrase applied to the benefits that were supposed to flow from the Reagan tax cuts of 1981, is now appropriately applied to the whole economy. This is because during the era of the silent depression the upper 20 percent of the population experienced unchallenged prosperity and affluence, while the remaining 80 percent struggled to stay afloat economically. John Kenneth Galbraith says that what has emerged in American society in these years is a "culture of contentment," one in which the roughly 20 percent at the top of the economic pyramid have achieved *de facto* economic and political control of the nation.[2] The growing inequality in the distribution of income, plus the extreme—and increasing—inequality in the distribution of wealth, gives the "contented fifth" at the top enormous economic and political power. This is why there has been so little concern in Washington about the emergence of a silent depression, with its adverse effect upon large numbers of American families.

To put the silent depression and its impact upon Americans and their families in broader perspective, flash back to September 5, 1945, when General Douglas MacArthur accepted the surrender of Japan in Tokyo Harbor on the deck of the battleship

Missouri. America was at a peak of military, economic, and political power unmatched by any nation in history. World War II, tragic as it was, ended the Great Depression that had thrown millions out of work and sapped America's economic strength for ten dismal years after the stock-market crash of 1929. Between the outbreak of war in Europe in 1939 and its end in 1945, American production of both war and civilian goods had nearly tripled, while unemployment largely disappeared.[3] Unlike the retreat into isolation and "normalcy" after World War I, America in 1945 threw its energy and economic power into the task of creating a sound postwar political and economic order. After an emergency loan to Great Britain and a package of economic and military aid to Greece and Turkey at the start of the Cold War in 1947, the American government in 1948 launched the Marshall Plan for the economic reconstruction of Europe. Named after Secretary of State George C. Marshall in the Truman administration, the plan was a bold and imaginative venture in which America supplied needed money and material resources to help in rebuilding the war-shattered economies of Western Europe.[4] The quarter-century after the end of World War II turned out to be golden years for the market-based capitalistic economic systems of the West.[5] Economic growth, plentiful jobs, and low inflation were the norm; there were a few slumps, but, in contrast to the misery of the 1930s, they were mild and short. Sir John Hicks, a distinguished economist and Nobel laureate, described the years of prosperity following World War II as the "Age of Keynes." Indeed, John Maynard Keynes, the great English economist, had changed in a fundamental way how governments, economists, and informed citizens think about the economy and the way it works. Most Western governments followed Keynesian policies, which, they believed, spurred economic growth and kept unemployment low.

THE EMERGENCE OF
THE AMERICAN DREAM

After two and one-half years of transition from a wartime to a peacetime economy, America's "Age of Keynes" took off. From 1948 through 1973, the American economy grew at an annual average rate of 3.7 percent, a figure identical with the nation's long-term historic average for growth.[6] During these years, slumps were infrequent and mild, causing only a slight interruption to the steady growth in jobs and a rising standard of life for most American families.

The post–World War II experience of steady growth, abundant jobs, and low inflation shaped what we know as the "American Dream." The meaning of this idea, one intuitively understood by most Americans, is easily stated. At its core is the expectation that by dint of personal effort—hard work, education, saving, and playing by the "rules of the game"—one's economic well-being will steadily improve. Government is there primarily to help when people fall onto hard times through circumstances beyond their control. Obviously, the meaning of "hard times" that require help from government has changed as the complexity of the economy has changed, but, nonetheless, the economic ethic that undergirds the American Dream remains strongly individualistic.

There is a further set of expectations in the American Dream. First, a secure and steady job at good wages that steadily improve, not just in terms of money but in their purchasing power. Second, home ownership. Third, the affordability of an increasing number of things that may make life easier and more enjoyable—automobiles, washers, driers, microwaves, air conditioners, radios, TV, VCRs, power mowers, snow blowers. Fourth, an array of fringe benefits—paid vacations, generous pensions, and adequate health care, to name the most important. Fifth, travel and leisure, both of which require a growing amount of "discretionary income"—income one is free to spend without constraint. Sixth, college for the kids, and the hope and belief that the children's economic life will be better than their parents'. Finally, upward mobility. If not already in the "middle class," people and families on the lower rungs of the economic ladder expect to move into the middle class, while many in the middle class expect to move into the ranks of the affluent, and even, if lucky, to join the rich. Thus, we have a bundle of psychological expectations that form the essence of the American Dream. The long prosperity of the Age of Keynes made this dream a reality for increasing numbers of American families.

A TIME OF DISCONTENT

The story of the unraveling of the American Dream for many, if not a majority of, Americans and their families emerges from the statistics compiled by the Department of Commerce, the Bureau of Labor Statistics, and the Bureau of the Census. The story also has been told—and often told superbly—in the nation's major newspapers and business and news magazines.

In May 1991, Marley Kendall, a fifty-five-year-old bus driver in Minneapolis lost his job. Two weeks later, his wife, Frances, forty-five, lost the job she had held for fifteen years when the state of Minnesota, pinched by the recession, closed down the unemployment claims office where she worked. No expectation of the American worker has been more battered by the vicissitudes of the economy over the last twenty years than the hope for a secure job with wages that increase steadily in both dollar value and purchasing power. As Frances Kendall told a *Time* reporter, the upheaval of seeing their son having to drop out of college, losing their home, and possibly having to leave Minnesota like modern-day "okies" to find work somewhere in the Sunbelt was "especially painful when you have worked all your life and want something for your later years."[7] Happily, the Kendall story ended, after a year of fretting and worry, upon a less somber note. Marley Kendall finally found a job with a mining company in northern Minnesota, and Frances Kendall was recalled to another job with the state.

Millions of other workers and their families have shared the Kendalls' experience. According to the Bureau of Labor Statistics (BLS), of the three million workers laid off between July 1990 and the end of 1992, only 15 percent expected to return to the same job.[8] In past recessions, an average of 44 percent of workers expected to be recalled. Thus, many jobs have permanently disappeared. Unlike earlier post–World War II recessions, the 1990–91 slump hit white-collar workers and managerial employees harder than blue-collar workers in manufacturing and construction. Older workers—those between thirty-five and fifty-four—were especially hard-hit, experiencing layoffs at about twice the rate for workers in this age group in earlier recessions. Many of these workers are finding that the skills they developed during their years of employment are no longer needed because of advancing technology, or that they are overqualified for the jobs that are available.

The official BLS jobless numbers seriously *understate* the actual unemployment situation. The government fails to include in the jobless total "discouraged" workers—people who have given up trying to find a job and are no longer counted as a part of the labor force. In addition, no adjustment is made in the jobless numbers to reflect the large numbers of people working part-time who want to work full-time but can't find a full-time job. The number of people in this category was 31.6 percent higher in December 1992 than when the recession started in July 1990.[9] If these numbers are factored in, plus the admitted undercounting of the unemployed—California officials claimed that the jobless count in 1991 for their state was 350,000 too low, and New York officials said that the BLS underestimated the unemployed in the Empire State by 138,000—the "real" unemployment rate would be between 10 and 11 percent, a figure significantly above the official rate of 7.6 percent reported in mid-1992.

The corporate buzz word of the late 1980s and early 1990s

has been "downsizing," as top management in the nation's corporate giants slashed payrolls in a frenzied effort to cut costs and boost productivity in the face of increasingly tough global competition. Among major American corporations planning further cuts in their salaried employees are Du Pont, McDonnell Douglas, Pratt & Whitney, Sears, Eastman Kodak, Grumman, Boeing, General Motors, American Airlines, American Express, ITT, IBM, and many more. A survey of eight hundred companies by the American Management Association found that one out of four was planning continued work-force reductions through at least mid-1993.[10] For thousands of middle managers in corporate America, this meant a one-way ticket down the economic scale, sometimes out of the middle class into poverty. Since mid-1980, over two million middle-management jobs have been permanently eliminated. As a *Business Week* cover story said, "Behind the curtained windows of comfortable suburbs such as Fairfield County in Connecticut, in Lake Forest outside of Chicago, and Danville near San Francisco, stunned families are discovering that the social escalator is going down for the first time since the Great Depression."[11] The 1990s, *Business Week* fears, may become the age of the "dumpies"—downwardly mobile professionals—struggling to stay in the upper end of the middle class.

One such "dumpie" is Allen Stenhouse, whose twenty-four-year career in insurance ended when he lost his $50,000-a-year job as manager of the health-care department in a medium-sized corporation. Despite taking dozens of interviews, sending out hundreds of resumes, and resorting to reliable placement agencies, Stenhouse did not find a new job that matched his managerial skills and experience. After losing his wife through divorce, most of his savings in an ill-fated effort to start a financial-consulting firm, and his condo through foreclosure, Stenhouse in early 1992 was living in a small apartment, dependent upon disability payments (for depression) from Social Security. Admittedly an extreme case, Stenhouse's fate nonetheless reflects "the specter of downward mobility . . . haunting legions of once secure

professionals. They face permanent loss of the income, posses-
sions, and status long considered the defining elements of middle
class life."[12] Corporate buyouts of older workers through early-
retirement plans have become a commonplace feature of corporate downsizing, but the results are far less salutary than we may
believe. Many older workers discover they are neither psycholog-
ically nor financially prepared for early retirement. As one executive of a human-resources-consulting firm told a *Fortune* reporter,
"Somewhere about 18 to 24 months down the line, they (early
retirees) often discover two things. First, they need money. Second, they are bored out of their skulls."[13]

The 1990–91 slump wreaked further havoc on the American
family, already battered by the strains of the silent depression.
As happened during the Great Depression of the 1930s, marriages and births declined while divorces rose. Economic research
shows that, for every increase of 1 percentage point in the unemployment rate, the number of divorces jumps by approximately
ten thousand.. Although detailed statistics are scanty, the numbers available show that child and spouse abuse, and family
breakups without divorce, also rise during hard economic times.
Child support from absent fathers, never very dependable in the
American economy, becomes even scarcer, and adoption rates
drop.[14]

It is much the same story for millions of families across the
whole spectrum of expectations that constitute the American
Dream. Pensions that workers thought secure are seriously
underfunded or threatened with insolvency, because of bankruptcies or because pension funds were raided during the frenzied
corporate-takeover-and-buyout days of the 1980s. Concerning
health care, not only are an estimated thirty-five million or more
Americans without any form of health insurance, but a series of
recent decisions in the federal courts have given employers that
act as insurers (nearly 70 percent of employers are "self-insured")
power to cut back on existing coverage or skimp on coverage in
the first place.[15] Many workers are shocked to discover that their

health-insurance coverage evaporates just when they need it most. As for home ownership, younger families find themselves increasingly priced out of the house-buying market, although low interest rates in early 1993 eased the situation somewhat. In the 1950s and 1960s, it took about 15 percent of a young family's income to pay the principal and interest on a mortgage. Now this percentage has doubled to more than 30 percent, with little likelihood that it will fall significantly anytime soon. The Economic Policy Institute in Washington, D.C., estimates that 90 percent of the nation's renters cannot get together enough money to make the down payment on a medium-priced home ($79,000 in 1991). Further, the prospects for continued increases in the real value of the family's equity in its home, as happened from 1950 through the early 1980s because of inflation, is far less likely in the 1990s.[16] For an overwhelming majority of Americans, the equity in their home is the family's *major* form of wealth. Thus, the prospects for significant increases in net family wealth for most American families over the rest of this century are not good. It is much the same story for a college education. Not only have tuition and other costs been rising sharply, but tighter financial-aid standards have hit many middle-class families hard. In the late 1970s, the average federal packet of financial aid covered slightly more than 80 percent of tuition costs, according to the National Education Association. By the early 1990s, this figure had slipped to 60 percent.

Late in 1991, the speaker of Japan's parliament, Yoshio Sak-urauchi, and Japan's prime minister, Kiichi Miyazawa, set off a firestorm of anger and protest in America with their respective comments that Americans were "lazy," and "may lack a work ethics." Perhaps. In a book published about the same time, Juliet B. Schor, a Harvard economics professor, argued the opposite.[17] Rather than being lazy and lacking a work ethic, Americans have experienced a substantial increase in the number of hours of work over the last twenty years. The increase in time worked—which amounted to an extra month per year between 1969 and 1989—

was not, according to Professor Schor, a voluntary act. For at least 80 percent of the work force, it has been the only way that workers could maintain living standards in the face of a decline in the purchasing power of their wages. Thus, for many workers, another part of the American Dream—more leisure time—has slowly slipped away.

WHAT HAS GONE WRONG?

Both the anecdotal kind of evidence just surveyed, and the scholarly evidence gleaned from the torrent of numbers flowing out of Washington, tell us clearly that the economy in the early 1970s slid into an era of economic stagnation that is without precedent in our economic history. In 1929, the economy suffered an economic heart attack—a sharp, sudden crash. The worrisome economic malaise that besets the economy today is more like a slow-growing and insidious cancer, hard to detect, but deadly if not discovered in time. As happens with cancer in a person, a general sense of unease and discomfort may be present before the disease is discovered. So it is with the economy. Americans tell the polltakers that "we are on the wrong track," but they are unsure what has gone wrong. We should not push the medical analogy too far, because nations, unlike persons, rarely die economically. But we may be in for a long period of stagnation and subnormal economic performance unless we take corrective action.

Will all this change because the Democrats have recaptured the White House and are strongly in control of both houses of the Congress? Will the American Dream again become reality for a majority of Americans and their children? Perhaps. But we shall have to wait and see. Persons with enormous power and influence who find the *status quo* to their liking are in ample supply in both political parties. Because the causes of the silent depression have become so deeply embedded in America's economy and society, the Clinton administration must muster extraordinary imagination, vision, and political courage for the *whole* of its first term if it is to discover and carry through needed changes. One fact is clear. The changes needed must have strong support from the American people. Unless Americans understand fully what has happened to their economy, and why it has happened, this support won't be there. A major reason for writing this book is to provide that understanding.

CHAPTER 2

·

·

·

·

Diagnosing the
Silent
Depression

Throughout American history, words like "panic," "crash," "slump," "recession," and "depression" have been used to describe symptoms of economic hard times. The "business cycle"—the formal term economists use to describe the ups and downs of economic activity—has been studied and measured since the early nineteenth century. In the United States alone, there have been thirty-two measurable business cycles since 1854.[1] The biggest strides toward understanding the business cycle, however, came in the 1930s. It was the Great Depression of the 1930s that demonstrated the clear necessity for a correct, numerical accounting of what was happening to jobs, to production, to people's incomes, to taxes, to spending and saving, and to other indicators of economic activity. World War II, with the demand it brought for extensive economic mobilization, gave added force to this development. Thus, by 1945, the United States, like most other modern nations, had developed comprehensive and highly useful systems of national accounts designed to reveal in great detail the performance of the economy.

Another development, of equal importance, that emerged

from the trauma of the Great Depression was a revolutionary change in the way economists think about the whole economy. This change was in the realm of economic theory, springing almost entirely from the creative mind of the great English economist John Maynard Keynes. Keynes developed a basic theory that not only accounted for the catastrophic slump of the 1930s, but was general enough to explain the ups and downs of economic activity always present in systems of market capitalism. The full title of Keynes's monumental 1936 work is *The General Theory of Employment, Interest and Money,* usually called *The General Theory.*[2] Keynes's book opened the door to showing governments what they might do to smooth out fluctuations in economic activity, thereby improving the economy's overall state of health. National income accounting played the practical role of putting clothes on the bare bones of Keynes's theoretical ideas. Theory has its place, but without solid numbers that record what is happening, we can't get very far in prescribing what is to be done when the economy falls ill.

Despite more than fifty years of statistical and theoretical work, we find ourselves in the 1990s without a good definition of recession or depression. Recently, "recession" has been the most frequently used term to describe a downturn in economic activity. Since World War II, the word "depression" has not been fashionable and is used primarily to describe the deep slump of the 1930s. Occasionally, the news media have described economic conditions in parts of the country as being "depressionlike," as happened when the farm states were facing very tough economic times in the early and mid-1980s. Fashionable or not, the appropriate term for the economy today is "depression," even if it is a silent one, as the pages that follow will show.

MEASURING RECESSIONS
AND DEPRESSIONS

What is the difference between a recession and a depression? How is a recession or a depression measured? There is a witticism to the effect that a recession exists when your spouse loses his or her job, but a depression exists when you lose your job. Joking aside—and oddly, perhaps—the United States government, which compiles virtually all the statistics by which we measure the economy's state of health, does not have an official definition of "recession" or "depression." Among economists, too, no general agreement exists on how to define or measure recessions and depressions.

Agreement exists, however, on the proposition that a recession or a depression, however defined, interrupts the economy's progress. Interruptions happen whenever output goes down and people are thrown out of work. They also happen when *real* income (money income adjusted for inflation) stops growing, or productivity growth falters. If the real income of a worker or a family stops growing, economic progress for that worker or family is interrupted. If this happens to enough people over a long enough period, progress for the whole economy is interrupted. It follows logically that when this happens the economy is in a depressed state.

Using measures of the *real* income of workers and their families as the crucial criterion for defining the true state of health for the economy leads to a startling conclusion: the American economy has been in a depressed state since 1973—the last twenty years! Since four-fifths of American families have experienced falling or stagnant *real* incomes over these years, "depression" is the correct word for describing our situation. The paradox of the silent depression is that hard economic times have hit a majority of American families during years when the conventional measures of recession or depression—measures regularly reported in the news media—do not tell us that the economy is depressed.

What are the conventional measures? Essentially there are two, one involving output and the other jobs.

The definition most widely accepted and closest to an official definition for bad economic times is one developed and used by the National Bureau of Economic Research (NBER), a private but highly prestigious research institute located in Cambridge, Massachusetts. The National Bureau's definition is short and direct. A recession exists whenever the rate of growth for output declines for two consecutive quarters—that is, for six months straight. Since the end of World War II—and not counting the 1990–91 cycle—there have been eight downturns in the American economy. These post–World War II slumps averaged eleven and a half months in length, in contrast to the forty-three months of economic decline between August 1929 and March 1933.[3]

The Business Cycle Dating Committee (composed of seven economists) of the NBER is responsible for determining both the beginning and the end of recessions (or depressions). The committee, chaired by Robert Hall of Stanford University, established that the 1990–91 slump began in July 1990. Unfortunately for former President Bush, the committee did not meet until after the November 1992 presidential election to report that the recession had "officially" ended in March 1991. The committee said that the end of this recession was particularly difficult to pinpoint, because some of the measures used to determine the bottom of a slump didn't show improvement until much later. Unemployment, for example, continued rising to a high of 7.8 percent in June 1992, and then fell slowly to 7.0 percent by the end of the year.

The NBER does not say precisely what is the difference between a recession and a depression. It is a matter of judgment, depending upon the length and severity of a particular downturn. There is agreement in the economics profession that, because of their relative mildness, the slumps since World War II should be labeled "recessions," not "depressions."

Technically speaking, the second conventional measure closely associated with recession or depression is the unemployment rate, the percent of people in the labor force who are not working but are actually looking for work. As stated earlier, the "official" unemployment rate does not include persons who have become discouraged and thus are no longer seeking employment, nor does it adjust for people who are working part-time but want to work full-time. These are serious deficiencies in how the government measures unemployment. The labor force consists of all persons sixteen years of age or older who are either at work, looking for work, or unemployed. Surveys taken monthly by the Bureau of the Census, a part of the U.S. Department of Commerce, estimate the number of unemployed.

Does the federal government specify recessions and depressions in terms of unemployment rates? The answer is both yes and no. A law on the books says "full employment" exists if the unemployment rate for all workers age twenty and older is no greater than 3 percent. This definition appears in the Full Employment and Balanced Growth Act of 1978 (also known as the Humphrey-Hawkins Bill). So, presumably, if unemployment for workers age twenty or over goes above 3 percent, the economy is in a recession (or depression). Unfortunately, no administration has paid the slightest attention to this act, even though the goal of a 3-percent unemployment rate was supposed to have been achieved five years after it became law. Practically speaking, the federal government does not use an unemployment rate to define a recession or a depression.

What about the economists? Can they decide among themselves how much unemployment signals a recession or a depression? Again the answer is no. Economists agree with the commonsense proposition that output and unemployment move together—when output falls, jobs are lost, which means hard times. They also agree that employment of 100 percent of the labor force never happens. There are always some people temporarily not working for a variety of reasons—they are taking time off to look for a better job, they are in school, or their work is seasonal.

This makes for an unusual, seemingly contradictory definition of "full employment." Economists define it as an unemployment rate low enough that practically anyone who wants work can find an acceptable job. But stimulating the economy enough to achieve jobs for every single person in the labor force might push inflation to an intolerable level, because tight labor markets put strong upward pressure on prices. Unfortunately, the vague definition used by economists doesn't tell us what *rate of unemployment* equals full employment. In the 1960s, the Kennedy and Johnson administrations designated 4-percent unemployment as a full employment target. Since then, however, other administrations have either moved the rate upward to as high as 5.5 percent, or dropped altogether the idea of using a precise number to measure full employment. This is where the matter now stands.

The two measures most commonly used to determine the nation's economic health—changes in output and the unemployment rate—are a direct legacy of both Keynesian economics and the Great Depression of the 1930s. This book does not argue that these measures are in error. Rather, it argues that they are insufficient as measures of the economy's basic state of health, though they have served this purpose well in the past and remain important.

ALTERNATIVE DIAGNOSTIC MEASURES

Using changes in unemployment and output as measurement tools rests upon an implicit assumption that there is a close correlation between these standard measures and the economic well-being of the average citizen and his or her family. This was close to reality for at least a quarter of a century after World War II—a period of growth, low unemployment, and stable prices that meant prosperity for most citizens. Today the correlation between the conventional way in which we measure the economy's ups and downs and the prosperity of families in America is no longer so close. Although these standard measures remain useful, they must be supplemented with measures that offer greater insight into the actual economic health of workers and their families, irrespective of short-term changes in either the employment level or output.

The measure that will do this is the purchasing power of the income of the average worker and the worker's family. Again, economists call this *real* income, or income adjusted for inflation. Why use real income to diagnose the state of health of the economy? The answer is straightforward. It is the purchasing power of our incomes that determines our true living standards, no matter what work we do or where we live. A $35,000 annual income in 1993 is not the same as a $35,000 income in 1983, because prices have gone up by 40.8 percent in this period.

At its best, economics has as its ultimate focus the material well-being of the individual (and the individual's family). Adam Smith wrote his economic classic, *The Wealth of Nations,* as a challenge to Mercantilism, the prevailing economic philosophy of the eighteenth century. Mercantilism placed the economic welfare of the state above that of the individual. Smith believed that the individual, not the state, should be at center stage. If we adhere to the spirit of Adam Smith, economic progress ought to be defined as a rising standard of material living for as many people as possible. It follows, therefore, that, if the *real* income for the individual and his or her family stops growing, then economic progress stops as well. Smith also believed that the individual, pursuing self-interest in his or her search for maximum economic well-being, would bring the maximum benefit to the state—that is, society.

THE SILENT DEPRESSION IN NUMBERS

Evidence for the silent depression in the American economy since 1973 rests upon three sets of numbers. The first involves changes in *real* weekly earnings for individual workers in the private nonagricultural economy since 1947, and the second involves changes in family income measured in constant dollars over the same period. These two diagnostic measures tell us what has happened to the purchasing power of a majority of American workers and their families in the near half-century that has elapsed since the end of World II—it rose until 1973 and has been declining or stagnant since then. The third set of numbers does not measure income directly, but is the most basic diagnostic statistic used by economists to understand the condition of the economy. This is productivity, the amount of output (goods and services) that a worker produces on the average during a stipulated period of time. An hour is the usual basis for measuring output, although productivity can be measured annually as well. The number that is crucial to our analysis is the average annual rate of change in productivity over the period 1947–92. As Professor Paul Krugman of MIT has said, "Productivity isn't everything, but in the long run it is almost everything."[4] In sum, productivity is the ultimate determinant of the economic well-being of the individual, the family, and the nation. Here again, 1973 marks a crucial turning point.

Figure 1 shows what happened to weekly earnings for individual workers from 1947 to 1991. Technically, this figure measures average weekly earnings in constant (that is, inflation-adjusted) dollars for production (nonsupervisory) workers in the private nonagricultural economy. These numbers represent about 80 percent of employed workers in the American economy.[5] The years from 1947 through 1973 were boom years. *Real* weekly earnings grew at an annual average rate of 1.9 percent, a rate that meant steady economic gains for a growing number of Americans. The generation that survived the Depression and

FIGURE 1 *Real Weekly Wages* *

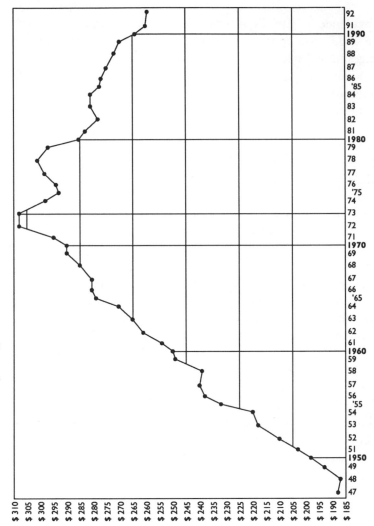

*In constant 1982–84 dollars.

SOURCE: *Economic Report of the President* (Washington, D.C.: U.S. Government Printing Office), 1991, 1993; Bureau of the Census, Current Population Reports, ser. P-60, no. 180, 1992.

fought in World War II became accustomed to regular, substantial, and uninterrupted improvements in their material standard of life.

Abruptly, and for reasons that are not fully clear, the trend line after 1973 for constant-dollar weekly earnings turned negative. An average worker earned $354.66 in 1991, compared with $145.39 in 1973. But the buying power of those earnings when measured in constant (1982–84) dollars dropped from a post–World War II peak of $308.03 in 1973 to $279.56 during the 1982 recession. Even during the much-praised expansion of the Reagan-Bush years (1983–91), *real* wages slipped further, to $260.37 in 1991. Thus, as the 1990s began, the buying power of the earnings for a typical worker was 15.5 percent *below* what it had been eighteen years earlier! Since the watershed year of 1973, the constant-dollar value of an average worker's weekly earnings has *fallen* at an annual rate of 0.9 percent.[6] For large numbers of working Americans, dreams of home ownership, better cars and appliances, vacations, and college for the kids gradually slipped away.

A similar story, although not so harsh, unfolded for family income. Here the technical measure we'll look at is median family income, which measures income at the midpoint after arraying all incomes from the lowest to the highest. It is more representative than average income, because in any average a few extremely high numbers pull the figure up, giving a distorted picture of what is typical in any situation. Real family income is a broader measure than the weekly wage, because it includes not just the income of production workers, but the income of the family from all sources, including all family members who work. Figure 2 traces the growth of median family income in constant dollars from 1947 through 1991. As with *real* weekly wages, median family income in constant (1982–84) dollars grew briskly from 1947 through 1973.[7] In these years, the annual average rate of growth was 2.8 percent, which would double family income every twenty-five years—about a generation. This experience led the

FIGURE 2 *Real Family Income*

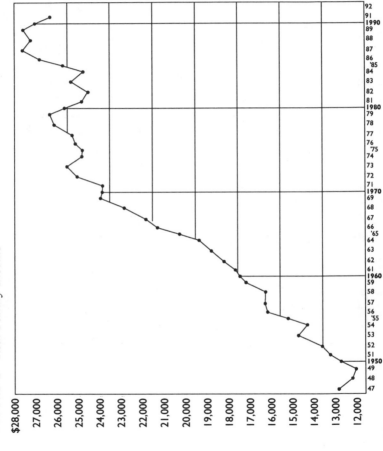

* In constant 1982–84 dollars.

Source: Bureau of the Census, Current Population Reports, ser. P-60, no. 167, 1990, updated.

generation that came of age in the Depression era and World War II to believe that children in America should do better economically than their parents.

The annual average rate of growth for *real* median income of the family between 1947 and 1973, 2.8 percent, is significantly higher than the rate of growth for *real* weekly earnings of the individual, 1.9 percent. Several factors account for this difference. Family income includes the income of high-salaried managerial and professional workers, who make up roughly 20 percent of the work force. It also includes income from property (rents, dividends, and interest) as well as from work. The most important factor explaining the difference is the entry of wives and mothers into the labor force to supplement the family income. This development began almost immediately after World War II, but the *rate* at which women entered into work accelerated sharply in the 1970s.[8] The effect of working wives and mothers on family income has been dramatic. In 1950, for example, when only one-third of all women worked, the income of families in which the wife or mother worked outside the home was 21 percent greater than the income of families in which the wife did not work outside the home. By 1991, when 57.3 percent of women were working outside the home, families with working wives and mothers had incomes 60 percent greater than those in which only the husband or father worked.[9] This change is explained primarily by an increase in the number of wives and mothers at work, not an increase in the wages of women compared with the wages of men. Over the long haul, it is not a sustainable source of gain for the family's income, because sooner or later the economy will run out of wives and mothers to put to work.

As with *real* weekly wages, the gains in inflation-adjusted income for the American family came to an abrupt halt after 1973. Unlike *real* weekly earnings, however, the rate of growth for median family income did not turn negative. But it slowed to a mere trickle, as the average annual rate of increase for the eighteen years from 1974 through 1991 dropped to a minuscule

0.18 percent. At this rate, it would take nearly four centuries for constant-dollar family income to double! Working wives, mothers, and even children saved *real* family income from an actual decline during these years. This near stagnation in family income explains why many of the baby-boomers and the generation that reached working age within the last decade doubt that their living standards will ever reach those of their parents, let alone exceed them.

Now we come to productivity, in many ways the most critical number of any that we shall consider. If there is a single proposition upon which all economists can agree, it is that higher productivity is the key to an improved standard of life. Figure 3 charts annual average rates of change in American productivity from 1948 through 1991. In general, the figure reveals a slowing in the long-term trend in productivity growth, but, as with the weekly wage and family income, the really sharp break in this trend line came after 1973. Between 1948 and 1973, average output per hour for workers in the nonfarm business sector grew at an annual average rate of 2.5 percent. The practical meaning of this number is that during each of these years a typical worker produced 2.5 percent more goods and services for each hour he or she was at work.

Productivity measures more than the skill of the individual worker; it includes everything—machines, technology, managerial skill, education, even buildings—that affects the worker's efficiency. It is an average, obtained by dividing the total output during a period by the amount of work taking place in that period. The productivity of a typist, for example, will increase if a better machine becomes available, even though there is no change in the basic skill of the typist. A worker with a bulldozer is more productive than is a worker with a shovel, even though more skill is required to use a bulldozer than a shovel. For our standard of life to improve, we must produce more goods and services each year, especially if population is increasing. We can produce more by having more people at work, but it is much more important

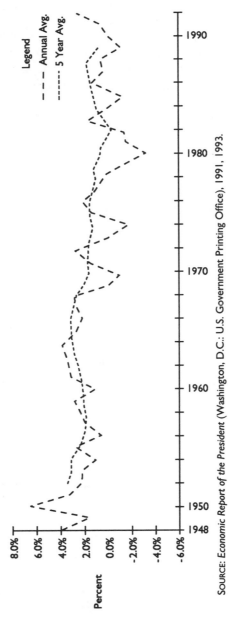

Figure 3 *Rate of Change in Productivity: 1948–1992 (in percent)*

SOURCE: *Economic Report of the President* (Washington, D.C.: U.S. Government Printing Office), 1991, 1993.

to achieve these gains by improving the efficiency—that is, the productivity—of the work force. In fact, if productivity had not increased over the nation's history, it would not have been possible to reduce the average hours of work each week while at the same time producing more goods and services.

After 1973, the watershed year that marked a change in the basic health of the American economy, productivity growth took a nose dive. From 1974 through 1991, the annual average rate of growth in output per hour in the nonfarm business sector dropped to 0.7 percent, a 72-percent decline in the growth rate for this key indicator as compared with the earlier period.

Why did this happen? The answer remains one of the great economic mysteries of our time, a mystery explored more fully in later chapters. However, the decline in the rate of growth of productivity is real—all too real—and is the main reason why there has been deterioration in *real* wages for nearly the last two decades. The silent depression won't disappear until we restore productivity growth to its historic, long-term trend.[10]

Another way to underscore the importance of productivity growth is to ask how long it will take output per worker to double at these two different rates. The "rule of 70" provides an answer to this question. To find out how long it takes for any quantity to double when it is growing at a particular rate, divide 70 by that rate. Thus, if output per worker is growing at an annual average rate of 2.5 percent, it will take 28 years for this average to double ($70 / 2.5 = 28$ years). This represents a generation, and is in line with the historical, long-term performance of the American economy. Contrast this to a productivity growth rate of 0.7 percent. When we apply the "rule of 70" here, we discover it will take 100 years for output per person to double ($70 / 0.7 = 100$), or more than 3.5 times longer. If productivity growth stays below its historic trend, the future prospects for the American economy are grim.

Before we leave the topic of productivity growth momentarily, it is important to clarify a matter where there may be some misunderstanding. What I have been discussing is the *rate* at which the nation's productivity has been growing, not the actual or absolute level of production per worker. At times, there is confusion on this point in the news media. America's average output per worker has not fallen—our productivity in this absolute sense remains the highest in the world. Where we have fallen behind the Germans, the Japanese, and others is in the *rate of growth* of productivity.

To illustrate this point, the average output per year for an employed worker in the United States was $18,702 in 1947 as measured in 1982 prices. By 1973, this figure had climbed to $32,259, a 72.5-percent increase in goods and services produced per employed worker in a year. In 1990, the output-per-employed-worker figure stood at $35,244, only 9.3 percent higher than the 1973 figure.[11]

Output per employed worker per year is also a measure of productivity, but one that uses a different time period—the calendar year. The time period used in figure 3 is an hour. Productivity measured on an output-per-employed-worker-per-year basis grew more slowly than did productivity measured on an output-per-hour basis for both the major time periods analyzed in this chapter. Between 1947 and 1973, output-per-employed-worker per year grew at an annual average rate of 2.1 percent, whereas during the 1974–90 period this rate dropped to 0.5 percent. These rates are below the growth rates for output per hour for workers. Why is this? Primarily it is because the average hours worked per week have fallen. In the 1947–73 period, people worked on the average 38.7 hours per week; during the 1974–90 period, this average fell to 37.3 hours, a drop of 1.4 hours per week on the average.[12] Since what is produced depends upon both productivity gains and the number of persons at work, any decline in the average time spent at work will offset to some extent any gains in productivity.

There remains one final question to discuss before concluding this chapter. A measure widely used in the press and on television for judging the economy's health is per-person (per-capita) disposable income, measured in dollars of constant purchasing power. Disposable income is basically a measure of take-home pay, the amount of money people have to spend out of their inflation-adjusted money income from all sources after paying taxes. Economists regard it as another good diagnostic measure of the individual's economic well-being.

Per-capita disposable income has grown almost continuously, even after the watershed year of 1973. This prompts the following question: if on a per-person basis everyone has enjoyed more *real* spending power year after year over the entire post–World War II period, isn't the silent-depression thesis invalidated? The answer to this question is no—for two reasons. The first involves what has happened to the rates of growth for *real* per-person disposable income during the postwar era, and the second concerns the appropriateness of using this figure to measure economic progress.

Although it is true that *real* per-capita disposable income has grown continuously since 1947, it is also true that there was a sharp slowdown in the *rate* at which this income measure grew after 1973. Between 1947 and 1973, *real* disposable income per person rose at an annual rate of 2.6 percent, which would allow the doubling of take-home pay every generation. Between 1974 and 1991, however, the growth rate dropped to 1.3 percent, only 50 percent as high as it was in the earlier period. At the latter rate, it would take fifty-four years for take-home pay to double. This slowdown in the growth rate for *real* disposable income on a per-person basis reinforces the silent-depression argument, even though the growth rate remains positive.

How is it possible for the rate of growth for disposable income in the 1974–90 period to be higher than the growth rate for worker productivity in the same period? The answer is that disposable income includes income from transfer payments—Social Security benefits, unemployment compensation, public assistance—in addition to income from work. Income from work stems directly from productivity growth, whereas transfer income depends upon government policy. In the 1970s, there was an explosive growth in transfer spending by the federal government.[13]

The second objection to the use of per-capita disposable income as a measure of economic progress is more fundamental. Per-capita disposable income is a flawed measure. Because it is an arithmetical average, high-income persons have a disproportionate influence on the overall picture. This was especially true in the 1980s, when the income of families in the top tenth of the population grew many times faster than the income of all other families. The gap between the income of families at the top and the rest is so enormous that including them in the picture results in a significant upward bias to the overall average. For example, in 1990, families in the top 5 percent received 17.4 percent of all family income, a larger share than the 15.4 percent received by the bottom 40 percent of families. The average 1990 income of families in the top 5 percent of the income scale was $148,124 (in constant 1990 dollars), fifteen times greater than the average income of $9,833 for the bottom 20 percent of families.[14]

In March 1992, a squabble erupted between Paul Krugman, The New York Times, and The Wall Street Journal over the distribution of the gains in real income by families in the 1980s. The origin of the controversy was a story in the Times in which Professor Krugman was quoted as saying that Congressional Budget Office (CBO) figures showed that the upper 1 percent of families got 60 percent of the gain in income during the 1980s. Several weeks later, The Wall Street Journal got into the fray, challenging the accuracy of Professor Krugman's figures, and quoting Robert D. Reischauer, CBO director, to the effect that Professor Krugman's 1- and 60-percent figures were based on his interpretation of CBO numbers, not any calculations carried out by the CBO.[15]

What actually happened to the distribution of 1980s income gains? This distribution was skewed heavily toward families at the top of the income scale, but not to the extreme degree suggested by Professor Krugman. According to numbers from the

Bureau of the Census, the total increase in income received by families between 1980 and 1990 was $533.5 billion (in constant 1990 dollars). Families in the top 20 percent got more than one-half of this total, 55.9 percent, as compared with the mere 2.3 percent that went to families in the bottom fifth.[16] This lopsided development contributed to the worsening of the distribution of income among families in the 1980s.

A SUMMING UP

The numbers just presented diagnose a serious and long-lasting deterioration in the basic economic fortunes for large numbers of American families. Figure 4 shows the percentage changes in annual average growth rates for 1947–73 compared with 1974–91 for six key measures discussed in this chapter. Here in a nutshell is the silent-depression story.

These adverse changes must be viewed and analyzed apart from the 1990–91 recession. Rather, they should be understood as the backdrop against which the most recent cyclical drama in the American economy played itself out. The causes for this deteriorating situation go well beyond the usual factors that economists point to in explaining cyclical ups and downs. Realization of this is growing among the public and policy-makers, a fact reflected in numerous stories in the news media about the abnormal sluggishness of the economy, even though it was, in the winter-spring of 1992–93, supposed to be recovering from the 1990–91 slump. USA Today, in midsummer 1992, used the catchy phrase from a well-known television beer commercial, "It doesn't get any better than this," to introduce a front-page cover story on how the "slow grow '90s" are going to follow the "go-go '80s." In The Wall Street Journal, Lawrence A. Hunter, deputy chief economist for the U.S. Chamber of Commerce, warned that the United States is facing a "never-ending recession," with subnormal growth rates extending through 1996 and beyond.[17] Polls have consistently shown that an overwhelming majority of

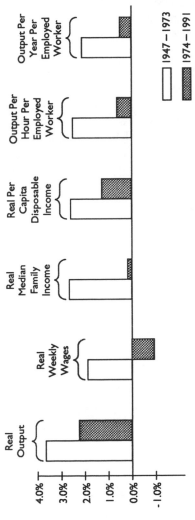

FIGURE 4 *Comparative Annual Average Growth Rates for (1947–1973) and (1974–1991)*

Growth rates for six measures of current progress worsened significantly in the 1974–1991 period as compared to 1947–1973.
SOURCE: *Economic Report of the President* (Washington, D.C.: U.S. Government Printing Office), 1991, 1992; Bureau of the Census, Current Population Reports, ser. P-60, no. 180, 1992.

Americans fear that something is fundamentally awry with the American economy, that the nation is on the wrong track. These fears undoubtedly contributed to the decisive electoral vote margin of President Clinton's victory.

So the cure for the nation's economic condition will not be found in the standard measures economists usually recommend for ending a recession or promoting growth—tax cuts, more government spending *per se,* lower interest rates, or pumping more money into the economy. Fundamental changes are needed, a fact recognized by President Clinton, and a topic addressed in detail in later chapters in this book. In the following chapters, human dimensions are added to these numbers by a careful look at how they have affected the fate and fortunes of Americans and their families.

CHAPTER 3

The Shrinking of
the Middle
Class

Before the 1990s, the usual pattern in a recession was for workers to lose their jobs, suffer through a period of idleness, and return to work—often to the same jobs lost earlier—when the economy began to recover. As the economy turned sluggish after the 1980s, then slipped into the 1990–91 recession, this scenario changed. Workers lost their jobs, but the jobs they lost often disappeared. What happened to Larry Weikel, a native of Spring City, Pennsylvania, is an experience shared by millions of other workers in the recession of 1990–91.

In 1966, Larry, a high-school graduate discharged after four years in the Air Force, returned to his hometown, where he took a job with the Diamond Glass Company, a family-owned business founded in 1874. Larry played by the "rules" of the 1950s and 1960s—making a commitment to a company in exchange for a steady job with a good salary, health-care benefits, and a pension. For Larry and millions of other blue-collar workers, this was the ticket to middle-class status and realization of the American Dream.

Twenty-four years after Larry started with Diamond Glass, in

August 1990, the plant where he worked shut down, leaving him and nearly three hundred other employees unemployed. After losing his job, and being abruptly dumped out of the middle class, Larry went to work part-time in a store run by his brother-in-law. His wife's $6-an-hour job in a sewing factory helped keep the couple barely above the poverty level. Fortunately, as Larry mused to *Philadelphia Inquirer* reporters Donald L. Barlett and James B. Steele, his children are grown, so "All I have to do is make enough money to feed my wife and myself." Yet the experience left Larry bitter. "It seems like I prostituted my whole young life to that company, and then they turn me out to pasture. . . . I was always working. And then they turn around and do something like that to you."[1]

Between 1966 and 1990, the Diamond Glass Company went public, changed its name after a management buyout, borrowed heavily to buy out competitors, and ultimately was sold to a larger competitor when unable to service its debt. The larger firm, itself a survivor of a leveraged buyout, closed many plants that the onetime family business had acquired in its heady expansion days. Like Larry Weikel, several thousand workers saw their precarious hold on a middle-class standard of life slip away as they went from $15-plus-an-hour factory jobs to making $6 an hour or less in the service sector.

Midway through the go-go years of the debt-fed 1980s expansion, the fate of Larry Weikel and thousands of other workers began to cast a shadow over President Reagan's rosy "Morning in America" theme. Increasingly, stories and articles appeared in the press and weekly news and business magazines about economic threats to America's middle class. Editors and writers feared that this bastion of stability in a turbulent world was being ground down between growing numbers of rich at the top and poor at the bottom.

"Middle Class Squeeze," read the headline for a 1986 *U.S. News & World Report* cover story. "Is the Middle Class Shrinking?" *Time* asked in November 1986, in a lead story in its Economy and Business section. "American Dream Comes Crashing Down" was the headline for a 1987 wire-service article by Gary Shilling, economist and owner of a leading economic-consulting firm. In *The Washington Post*, "America's Middle-Class Meltdown" was the headline on a 1991 article by Richard Morin, director of polling for the newspaper. On the other side, *Newsweek's* Panglossian economic columnist, Robert Samuelson, sought to reassure the worried, writing in 1985 about "The Myth of the Missing Middle."[2] There is no precise definition for the middle class. Nonetheless, the concept is helpful, especially for making the transition from trends in wages and family incomes at the national level, as discussed in chapter 2, to a more specific focus on what has been happening to the family in America. In this chapter, I examine the squeeze that America's middle class has experienced since 1973. Chapter 4 takes a look at how specific kinds of families have fared economically in the last two decades.

THE IMPORTANCE OF THE MIDDLE CLASS

Americans are uncomfortable with the idea of class, unless talking about the "middle class"—the one idea of class that Americans are willing to acknowledge and discuss. Belief in the middle class is so much the quintessence of American economic, social, and cultural life that in polls 80 to 90 percent of Americans consistently describe themselves as "middle-class." This is just as true for families barely above the poverty level, struggling to keep afloat, as it is for families about to nudge their way into the millionaire income bracket. Rising concern over the worsening economic fortunes of middle-class Americans was a first sign of a growing public unrest about the rosy promises of the Reagan Revolution. As *U.S. News & World Report* noted in 1986, the best year of the Reagan boom, "America's middle class is in a fix. After decades of rising living standards, many in the middle now find they are clambering up a descending economic escalator."[3]

In an in-depth analysis, Barbara Ehrenreich—in her 1989 book, *Fear of Falling*—explored the worries that beset the professional middle class, a broad array of educated, well-paid people who make up about 20 percent of the working population. Schoolteachers, professors, doctors, lawyers, engineers, government bureaucrats, scientists, middle-management executives, and writers are members of the professional middle class. Their importance outweighs their numbers, for they are the trendsetters, the source of creative ideas needed when society changes direction. Their anxieties are more than economic, says Ms. Ehrenreich, because they are in fear of "growing soft, of failing to strive, of losing discipline and will."[4]

The daily press, weekly news and business magazines, television, and popular writers serve as society's radar, spotlighting troublesome problems in the nation. Subsequently, problems brought to light by this process become the subject of detailed scholarly investigations, which, ultimately, may become the basis for political action if that is the appropriate way to deal with the problems. This process is slow and cumbersome, but it is usually the way things get done in a democracy. To illustrate, solid statistical evidence on the economic troubles of the middle class is only now becoming available, though the media began focusing their radar on these problems in the mid-1980s. Political action lies farther down the road.

When the 1992 presidential campaign got under way in late 1991, fears for the fate of the middle class were high on the list of concerns of the presidential candidates. They talked about the virtues of a middle-class tax cut as a quick fix for the ailing economy, although no one seeking the presidency was specific about who belonged to the middle class. *U.S. News & World Report* commented acidly that President Bush redefined the middle class as "anyone who votes."[5] Most economists, including Alan Greenspan, Chairman of the Federal Reserve System, warned against a hasty and ill-conceived tax cut that would do little, if anything, to correct the fundamental, underlying ills of the American economy. These worries were unnecessary. By March 1992, the tax-cut idea was dead in the water. Congress and the administration could not agree on how taxes should be cut. Nonetheless, and in spite of the economy's short-term ups and downs, the fate of the middle class is something Americans will fret about for the rest of the century.

WHAT IS THE MIDDLE CLASS?

Before we answer questions about the economic fate of America's middle class, the phrase needs to be carefully defined. The fact that on any given day 80 to 90 percent of Americans regard themselves as members of the middle class only tells us how strongly embedded is the middle-class ideal in the American psyche. For a practical, working definition, we need more. Economists and government number crunchers don't have an accepted statistical definition of the "middle class" resembling the numbers they use to measure production or unemployment. This is hardly surprising, since middle-class status is as much a sociological and cultural condition as an economic one. One observer, economist Larry Lindsey of Harvard, has said that the numerical boundaries of the middle class cannot be defined, since it is essentially a state of mind. "A middle class person is someone who expects to be self-reliant, unlike the upper class with its unearned wealth or the lower class with its dependency on society."[6] The liberal-left opinion journal The Nation calls the idea of the middle class a "useful myth," designed to divide politically the working class—which the magazine says is the real majority.[7] These latter viewpoints are colorful, but they do not help measure the economic fate of the middle class. There is a need for accurate measures of the limits, size, and membership in this group.

Essentially, there are only two ways of using *numbers* to define the middle class, both of which we shall explore.

The first is simple but arbitrary: it fixes a percentage of the population as "middle-class," letting the income range vary. By this definition, the middle class includes the middle three-fifths (or 60 percent) of families. In economics, there is a long-standing practice of measuring the distribution of society's income among persons or families by arraying persons or families by fifths (quintals), from the highest to the lowest, then calculating the share of income received by each fifth. This approach sees society's total income as a gigantic pie divided into five pieces, although the pieces are not of equal size.

Defining the middle class as the middle three-fifths of families makes no judgment about the upper and lower limits of the middle class in terms of dollars. Statistically, the middle class is always the same—the 60 percent of families in the middle range of the income-distribution scale. The upper class is the 20 percent of families at the top, the lower class the 20 percent at the bottom. This approach can't tell us if the *proportion* of families described as middle-class is changing—by definition, it is always 60 percent. What it does show is whether the middle class is changing in terms of its share of the income pie. Since it is also possible to calculate the average income and the range of income for each fifth of the income pie, the individual family can discover where it stands—inside the middle class, above it, or below it. This is useful information, but doesn't give us the entire picture of what has been happening to the middle class.

The second way of defining the middle class is tougher and more controversial, but it is an approach that must also be used to avoid designating the middle class as an arbitrary percentage of all families, and to learn, also, what happened to these families over time. In this approach, the middle class consists of families whose income lies between designated upper and lower income limits measured in dollars. Defining the middle class by specified income levels allows the percent of middle-class families to vary over time. We can find out if the middle class is growing or shrinking. The drawback of this approach is that it does not tell us anything directly about the share of the total income received by middle class families—how big a piece of the income pie is going to the middle class. It is also arbitrary in that the actual lower and upper dollar limits chosen are a matter of judgment. To answer the question raised by the title of this chapter—is the middle class shrinking?—we need information not only about the number of families that belong to the middle class, but also about what has happened to the distribution of income between the middle, the lower, and the upper classes. So our analysis must draw upon both approaches.

At first glance, it ought to be easy to discover if the middle class is shrinking. Unfortunately, this is not so. Measuring the size and economic fate of America's middle class is complex, and both politically and economically controversial. Lurking not far beneath any discussion of class in America is the fear of "class warfare," a fear that is all too easily—and readily—exploited by politicians. However, the issues involved should be sorted out, because society needs practical and useful answers to this important question.

In a 1975 essay, written long before the current furor began, Robert Heilbroner challenged the idea that America consisted of one big, happy middle class. He argued that the middle class covered families with an income between $15,000 and $32,000, a range that included only 35 percent of the families in the nation.[8] Heilbroner's statistical definition of the middle class only took in families whose income exceeded the median family income, which was just under $14,000 in 1975. He excluded most working-class families, defined as families with incomes between $6,500 and $15,000. Membership in the middle class, according to Heilbroner, consisted primarily of professionals—doctors, lawyers, airline pilots, managers, and proprietors. Heilbroner did not attempt in his essay to determine whether the middle class had changed in size over any distinct period.

Recent academic efforts to define the middle class cover a much larger segment of the American population. Membership in the middle class includes not only professionals but also blue-collar workers, civil servants, some clerical workers, middle managers, and salespeople. Income, not occupation, is the primary determinant of middle-class status. Katherine Bradbury, an economist at the Boston Federal Reserve Bank, in a major study covering the years 1973 through 1984, included in the middle class families with an income between $20,000 and $49,999 in constant 1984 dollars.[9] A later study by two economists with the Bureau of Labor Statistics, which covered the 1979–88 period, kept the lower limit of the middle class at $20,000 but raised the upper limit to $56,000 (in 1988 dollars).[10] One conclusion that emerged from these and other studies was a rough rule of thumb to the effect that the middle class includes between 40 and 60 percent of the total number of families. This is not very precise, but, since setting the upper and lower dollar limits is a matter of judgment, it is not surprising. Besides, as society's income increases over time, the upper and lower limits must change.

IS THE MIDDLE CLASS SHRINKING?
A SNAPSHOT PICTURE

Initially, we shall tackle the debatable question of whether the middle class is shrinking by specifying it as a range of incomes. We will define the "middle class" to include all families with an income between $25,000 and $75,000 (in constant 1990 dollars).[11] These income ranges are higher than in earlier studies, but the changes are in order, because incomes have increased since the earlier studies appeared. Difficult problems exist, of course, in setting income limits for the "middle class" in a nation as big and diverse as the United States. In New York City, for example, an income of $75,000 for a family of four would put that family far down in the ranks of the middle class. In Mississippi, on the other hand, such an income would nudge the family into the lower ranks of the rich. These problems aside, the advantage of this approach is its simplicity: we have to deal with only three income classes—upper, middle, and lower.

Table 3-1 shows in percent the number of American families in each of these three classes in 1973 and 1990. This is a "snapshot" (the technical term is "cross-section") picture, because it depicts the situation at two different points in time. By way of a benchmark, median family income in 1990 was $35,353, which puts the lower limit of the middle class as defined here at 70.7 percent of the median, and the upper limit at 212.1 percent. The poverty-level income for a family of four in 1990 was $13,359, so the threshold level for entry into the middle class is significantly above the poverty level. This is as it should be. Families with incomes between the poverty level ($13,359) and lower threshold for the middle class ($25,000) belong to the "working poor."

TABLE 3-1 *Distribution of Families by Income Class: 1973 and 1990 (in percent)*

Income Class	Percent of Families in:		Percent Change
	1973	1990	
Upper: Above $75,000	8.6%	12.3%	+43.0%
Middle: $25,000–$74,999	59.7	54.5	−8.7
Lower: $0–$24,999	31.8	33.3	+4.7

SOURCE: Bureau of the Census, Current Population Reports, ser. P-60, no. 174, *Money Income of Households, Persons, and Families in the United States: 1990*, p. 199, table B-3.

What follows from these figures? Given the assumed boundaries of $25,000 to $75,000, the middle class has shrunk in size since 1973. In percentage points the drop is 5.2, which is equal to an 8.7-percent decline in its *relative* size. The numbers also show polarization—more rich and more poor, and fewer between! These findings are in approximate agreement with the two academic studies mentioned earlier with respect to the decline in the size of the middle class.

What table 3-1 does *not* show is whether the distribution of total income between the lower, middle, and upper classes changed over this period. As Bradbury said, "The fact that American society has become less 'middle class' would not be a source of concern if families generally were becoming richer."[12] They are not, however. Family income measured in constant dollars grew very little between 1973 and 1990, but income inequality between families worsened. Table 3-2 shows this.

The table tells two stories. First, between 1973 and 1990 the distribution of income among families—how we cut up the income pie—became sharply more unequal. In 1973, the top 20 percent of families got 41.1 percent of the total income, but by 1990 their percentage share had climbed to 44.3 percent, a 7.8-percent increase in their relative share. Families in the other four-fifths saw the relative size of their slices of the pie shrink. Second, the numbers also confirm the shrinkage of the middle class, when the latter is defined by the income share received by the middle three-fifths of families. In 1973, the combined proportion of income received by the middle 60 percent of families was 53.4, but by 1990 their share had fallen to 51.2 percent, a decline of 4.1 percent in the relative size of the middle-class piece of the income pie.

Another way to underscore the *degree* to which the distribution of income among families has become more unequal is to compare the ratio of the average income of families in the top 5 percent and upper fifth with the average of families in the lower fifth. In 1973, families in the top-5-percent bracket had an aver-

TABLE 3-2 *Distribution of Family Income by Fifths (Quintals): 1973 and 1990 (in percent)*

Income Group	Share of Income in:		Percent Change
	1973	1990	
Top* 5%	15.5%	17.4%	+12.3%
Top Fifth	41.1	44.3	+7.8
Fourth Fifth	24.0	23.8	−0.8
Third Fifth	17.5	16.6	−5.1
Second Fifth	11.9	10.8	−9.2
Lower Fifth	5.5	4.6	−16.4

*Included in the top fifth.
SOURCE: Bureau of the Census, Current Population Reports, ser. P.-60, no. 174, *Money Income of Households, Families, and Persons in the United States: 1990*, p. 216, table B-13.

age income 11.3 times greater than families in the bottom fifth. By 1990, the income of the top families was 15.1 times larger, a 33.6-percent increase in this ratio. For families in the upper fifth of the income scale, their income in 1973 was 7.5 times greater than the income of families in the lower fifth. By 1990, this differential had risen to 9.6, a 28.0-percent rise in the ratio.[13]

We still do not have the full story of what has happened to the middle class as defined by the income ranges shown in table 3-1. Although there is a presumption that the relative gain shown for families at the top of the income scale in table 3-2 came at the expense of families lower down the scale, this is still only a presumption. The numbers in table 3-2 can't tell us exactly what happened to the income share received by families with incomes between $25,000 and $74,999 (in 1990 dollars). To put this last piece of the puzzle in place, help comes from an unexpected source—tax data from the Internal Revenue Service. If total money income is allocated to the income classes shown in table 3-1, using adjusted gross income as reported in tax returns, we find that in 1973 middle-class families received 57.7 percent of total income. By 1990, the middle-class share of the income total had fallen to 49.7 percent, a 13.9-percent relative decline. Tax-return figures show that the upper class's share of the income total went from 21.4 percent in 1973 to 29.8 percent in 1990, a 39.3-percent gain in the relative size of their piece of the income pie. [14]

Recent numbers from the Bureau of the Census confirm these basic findings. In a report issued in December 1991, the Census Bureau, using a technique that considers changes in the size of the family, found that the percentage of persons living in middle-income families dropped from 69.0 percent in 1969 to 63.3 percent in 1989, an 8.3-percent relative decline in the size of the "middle." This percentage change is almost the same as the percentage change shown in table 3-1, though the boundaries for the middle class used in the latest Census Bureau study differ from those in table 3-1. From 1969 to 1989, the proportion of persons in low-income families rose from 17.9 to 22.1 percent of the total, while the proportion of persons in high-income families jumped from 10.9 to 14.7 percent of the total, a 34.9-percent *relative* gain. The income limits used for the middle class in this Census Bureau study were $18,576 and $74,304. [15]

So what do we have? Numbers from the Bureau of the Census and the Internal Revenue Service confirm the widespread, anecdotal evidence on the shrinking of America's middle class. Not only has the middle class shrunk as measured by the number of families, but the share of the income pie going to the middle class has shrunk even more.

What these "snapshot" numbers don't reveal is the process through which the shrinkage has taken place. Snapshot numbers provide information only on the *net* changes that have taken place between the income classes. America has always been a society characterized by economic mobility—both upward and downward. Snapshot numbers do not reveal mobility. Needed is information about the actual movement of families into and out of the middle class. Besides snapshot information, we need "moving-picture" numbers showing the middle class in motion.

IS THE MIDDLE CLASS
SHRINKING? A MOVING PICTURE

Economic mobility—the movement of persons and families up and down the economic ladder—is the key to understanding changes in the size of the middle class. "Mobility" usually refers to changes in income, but the idea also applies to occupational changes. Upward mobility occurs when a person or a family moves into a higher income or occupational class. Downward mobility is the reverse, a fall to a lower income or occupational level. Thus, mobility is a two-way street. Persons and families can either climb to a higher level on the economic ladder, or slip down to a lower rung. Mobility may be *intragenerational,* which means moving up or down the economic ladder within the time span of a generation, or one person's lifetime. There is also *intergenerational* mobility, movement across generations. Comparison between the economic prospects and attainments of a parent and a child involves intergenerational mobility. Both types of mobility are relevant to the shrinkage of the middle class during the last twenty years.

Mobility is a four-way proposition when it concerns changes in the size of the middle class, since both upward mobility and downward mobility have two dimensions. Upward mobility happens when people and families move either from the lower class into the middle class or out of the middle class and into the upper class. Downward mobility, the fearful thing that has swept through the middle ranks of corporate middle managers and the middle class generally since the mid-1980s, means moving from the upper to the middle class, or from the middle to the lower class. *Busi-*

ness Week compares downward mobility to the stages of dealing with death—"you deny the reality of job death, you suffer, you grieve, adjust your values, and then act to recover."[16]

These transitions—flows of people and families between classes—take place continuously. To get a complete picture of what happened to the middle class between 1973 and 1990, it is necessary to combine the information obtained from snapshot studies with information that shows the magnitude over time of the flow of people and families between classes.

Information on the magnitude and direction of upward and downward flows between classes is available through research done at the Survey Research Center of the University of Michigan. For more than two decades, researchers at this center have been tracking the economic fortunes of persons in more than five thousand families. This research, involving over forty thousand individual family members, results in a continuous picture—a "moving-picture"—of what is happening economically to these families and their members over this period. Over the years, the composition of families and their economic fortunes change for many reasons—through death, through birth, through marriage, through divorce, through children leaving home. Divorce, for example, is the major reason for drastic changes in the economic well-being of families made up of small children and women. These changes, which often thrust a family into a different income class, cannot be uncovered through "snapshot" studies. For this, studies like those being done at the Michigan center are necessary.

The Michigan studies yield solid numerical evidence that documents two major developments affecting millions of families. First, the "moving-picture" evidence coming from these studies reinforces other evidence on the shrinkage of the middle class. Second, they show that significant changes in mobility have taken place, especially during the 1980s. The last decade saw an *increase* in downward mobility and a *decrease* in upward mobility, developments that run counter to deeply held aspects of the American dream.[17]

A quarter-century of research by the Survey Research Center shows that there has been since the mid-1960s a persistent "withering of the middle class." Thomas Smeeding, economics professor at Syracuse University and a key participant in this research, says, "What we are looking at is a permanent decline in the size of the middle class."[18] According to the Michigan study, the proportion of prime-working-age adults (twenty-five to fifty-four years old) living in middle-class households fell from 60 percent in the late 1960s to about 51 percent in the late 1980s, a more drastic decline than shown in table 3-1.[19]

Conservatives rarely show concern about findings of greater inequality, or a shrinkage in the size of the middle class, believing that America's class structure remains highly fluid. The United States, argues Bruce Bartlett, former Treasury official in the Bush administration, has a class structure that won't stay put, which is why the "American people have never sympathized with class warfare."[20] Statistically, a class structure "that won't stay put" means that over time the number of people and families climbing up the income ladder are roughly equal to those who tumble down.

During the late 1960s and the 1970s, according to the Michigan study, this was essentially true—shifts into and out of the middle class canceled each other out. But after 1980, this was no longer the situation. The dynamics of income mobility became more complicated, no longer favoring middle-class stability, or upward mobility for large numbers of families.

At the lower stages of the income ladder, mobility shifts in the 1980s saw more families fall out of middle-class status into the lower income ranges, and fewer families climb up the income ladder from the bottom rungs toward the middle. Specifically, before 1980, according to the Michigan studies, 35.5 percent of low-income individuals moved into middle-income groups, but after 1980, the number dropped to 30.4 percent. This is a 14.4-percent decline in upward mobility after 1980. Until recently, as a *U.S. News & World Report* cover story reported, failure to move upward toward realization of the American Dream was seen as a disturbing aberration, limited largely to families headed by poorly educated single women.[21] Belatedly, it is recognized that upward mobility is no longer possible for millions of American workers. During these same years, fallout from the middle class jumped from 6.2 percent (from 1967 to 1980) to 8.5 percent after 1980, a 37.1-percent increase in downward mobility.[22] The combined effect of these two changes in upward and downward mobility at the lower end of the income scale was to make for more inequality during the 1980s in the distribution of income and swell the ranks of the working poor.

At the upper end of the income ladder, the situation is more complicated. After 1980, the percentage of prime-age men and women moving from middle- to high-income status actually increased, from 6.3 to 7.5 percent. This, as the researchers for the Michigan study said, is the "good news that late 20th-century America offered abundant opportunity for the upper middle class."[23] The bad news, though, is that downward mobility out of the upper-income range is much greater than mobility upward. For the twenty years of the Michigan study (1967–87), 29.7 percent of high-income individuals fell out of the upper income bracket of the Michigan study, while only 6.7 percent of middle-income individuals climbed into the upper bracket. The lower and upper income boundaries for the Michigan study were $18,500 and $55,000 respectively (in 1987 dollars).[24] These are the numbers behind the tragedy of Allen Stenhouse and other "corporate castoffs . . . struggling just to stay in the middle class."[25]

Prime-working-age adults with the greatest chance to move from the middle to the upper class are found in families headed by a person with a college education and well-educated single women. Upward mobility is least for young families—families in which the head was under thirty-five—and for blacks. Downward mobility from the middle to the lower class was greatest for black families, for families headed by a woman, and for families with a head less than thirty-five years old. As might be expected, changes in personal wealth—assets minus debts—followed closely the changes in family income, being greatest for families climbing into either the middle or the upper classes.

The current epoch, the researchers on the Michigan project conclude, is a "time marked by a significant increase in real income and wealth for those with already high incomes and substantial wealth." This would be a desirable outcome if the trend were for upward mobility across the income distribution spectrum, but "large sustained income gains are apparent only for the yachts— not for the tugboats or rowboats."[26]

There is another dimension to mobility that is not explored in the Michigan studies, one that has extremely serious implications for the kind of society toward which America may be moving. This is *occupational* mobility. Involved here is movement between occupations, which usually comes about when children move into occupations that differ from their parents' occupation with respect to both income and status. In an open society with equality of opportunity, upward occupational mobility ought to increase. Gains in occupational mobility would show up in an increase in the number of children who move into occupations above the income and status level of their parents.

This is not happening, according to David Gordon, economics professor at the New School for Social Research. Rather, the reverse is the case, particularly with respect to managerial and professional jobs. Increasingly, according to Gordon, there is similarity between the occupational status of parents and children. This has come about in part because rising tuition, coupled with less public assistance, is closing the college door to many children from low-income families. Families at the top are in much better financial position to give their children the college education that makes possible entry into high-paying jobs in management and the professions. This means, Gordon fears, a more rigid class structure, one in which upward mobility for three-quarters of American families is being squeezed, not only for the families now, but for their children in the future.[27]

A CONCLUDING COMMENT

The 1980s marked a significant break with the past trends. Upper-class families enjoyed large income and wealth gains, while poverty rates remained high and upward income mobility declined among families in the lower class. Many of these families are among the "working poor," trapped in low-pay, low-skill, no-future jobs from which there is no easy escape. The withering of America's middle class is not the stuff of high drama, with the good guys and the bad guys easily identified. It is more like a puzzle with many pieces that must be brought together before a clear picture emerges. Once all the pieces are in place, the picture is one in which, for millions of Americans and their families, the nightmare of downward mobility is a reality. This is a major consequence of the ongoing silent depression. Ultimately, the forces that have battered the middle class over the last two decades touch home at the level of the family, still the most important economic and social unit in American society.

CHAPTER 4

- ●
- ●
- ●
- ●

The Stressed-out American Family

In the 1950s, the word "family" evoked the "Ozzie and Harriet" image, a family in which the father worked, the mother tended the children, the house, and the pets, and they all dwelt together in harmony in middle-class comfort in a colonial house on a tree-lined suburban street. As television advertising and some sitcoms still proclaim, this remains the ideal for many Americans. Reality, though, is different.

As happened with the middle class, the economic and social turbulence of the last two decades brought stress and change to the American family. The speeches at the 1992 Republican convention and the bitter exchange over "family values" during the presidential campaign attest that an intense emotional struggle is going on in America over the definition of the family. Those on the conservative right cling tenaciously to the two-parent family as the cultural norm, the true source of family values in American life. On the liberal left, the demand is for a broader definition, one that recognizes unmarried couples as well as gays and lesbians living together as a family, both morally and legally. Given the intensity of feeling by the participants in the cultural struggle over the "true" nature of the family, the issue is not going to disappear soon.

In the more traditional sense, the family is still the primary unit in American social and economic life, although most families today don't resemble the "Ozzie and Harriet" ideal of the 1950s: in 1990, 83.9 percent of Americans lived in families.[1] As used here, the word "family" is the Census Bureau definition: a group of two or more persons related by *birth, marriage,* or *adoption* who live together. What of the 16.1 percent of people who don't live in families defined this way? They consist primarily of the institutionalized population, members of the armed forces and their families living outside the United States, and persons living alone, people the Census Bureau describes as "unattached individuals."

Because the family and its values are cherished by an overwhelming majority of Americans, family income is a key measure of the economy's real well-being. As we will find, the elderly have been much better off since 1973, the poor are no better off, and the middle class is putting both parents to work with little overall gain in well-being.

THE CHANGING AMERICAN FAMILY

Demographers who study the American family find it convenient to classify families into five categories: families with children under eighteen; married couples with children; single-parent families; nonelderly childless families; and elderly families. Married couples with children and single-parent families are subsets of the first category. Details of changes in families between 1973 and 1990 are shown in table 4-1.

Census Bureau numbers show drastic changes in the American family over the last two decades. Families with children are still in the majority within America, but just barely so. Their numbers increased the least between 1973 and 1990—11.4 percent—for any of the five basic categories of families. Worrisome,

TABLE 4-1   *The Structure of American Families: 1973 and 1990 (in thousands and in percent)*

Type of Family	1973	1990	Percent Change
Total Families	55,053	66,322	20.5%
Families with Children	30,977	34,503	11.4
Percent of Total	56.3%	52.0%	
Married Couples with Children*	25,983	25,410	−2.2
Percent of Total	47.2	38.3	
Single Parents*	4,994	9,093	82.1
Percent of Total	9.1	13.7	
Nonelderly Childless Families	16,489	20,919	26.9
Percent of Total	29.9	31.5	
Elderly Families†	7,540	10,900	44.6
Percent of Total	13.7	16.4	

*Subset of first category, families with children.
†Head of family is over sixty-five.
SOURCES: Bureau of the Census, Current Population Reports, ser. P-60, no. 174, *Money Income of Households, Persons, and Families in the United States: 1990*, p. 56; and ser. P-60, no. 175, *Poverty in the United States: 1990*, p. 20.

too, is the fact that married couples with children are losing ground as a percent of families. Their numbers dropped by 2.2 percent between 1973 and 1990, making them the only type of family that actually declined in numbers over the period. On the positive side, married couples with children accounted for 73.6 percent (in 1990) of families with children. Also, in 1989, according to the Joint Economic Committee of the Congress, 54.5 percent of the nation's population lived in families with children under eighteen.[2] The traditional married couple with children is still the most important type of family in the nation, so its economic well-being is a major determinant of the nation's economic health.

The most disturbing fact coming from the Census Bureau is that the number of single-parent families grew far more rapidly in the 1973–90 period than that of any other type of family: by a staggering 82.1 percent. Women head most single-parent families, one-third of which were below the poverty line in 1990. Further, there has been little progress in lifting these families out of poverty over the last two decades.[3] In 1990, the percentage of single-parent families headed by women in poverty was only 1.2 percentage points below the 1973 figures for such families.

The second-fastest-growing type of family is the elderly one, which increased by 44.6 percent between 1973 and 1990. For a family to be classified as "elderly," one member must be sixty-five years of age or older. The decrease in the incidence of poverty among elderly families in America is one of the great success stories of the post–World War II era. In 1990, the poverty rate for elderly families was 6.4 percent, as compared with a poverty rate for all families of 11.1 percent.[4] Elderly families were clear winners with respect to income gains between 1973 and 1990. This was not so for elderly persons living alone: their poverty rate in 1990 was 24.7 percent, little changed from a decade earlier.

Finally, there are nonelderly families without children, a group that has not grown as fast as either the elderly or the single-parent families, but has significantly outpaced the growth of married-couple families with children. The percentage of nonelderly families without children grew by 26.9 percent between 1973 and 1990, a consequence of postponed marriages, a sharp drop in the birthrate after the baby boom ended (circa 1964), and the emergence of a "yuppie" life style among the most well-to-do of the baby-boomers. These are the major demographic changes that have occurred since 1973. Given the shrinkage in the middle class, plus the changes in the distribution of income between the lower, the middle, and the upper classes, the crucial question is this: what has happened to the income of these different types of families since 1973?

WINNERS AND LOSERS

A second dimension of the changing nature of the American family involves their incomes—what has happened to the incomes of the different categories of families since 1973? In this realm, Census Bureau findings reveal large differences in the percentage by which income in real dollars changed for different types of families (table 4-2). There has been a significant reshuffling of income between the different family types. As has already been established, society's income pie grew more slowly after 1973, but some types of families were more successful than others in increasing the size of their slices.

TABLE 4-2 *Income Growth Between 1973 and 1990 by Type of Family*

Type of Family	Percent Change in Income: 1973–1990*
All Families	5.7%
Families with Children	2.4
Married Couples with Children†	11.1
Single Mothers†	0.7
Nonelderly Childless Families	19.6
Elderly Families	32.8

*In 1989 dollars.
†Subset of families-with-children category.
SOURCE: U.S. House of Representatives, Committee on Ways and Means, *Green Book* (Washington, D.C.: U.S. Government Printing Office, 1992), pp. 1378–81, table 48.

Clearly, top prize in the income-redistribution sweepstakes over the last two decades goes to the elderly families. Their average income grew by one-third over this period (32.8 percent), the highest percentage growth for any of the five types of families being discussed. The elderly have done very well in American society over the past two decades. As *U.S. News & World Report* phrased it in a cover story, "If the 1960s were dominated by youth, the 1980s belong to the older generation," a generation that attained a level "of health and financial independence scarcely imaginable a generation ago."[5]

This success story is not to be explained wholly by the growth in Social Security, as some might be inclined to think. According to the House Ways and Means Committee, income from private sources—primarily property and pension income—grew almost as rapidly for elderly families as did government-transfer income, such as Social Security and Medicare benefits.[6] Many members of the generation that began to reach retirement age in the 1980s were children during the Great Depression, came of age during World War II, and entered the labor force as young adults in the 1940s and 1950s. As Frank Levy and Richard G. Michel point out in their book, *The Economic Future of American Families*, members of this generation were lucky to be in the "right place at the right time."[7] Many entered their most productive years in the work force during the 1950s and 1960s, periods of high employment and strong economic growth. As Levy and Michel also stress, today's retirees accumulated significant amounts of personal wealth, including homes that rose in value faster than prices, before the economy slipped into the doldrums of the last two decades.[8] The downside in the income picture for retired elderly families is the drop in interest rates since the early 1980s. Since 1989 alone, interest rates on short-term certificates of deposit, a favored form of financial "nest egg" for retired men and women, have dropped by almost 50 percent.

The housing experience of Frank and Marion Cava, a retired California couple, was not uncommon for the generation that came of age in the 1940s. In 1973, the Cavas sold for $75,000 the house for which they had paid $29,500 in 1958. With their profit, they paid cash for a $44,000 condominium in an "adult" community where similar units were selling for more than $145,000 in the late 1980s.[9] The ride up the postwar housing escalator put home ownership within the reach of three-quarters of the families in America now classified as elderly.

Nonelderly families without children had the next-highest gain in income between 1973 and 1990. Their income advance was 19.6 percent, significantly higher than the average gain of 5.7 percent for all families. In 1990, the average income for nonelderly families without children was $47,311 (in 1989 dollars), the highest income for any of the five categories of families being examined. The income of this group in 1990 was 47.6 percent higher than the average income for all families, which was $32,063 (in 1989 dollars). Higher earnings for women accounted for most of the income gains that nonelderly families without children experienced. For example, between 1979 and 1989, women's earnings jumped by 27.4 percent, while the earnings of men rose by only 2.3 percent.[10]

Married-couple families with children ranked third in the increase in family income between 1973 and 1990. This group had the second-highest family income in 1990, $43,741 (in 1989 dollars), which was 36.4-percent higher than the average for all families. For this group, nearly all of the income gains between 1979 and 1989 resulted from higher earnings for women (53.8 percent), primarily from mothers already working, rather than more mothers coming into the work force. Men's earnings during this period rose by only 4.0 percent.[11]

Even though nonelderly families without children have the highest family income, and perhaps contrary to popular wisdom, these families do not have the highest percentage of working wives. This distinction belongs to married couples with children. In 1988, 65.0 percent of married women with children under the age of eighteen and a spouse present were working, compared with 50.5 percent for women with no children under the age of eighteen. For mothers with children under the age of six—mostly preschoolers—the rate was 57.1 percent, and for married women with children between fourteen and seventeen, the percentage working climbed to 73.0. Absentee mothers are a fact of life for the overwhelming majority of teenagers in America. Contrast the situation today with what it was in 1947, when only 18.6 percent of women with children under the age of nineteen were in the labor force, and of these, the figure for mothers with children under the age of six was but 12.0 percent.[12] The continued entry of mothers with children into the labor force has been one of the most extensive and, perhaps, socially wrenching changes of the entire post–World War II era.

If we judge "losers" to be families whose income gains were below the average for all families, then single-mother families are the big losers over the last twenty years. Families headed by a woman with no male present make up the overwhelming majority of single-parent families. In 1990, single-mother families equaled 84.8 percent of all single-parent families. Their actual number was 7.7 million, up 67.4 percent from the 4.6 million single-mother families in 1973.[13] Incomes for single-mother families increased by only 0.7 percent between 1973 and 1990. In 1990, the income of these families was $15,036 (in 1989 dollars), only 46.9 percent as high as the average income for all families. During the 1979–89 decade, the earnings of women who head single-parent families increased by 16.1 percent, but this was more than offset by a drop of 27.9 percent in the constant-dollar value of public-assistance (welfare) payments.[14]

Within the single-parent-family category, children are the real losers. In 1990, there were 13.4 million children living in poverty, which was 39.9 percent of the total of 33.6 million persons living below the poverty line in that year. The odds that a child will live in poverty are 4.5 times greater in a single-parent family than in a married-couple family. The sharp growth in the percentage of children living in poverty is the dark side of the success story for elderly families, a development that does not bode well for the nation's future. In 1973, the percentage of children living in families below the poverty line reached a post–World War II low of 14.4 percent. The poverty rate climbed back to 22.3 percent during the 1982–83 recession, and then dropped back to 20.6 percent in 1990.[15] This statistic is the source for the assertion that one child out of every five in America now lives below the poverty line. One major reason for the worsening condition of children has been noted—namely, the 27.9-percent cut in means-tested cash transfers in constant dollars ("welfare" payments) going to single mothers with children between 1979 and 1989.

AGE, EDUCATION, AND RACE

Families with children scored the smallest gains in average real income between 1973 and 1990 as compared with other types of families, but there were other family characteristics that played a significant role in separating winners and losers. In 1989, the Bureau of the Census of the U.S. Department of Commerce published a massive study of family and household income for the years 1947 through 1988. This study, written by Mary F. Henson, an economist with the Census Bureau, analyzed in great detail the impact of a variety of economic, social, and demographic factors on the distribution of income among persons, households, and families.[16] The most important of these are: (1) the age of the family head; (2) the educational level of the family head; and (3) the family's race.

The best and easiest way to analyze and understand how the age and education of the family head and the race of the family affect family income is to use a simple number. That number is the *ratio* of the median income for families having these characteristics to the median income for all families. This ratio tells us whether the median income of a family with a specific characteristic—say, headed by a high-school graduate—is above or below the median income for all families. By comparing changes in these ratios between 1973 and 1990, we can see the effect of the age and education of the family head and the family's race on the family's income, giving us a much more complete picture of which families emerged as "winners" or "losers" between 1973 and 1990 (table 4-3).

The basic story told by the Henson study is one of an increasing polarization among families based on the age and education of the head of the family. Surprisingly—especially in view of the widespread evidence that race relations are getting worse in the nation—the income gap between white and nonwhite families did not enlarge appreciably between 1973 and 1990. How can this be, particularly in view of the worsening conditions in the black ghettos of America's major cities? The answer is that income gains by middle-class blacks offset increases in poverty among black families trapped in urban areas.

Overall, though, there hasn't been any improvement: the income gap between black and white families remains just about where it was two decades ago. Median income of black families in 1990 was 60.6 percent of the median income for white families, compared with 60.3 percent in 1973. For Hispanics, the income gap with white families worsened, going from 72.3 percent in 1973 to 66.3 percent in 1990 (table 4-3). This development resulted from the increased migration of low-skilled Hispanic persons and families into the United States from Mexico and Central America over the last two decades.

Younger families—families in which the age of the nominal head is below thirty-four—are much worse off compared with similar families in 1973. Families whose heads are under twenty-four and also between twenty-five and thirty-four lost ground between 1973 and 1990. For both these groups the income dropped, whereas for families in all other age brackets income rose. The decline in income for families whose heads are under twenty-four was especially sharp. In 1973, the median income of these families was 62.6 percent of the median income for all

TABLE 4-3 *Ratio of Medium Family Income for Families in Specific Categories to Median Family Income of all Families: 1973 and 1990 (in percent)*

Family Category	1973	1990	Percent Change
By Age of Head of the Family			
Under 24 Years	62.6%	45.9%	−26.7%
25 to 34 Years	95.3	89.1	−6.5
35 to 44 Years	111.7	116.2	4.0
45 to 54 Years	118.3	133.4	12.8
55 to 64 Years	99.8	110.4	10.6
Over 65	50.2	70.9	41.2
By Education of the Head of the Family			
Elementary School*	70.5%	51.7%	−26.7%
High School†	103.3	94.6	−8.4
4 Years of College	144.5	154.0	6.6
5 Years or More of College	160.7	180.3	12.2
By Race of Family			
White	104.5%	104.4%	—
Black	60.3	60.6	0.5
Hispanic‡	72.3	66.3	−8.3

*Eight years of schooling.
†Four years of schooling.
‡Persons of Hispanic origin may be of any race.
SOURCES: Bureau of the Census, Current Population Reports, ser. P-60, no. 167, *Trends in Income by Selected Characteristics: 1947 to 1988* (by Mary P. Henson), pp. 56, 63, and 69.

families. By 1990, their incomes were only 45.9 percent of the general median.

Several factors account for the slow deterioration in the economic position of families headed by younger workers. Younger families are much more dependent on wage earnings than on property income, so they suffered particularly from the decline in the real value of money wages over the 1973–90 period. Also, capital income, primarily dividends and interest, grew much more rapidly than did labor income in the high-flying Reagan years.[17] Younger families were not in on the financial boom of the 1980s.

Though the high-paying, unionized jobs in the goods-producing sectors of the economy that disappeared were offset by new jobs in the services, most of the service-sector jobs paid far less than the manufacturing jobs lost. Terry Biddle, a forty-one-year-old resident of Beaver Falls, Pennsylvania, with a wife and three children, went through this cycle. A high-school graduate, he worked in a steel-tubing plant from 1969 until the plant closed in 1987, eventually earning $28,000 plus health insurance for himself and his family. After the tubing plant closed, he delivered pizzas for $3.50 an hour, studied auto mechanics in a local community college, and finally secured a job in a local auto-repair shop. In early 1992, he was earning $18,000 a year, which in inflation-adjusted dollars gives him only about half the purchasing power he had from his factory job.[18]

One of the ways in which younger families cope with low-paying jobs is by working at more than one job. Figures from the Bureau of Labor Statistics estimate between seven and eight million Americans work at more than one job, up from around four million at the end of the 1970s. Randal Bauer, a thirty-two-year-old husband and father in Omaha, in early 1992 quit his job as a finance manager for a car dealership to take on two other jobs. One was full-time with a telemarketing firm, the other part-time with a customer answering service. In total these two jobs, Bauer told an *Omaha World Herald* reporter, paid about the same as what he earned at the car dealership, but took fewer hours.

At the car dealership, declining car sales meant working longer for less commission.[19] The downside of part-time jobs is not only low pay—most are in the service sector—but few fringes benefits, such as health insurance, pensions, or unemployment insurance.

As for the other age groups, families headed by forty-five-to-fifty-four-year-olds continued to have the best incomes. These are the years of peak earning power for most family heads. The ratio for these families of income to overall median income went up by 12.8 percent, a greater gain than for families in any other age bracket except the elderly. It was the latter—families headed by persons sixty-five years old or older—which gained the most. For these families, the ratio of their incomes to median family income jumped by a staggering 41.2 percent between 1973 and 1990! Here is another statistic confirming the substantial progress made by elderly families since 1973. Still, elderly-family incomes remain significantly below the median for all families, 50.2 percent of that median in 1973, and 70.9 percent below in 1990. This is not necessarily bad. Since an elderly "family" usually has just two people with reduced material needs, it would be normal for their income to be below the median income for all families. What is disturbing is that elderly-family income is now greater than that of families whose heads are under twenty-four years of age. In 1973, families headed by persons twenty-four years of age or less had incomes 80.2 percent greater than did elderly families. By 1990, the income of elderly families was 54.4 percent greater than the income of the younger group. Here are the elements for intergenerational warfare.[20]

Perhaps the most alarming development revealed by the numbers from the Henson study is the growing polarization of American families in terms of the educational level of the head of the family. The gap between the college-educated and the elementary-educated, and between the college- and high-school educated, has grown much wider since 1973. Income for a family headed by a person with only an elementary-level education fell from 70.5 percent of median family income in 1973 to 51.7 percent in 1986, a drastic 26.7-percent decline! The same thing happened to families headed by high-school graduates, although the drop was not so severe: 8.4 percent.

Families headed by a college graduate with a four-year degree experienced only a slight increase in incomes. The rise in the ratio of their incomes to the median income was 6.6 percent. Families whose heads had five or more years of college did much better: the increase in the ratio for them was 12.2 percent. These changes reflect a concern widely discussed in the news media—namely, the increased training, education, and skill needed for getting and keeping better-paying jobs. The growing gap between the rich and the poor in America results from differences in education as well as the tax policies of the Reagan years that favored the rich.

To put these changes in further perspective, we can say that in 1973 a family whose head was a four-year-college graduate earned an income 104.8 percent greater than that of a family whose head had only eight years of grammar school. By 1990, the difference was 197.9 percent. In 1973, the family headed by a four-year-college graduate had an income 39.9 percent greater than the family whose head had only a high-school education. By 1990, the difference had grown to 62.8 percent. What is significant is not only the widening of this educational gap, but the fact that the gap widened more because of the deterioration of the incomes of families headed by persons with less than a college education, rather than large gains in the incomes of families headed by college graduates.

BEHIND THE NUMBERS: THE GOOD-JOBS / BAD-JOBS CONTROVERSY

The numbers just discussed underscore two growing income gaps in the American economy—a gap between younger families and older families, and a gap between families because of the education of the family's head. There is more to this matter than simply growth in the gap between the rich and the poor. Involved are some important changes in the demand for different types of labor, changes that arise out of other, primary changes in the character of the American economy.

The mediocre growth record in the median income for all families since 1973 does not present a puzzle. It is a consequence of the slowdown in productivity growth, a development that slowed the rate of growth of wage and salary income for most families. A more complex problem centers on the changes in family income linked to the age and education of the family's head. These stem from broad changes in the basic structure of the economy.

In 1973, slightly more than one-third of young male workers (thirty-four years of age or less) with only a high-school education had jobs in manufacturing, where the wages were about 75-percent higher than for jobs available to men of comparable age and education outside manufacturing.[21] In contrast, in 1973 only 20 percent of college-educated young men, again under thirty-four years of age, worked in the manufacturing sector.

These jobs in manufacturing are the "good" jobs of the good-job / bad-job controversy. A good job is one that pays enough to support a middle-class standard of living—a single-family home, one or more cars, paid vacations, job security with good fringe benefits, including medical care, and an expectation of steady improvement in one's standard of living.

Since 1973, there has been a continued loss of manufacturing jobs in the American economy, which has been especially devastating for the young, non–college-educated male workers. In August 1992, there were 9.9 percent fewer jobs in manufacturing than in 1973, though total jobs in the American economy had grown by 41.0 percent in this period.[22]

The brunt of this loss of manufacturing jobs has been borne by younger, not-so-well-educated workers. According to the research by Levy and Michel, there was a 30-percent drop between 1973 and 1986 in the proportion of male workers under the age of thirty-four with only a high-school education who were employed in manufacturing.[23] Interestingly enough, the proportion of college-educated male workers under the age of thirty-four employed in manufacturing remained constant over this period. This suggests that the demand for workers in manufacturing has been shifting toward those with more education, a development that helps explain the widening gap between families based upon the education of the family head. To put it another way, the "good" jobs available to workers with less than a college education have been slowly slipping away.

What happened to the younger, less-well-educated workers whose manufacturing jobs have been lost? Some, of course, found other jobs in the services sector, but, surprisingly, this shift was small. Levy and Michel found only a 4-percent increase between 1973 and 1986 in the proportion of under-thirty-four male workers with only a high-school education employed in the service sector.[24] Many left the work force; between 1973 and 1986, the proportion of male workers under thirty-four years of age with only a high-school education *not* in the work force jumped by an astonishing 133 percent![25] This is a major explanation for the decline in labor-force participation by male workers after 1973.

In addition, the excess supply of young, uneducated workers widened the wage gap between manufacturing and the kinds of employment in the services sector open to these workers. In 1973, average weekly earnings (in current dollars) in manufacturing were 72.6-percent higher than comparable earnings in retailing, often the refuge of the downwardly mobile. By 1990, earnings in manufacturing were 197.0 percent higher than in retailing.[26]

Because productivity growth in manufacturing recovered in the 1980s while it remained stagnant in the services, the demand for less-skilled labor in manufacturing was reduced even more. The Reagan administration made much of the increase in employment by more than fifteen million people between 1980 and 1988, but glossed over the fact that about half the jobs created in the 1980s were jobs of the kind that Douglas Copeland, author of *Generation X*, a novel of the adventures and misadventures of the twentysomething generation, describes as "McJobs"—low-pay, low-dignity, low-benefit, no-future jobs in the service sector.[27]

The magnitude of the good-jobs / bad jobs problem is reflected in a 1991 Bureau of the Census study on the number of workers with "low earnings," defined by the Census Bureau as annual earnings less than the poverty level for a family of four. In 1964, 24.1 percent of year-round, full-time workers were in low-earning jobs. This percentage figure fell to a postwar low of 12.0 in 1974, but since then, in 1990, it has climbed back to 18.0.[28]

The growing scarcity of good jobs—what *Fortune* magazine (August 24, 1992) describes as "solid middle class jobs, the kind that allow a single worker to be the family breadwinner"—is one of the toughest problems facing the Clinton administration in its first term. The conventional view, expounded by both candidates in the presidential campaign, is that more and better education and job training is the answer.

The truth is, the problem is not so simple. Consider this aspect of the productivity problem analyzed in chapter 2. Between 1973 and 1991, production of goods grew by 42.9 percent, while the number of people employed in goods production fell by 4.3 percent. This means that the problem of slow productivity growth is not to be found in the goods-producing sector. If 4.3 percent fewer workers can produce 42.9 percent more goods, clearly there has been a significant increase in worker productivity.

Now look at services. Between 1973 and 1991, the number of workers employed in the services sector (excluding government) increased by 64.1 percent, while the output of services grew by just slightly more, 66.0 percent. For all practical purposes, there was *no* increase in productivity in the services-producing sector of the economy during this period.[29] Service employment has been growing at a deceasing rate since the 1960s. In the 1960s, it grew at 3.4 percent annually, followed by 3.3 percent in the 1970s, and 2.7 percent in the 1980s. In 1990, the rate dropped to 2.0 percent, and turned negative (-0.5 percent) in 1991. The 1990–91 recession was the first slump since the end of World War II in which there was an actual decline in employment in the services sector. This is why it was a white-collar as well as a blue-collar downturn. The bad news in this is that solving the productivity problem—an absolute must if the nation is to work its way out of the silent depression—may hit service employment over the rest of the century in the same way that goods employment was hit in the last twenty years. This underscores the never-ending dilemma of productivity. Without strong gains in productivity, there cannot be major advances in living standards. But in the short run, productivity gains displace workers, some of whom will always find it difficult to find alternative, well-paying jobs. This is why public policies are needed that will help workers make the transition to new jobs whenever their old jobs are lost because the economy is becoming more productive.

What about education, particularly higher education? Isn't this the answer, especially since there is overwhelming evidence about the economic value of a college education. Unfortunately, the prospects for the college-educated may not be so rosy in the future as they have been in the past. A recent study by two economists in the U.S. Department of Labor, Daniel E. Hecker and Kristina J. Shelley, shows that the percent of college graduates in jobs that don't really require a college degree had almost doubled between 1970 and 1990, from 12 to 20 percent. Further, they expect this figure to rise to 25 percent by 2005.[30] Investing in human capital—especially higher education—will not necessarily lead to more high-paying good jobs, unless at the same time business and government develop policies that will use the skills of a better-educated work force.

Does this mean the Clinton administration has set for itself an impossible task? Not necessarily, but realism demands recognition that the task is far more difficult and complex than the easy rhetoric of a political campaign suggests. In the halcyon days of the Age of Keynes, stimulating the economy by increasing government spending or cutting taxes could be counted on to create good jobs, but this is no longer true. The link between output and good jobs is far less close than it was in the quarter-century after World War II. Perhaps we are facing a situation unprecedented in human history. Modern technology may allow us to produce as much output as needed for a decent standard of life for everyone with far fewer people employed in the conventional way in which we understand and measure employment. This would require, however, breaking the link between work as conventionally defined and income, something that will be difficult to accomplish.

"RUNNING FASTER TO STAY IN PLACE"

Among American families today, married couples with children are usually the most stressed economically. The numbers on age and education help explain this, although they don't tell the whole story. Census figures do not reveal directly the proportion of married-couple families with children headed by someone either under thirty-four years of age or with only a high-school education. If we use percentages that apply to *all* families, it is possible to obtain reasonable estimates of the number of married-couple families with children to which these characteristics of age and education apply. In 1990, for example, 26.1 percent of families were headed by persons under the age of thirty-four, and 38.5 percent by persons with four years of high-school education. Based on these numbers, a reasonable estimate is that about 20 to 25 percent of married families with children are headed by someone under twenty-four who has no more than a four-year high-school education.[31]

What has happened to families in general since the 1970s—sluggish income growth and a sharp increase in inequality—is mirrored in what has happened to married-couple families with children. In January 1992, the Joint Economic Committee of the

Congress published a report on changes during the 1980s in living standards for two-parent families with children, families that
account for 73.6 percent of families with children.[32] The report
does not make for cheerful reading.

Within this group, as in society generally, polarization between
the top 20 percent and the bottom 20 percent worsened. In 1979,
for example, the top fifth of married couples with children had
incomes 4.8 times greater than did families in the bottom fifth.
By 1989, the incomes of the top families were 5.8 times greater,
a widening of the differential by 20.8 percent.[33] Married-couple
families with children in the middle three-fifths gained relative
to the bottom, but by smaller amounts, on the average, than
those at the top. The average gain in real family income for the
middle three-fifths was 5.9 percent, in contrast to a gain of 18.9
percent for families at the top, and a loss of 3.5 percent for families at the bottom.[34]

Since 89 percent of the family income for married couples
with children comes from earnings from work, the economic
welfare of the family depends primarily upon how many hours
the parents work and how much they earn per hour. Bad news
about these two factors emerges from the Joint Economic Committee study. Husbands in four-fifths of these families saw their
hourly wages in constant dollars decline between 1979 and 1989,
by an average of 6.8 percent; only husbands in the top fifth gained,
by 7.8 percent.[35]

The picture is somewhat better for working wives and mothers. Although women in the bottom fifth lost ground in hourly
earnings, working women in the other four-fifths gained. For
women in the two top brackets, the gains were substantial, 20.5
and 27.8 percent respectively.[36] There was also some narrowing
of the hourly-pay gender gap during this period—the difference
between pay for women and for men went from 55 percent in
1979 to 64 percent in 1989. Most of this came because of the
decline in the hourly pay for men, not from significant increases
in the earnings of women.[37]

What really saved the income for the middle three-fifths of married-couple families with children from an actual decline—as happened to families in the bottom fifth—was longer hours of work for the women. Husbands, the Joint Economic Committee study found, did not work significantly more hours in 1989 than they did in 1979. Wives and mothers worked on an average 32 percent more hours in 1989 than in 1979, with the greatest increase—44.7 percent—for working wives and mothers in the bottom fifth.[38] Only in families in the top fifth did the total change in the earnings of wives and mothers result from more pay instead of more hours at work.

Are wives and mothers working by choice or by necessity? The question almost answers itself, given the facts just examined. Wives and mothers work by necessity, the Joint Economic Committee concluded. If choice were the primary reason wives and mothers entered the work force, the wives and mothers in the income bracket having the largest increase in pay would show the greatest increase in hours worked. Higher pay reflects expanded opportunities for women in the world of work, which should pull more wives and mothers into the work force. It didn't turn out this way. The greatest increase in hours on the job went to the income groups in which hourly pay increased the least, or even declined, as happened to the bottom fifth.[39] Thus, economic necessity, not choice and the opportunity for greater personal fulfillment through work, was the major force bringing wives and mothers into the paid labor force.

The reality is that most married-couple families with children find themselves running faster to stay in place. In fact, too many families cannot stay in place—maintain their real standard of living—even though they are running faster. The Joint Economic Committee explains this in two ways. It does so first by looking at changes in the family's *real* wage, and second by adjusting the wage to account for the added costs incurred when wives and mothers go to work.

If a family's total inflation-adjusted earnings in a year rise less than the increase in actual hours worked by members of the family, then the family's *real* wage has declined. When this happens, it takes more running (more hours at work) to stay in place (maintain a given level of *real* earnings). Using this standard alone, the Joint Economic Committee found that the lower 60 percent of married-couple families with children saw their standard of living drop between 1979 and 1989.[40] Even by running more these families were not able to stay in place.

When a wife and mother goes to work, the extra income is not all gravy for the family. Working brings with it added financial costs in addition to more money income. Transportation, child care, meals out, and more taxes are the major expenses a family faces when wives and mothers go to work. Thus, to get a true picture of the contribution to the family's economic well-being that results from a wife and mother's entering the work force, it is necessary, as the accountants say, to *net out* the added expenses from the added income. Doing this makes a bleak picture even bleaker. Citing research based upon the Census Bureau's Consumer Expenditure Survey, the committee says that the standard of living for the bottom 80 percent of married-couple families with children did not improve between 1979 and 1989, despite extra hours in the workplace each year.[41] As the Joint Economic Committee concludes, ". . . stagnation has given a majority of American families only unattractive economic choices," and unless profound changes are taken to raise the rate of growth in wages for both men and women, the "most likely forecast for the coming decade is for continued economic stress on a majority of American families."[42]

ACROSS THE GENERATIONS

A major element in the fading of the American Dream is the growing belief that children today will live less well than their parents, and that, in turn, their children may live even less well. The faith that each generation of Americans will live better than the preceding generation—a faith solidified by the good growth years of the 1950s and 1960s—is eroding for many families.

In 1988, *Time* dramatized the widening economic gulf between generations with a story about Bob and Carol Forrester, a blue-collar California couple, and their three children, Billy (age thirty-four, Peggy (age thirty), and Paul, (age twenty-six).[43] Bob and Carol, neither of whom went to college, were married in 1953, shortly before Bob went to work in a union job in the Los Angeles harbor. Bob Forrester is now a union official; his job in a unionized industry was his ticket into the American middle class. By 1962, the Forresters had three children and owned a three-bedroom house. As was the norm in the 1950s and 1960s, Carol did not work, but stayed home to raise the children. When *Time* did its profile of the Forresters in 1988, Bob was making $40,000 a year, lived in a house whose estimated worth was $300,000, owned two other houses and a lot, and could look forward to a retirement pension of $1,600 a month from his union plus Social Security. Bob Forrester's blue-collar success story was duplicated all across America in the twenty-five years of growth and prosperity that came to Americas after World War II.

For the Forrester children, who, like their parents, opted not to go to college, the economic world has changed drastically. For a while, it appeared that Billy, the oldest, might duplicate his father's success in a unionized industry. In 1979, he went to work "on the boats" in an $11-an-hour union job with full medical, dental, and pension benefits. He was earning $27,000 annually at the time he lost his job. His "good" union job disappeared when the company he worked for broke the union by hiring maritime workers from Louisiana at cheaper wages. With four children to support and house payments to meet, Billy is in business for himself as a gardener, an enterprise that nets him between $10,000 and $20,000 a year, much less than his previous earnungs and benefits.

The economic story for the Forresters' other two children is similar. Peggy, the middle child, is the manager of a retail clothing store, earning $25,000 a year. Two-thirds of her salary, she told the *Time* writer, goes for rent, household, and car expenses. The possibility of owning a house—medium-priced houses in her area were selling for over $180,000 in 1988—lies outside her dreams.[44] Her younger brother, Paul, who drives a delivery truck for a private mail company, lives with his wife in a modest one-bedroom apartment only a few miles from Paul's parents' home. Like his older brother, Billy, Paul keeps hoping to land, through the Longshoremen's Union, one of the increasingly scarce "good" union jobs in the harbor.

The Forresters' story is typical of many middle-class families. For men like Bob Forrester, coming into the labor force equipped with a high-school education in the early post–World War II years, a union job brought near-certain entry into a middle-class way of life. This is no longer the case for millions of the baby-boomer children born into such families—children like those in the Forrester family. Although the "yuppies" are the stereotype for the baby-boomers that fills the press and airways, they are but a tiny minority of the approximately sixty million "boomers" now living. In 1985, twenty-four million members of this 1946–64 population cohort had incomes of less than $10,000 per year; another twenty-five million, with at least a year of college, had incomes above $20,000 but less than $40,000. Yuppie income began at $30,000 for singles and $40,000 for married or living-together couples.[45]

The need for more education and the disappearance of "good" unionized jobs that required only a high-school education in many industries are the basic reasons for this change. The low growth in productivity that has plagued the economy since the early 1970s worsens the problem. Levy and Michel show how a continuation of these trends will play out across the generations. For children with a college education, the future is optimistic, but for those with only a high-school education or less, the picture is far less bright. For example, Levy and Michel examined the case of a father (age fifty-five) and a son (age thirty), both of whom had four years of college. They discovered that in 1986 the son, at age thirty, would be earning about $4,000 (in 1987 dollars) more than his father had earned at age thirty, twenty-five years earlier. This is the type of *intergenerational* upward income mobility for children over their parents' income that the post–World War II generation came to regard as "normal." Looking ahead, Levy and Michel projected that, even at the slower rates of productivity growth that characterized the economy in the 1980s, the college-educated son's income would be $1,700 higher than the best income the father would earn in his lifetime. With a higher rate of productivity growth (1.9 percent instead of 1.25 percent), the son's income in his best year would be $10,000 (in 1987 dollars) greater than the father's in his best year.[46]

It is a different story for a father and son who have only a high-school education. The son's earnings in 1986, at age thirty, would be about $18,000 (in 1987 dollars), only slightly more than his father earned twenty-five years earlier at age thirty. If the low productivity growth of the 1980s continues, the son's peak income will be almost 20-percent less than the peak income of his father. This is what was happening in the Forrester family. Even under the most optimistic scenario—that of productivity growth of 1.9 percent a year between 1986 and 2005—the thirty-year-old high-school graduate's income would just reach that of his father in his best year.[47] Living standards do not remain static, so an income in 2006 that was no larger in real terms than it had been twenty years earlier would mean a much lower standard of living than his father's for the son when he reached his earnings peak. For the twentysomething generation, children of the post-1964 "baby bust," the outlook is even bleaker.

One lesson Levy and Michel draw from their analysis is the fundamental importance of productivity. The expansion of the middle class and the upward mobility that characterized American society in the twenty-five years after World War II depended much more upon rapid economic growth than upon any significant reduction in income inequality among American families.[48]

Actually, the distribution of income remained practically unchanged from 1945 to the early 1970s. It is only within the last two decades that significant changes have taken place, all in the direction of greater inequality.

The numbers examined so far add up to the worst of two bad economic worlds—slower economic growth, and increasing inequality in the distribution of the nation's income. The shrinking of the middle class, in combination with an income pie that is growing much more slowly than people expected, has led to greater polarization in American society. This polarization affects the young and the old, the college-educated and the non-college-educated, the rich and the poor, and the white and the nonwhite. This is the raw material for bitter, divisive conflict in America. If slow economic growth and stagnant real wages continue for the rest of this century, it will take some extraordinarily creative and skilled political leadership to avoid an explosion.

CHAPTER 5

... And the Rich
Get Richer

I n the late afternoon of June 13, 1985, as half the city watched in fascination, a British Airways Concorde circled gracefully before landing at Omaha's Eppley Airport. Yes, Omaha, Nebraska!

The next day, crammed with a hundred excited Omaha and other Nebraska residents, the Concorde took off for its supersonic flight to London, where a fleet of Rolls-Royce limousines waited to convey the Midwesterners to several London luxury hotels for four days of sightseeing, shopping, and parties.

The occasion? Omaha centimillionaire Willy Theisen, founder and recent owner of the nationwide Godfather pizza chain— "I'll make you an offer you can't refuse"—decided to rent the Concorde and take a "few" friends to London to celebrate his fortieth birthday. The *Omaha World Herald* estimated the party cost more than $500,000.

Willy Theisen's Concorde-to-London party was a minor display of wealth in a decade for which President Reagan and First Lady Nancy set the tone at the inaugural balls in 1981. Wealth was chic. If you have it, display it. Not to do so was, well, almost un-American. As the *U.S. News & World Report* said in its September 28, 1981, issue, "Wealth is back in style. Poverty is déclassé. Mink coats are everywhere. . . ." In the 1920s, Calvin Coolidge, whose picture President Reagan displayed prominently in the White House, said, "The business of America is business." In the 1980s, the business of America was to make money fast, letting the world know how much you had made. For a time, the public's appetite for fact, fancy, and trivia about the glitter, the glitzy life, and financial extravaganzas of the Donald Trumps, the Michael Milkens, the Ivan Boeskys, the Carl Icahns seemed insatiable.

With the stock-market crash of 1987, the departure of the Reagans from the White House, and the recession of 1991–92, the bloom, the novelty, the open-mouthed admiration for the newly rich of the 1980s began to fade. " 'Stealth Wealth' Takes the Place of Conspicuous Consumption" was the headline on a *Los Angeles Times* story about the wealthy. Hit by crime, fearing soak-the-rich campaign rhetoric, chastened by shareholder revolts, the rich backed away from flaunting their wealth. In *The Wall Street Journal*, Robert Frankel, the forty-two-year-old head of a local luxury-car empire in Baltimore, mused, "In the '80s there seemed to be an open feeling: Go out there and do it. It's getting ugly now. It's almost to the point where you are embarrassed if you make money. That used to be the American dream."[1]

Beyond the headlines, beyond the public-opinion polls tracking how Americans feel at any moment about the rich in their midst, there is a more sober, enduring reality. While sagging incomes since the early 1970s brought pain and misery to the poor, and squeezed families in the middle, the "fortunate fifth" at the top of the income pyramid enjoyed mega-gains in their income and wealth. As noted by Kevin Phillips, a leading conservative writer and thinker, whose book *The Emerging Republican Majority* strongly influenced the policies of the Nixon administration, this was a major transformation, one in which definitions of the rich changed as radically as happened in the "Gilded Age" of the 1880s and the excesses of the 1920s.[2] What happened at the top—why it happened, who benefited—was not merely another dimension of the silent depression. It was a seismic upheaval in the distribution of wealth and income in America, one that will not be reversed by an anemic recovery from the 1990–91 recession.

From a historical perspective, the massive tilt in wealth and income toward the top is but another act in a political drama that is as old as the republic itself. It is the conflict and emotion that revolve around what William Greider calls "the buried fault line of American politics."[3] This is the question of the distribution of income and wealth—the fundamental issue of who gets what and why. At center stage is the federal government and its policies. Control of the central government is the key to having a major voice in determining the distribution of income and wealth. As with sex in the Victorian era, we know that this is the reality, but we seldom discuss it openly in our politics.

At times, the greed of the privileged at the top becomes excessive enough to bring on a major political reaction. Thus it was with the growth and flamboyant displays of wealth in the 1880s and the 1920s, eras that inspired Bryan populism and the Progressive Era in the 1890s and early twentieth century, and the reform legislation of the New Deal in the 1930s. The unanswered question now is whether the 1990s will see these events unfold once again—a time of greed followed by an era of reform. With the fading of the Cold War, the distribution of wealth and income *could* become the central issue of the 1990s. Yet this is not certain. The victory of Bill Clinton over George Bush in 1992 showed that the nation wanted change, but it is by no means clear whether the desire for change extends to income, wealth, and its distribution. The Clinton administration may nudge the economy somewhat more in the direction of less inequality in income and wealth distribution, although the top economic team in the new administration—Lloyd Bentsen at the Treasury, Leon Panetta at the Office of Management and Budget (OMB), Robert Rubin, head of the new National Economic

Council, plus Alan Greenspan, holdover chairman of the Federal Reserve System—seem to value deficit and debt reduction over income redistribution.

Even when the nation finds itself in one of its infrequent reform eras, there is reluctance to raise bedrock questions about the economic and philosophical legitimacy of the terms on which people own wealth and gain income. Also, given the stranglehold that the top fifth—Galbraith's "contented majority"—has on money, politics, and the economy, the events and mechanisms that might usher in a new reform era are unclear. In the 1930s, it was painfully obvious what had gone wrong—there were far too few jobs to make the economy work. World War II showed that under the right circumstances the government could create enough jobs to bring health to the economy. Now it is not so obvious what has gone wrong, or precisely what the government should do to restore the nation's economic health.

Nonetheless, a major consequence of the silent depression is the extensive upward redistribution of wealth and income that took place in the 1970s and 1980s. This issue is too vital for the health of the economy to remain forever on the back burner of our politics. Someday the American body politic will have to face the troubling question of "How rich is too rich?" If the matter of income and wealth distribution is to be brought out of the closet and placed upon the political agenda, public understanding of how drastically income and wealth have been redistributed toward the favored few at the top since the 1970s is an essential first step. So let's take a look at these issues.

HOW WE CUT UP THE INCOME AND WEALTH PIES

Sometimes there is confusion between income and wealth, even though the two are closely related, and measured in the same way—in money. Wealth is what we own at any particular time—measured in its money value—whereas income is the amount of money we get over a period of time—a week, a month, or a year. Wealth can be likened to the amount of water in a reservoir at any moment, income to the flow of water into the reservoir. When water leaves the reservoir through use or evaporation, the amount will change. Using the water in the reservoir is analogous to using our income through spending. If we spend less than our income, our wealth will grow, just as the water level in a reservoir will rise if less water flows out than flows in. Over the past several years, most people have probably seen the dramatic television pictures showing how many vital California reservoirs practically dried up because of drought—too little inflow of water from the streams, and too much outflow for household use, growing crops, and keeping grass green.

This simple analogy between water in a reservoir and wealth holds for a nation, but not necessarily for the individual and the family. A nation gets "wealthy" by merely not using up—spending—all of its income. The income of a nation is the actual goods and services produced by its citizens. Like nations, individuals and families get wealthy by not spending all their income (by saving), but they can become wealthy in other ways. The most common road to wealth is inheritance—being lucky enough to have chosen the right parents or grandparents. About 50 percent of personal wealth comes from inheritance, according to the scanty evidence available on how people get wealthy.[4] Capital gains are another source of wealth. The usual avenue is starting a new business, having it grow rapidly in its early years, and then selling it at a price far greater than the original investment. This was a common route to great wealth in the exploding world of electronics during the 1970s and 1980s. Getting wealthy by starting a business is no sure thing. Most small businesses fail. The laws of chance largely determine which businesses succeed and confer great wealth on their creators through capital gains.[5] Finally, lotteries make a lucky few people wealthy. Here the chances of success are infinitesimally small, but the hope nourished by millions of winning big someday keeps many states in the lottery business.

Measuring how the income and wealth pies are sliced—or, technically, the distribution of income and wealth—is not free of controversy, although there is general agreement on how it should be done. The disagreement comes over how to measure income or wealth, and what the results mean once measurements are made. As noted in chapter 3, the most common technique is to divide persons, households, or families into five groups of equal size (quintals), and then calculate how much of the nation's total income or measured wealth goes to or is owned by each fifth. Comparisons over time will tell us whether the slices of the income-and-wealth pie are becoming more equal in size, less equal in size, or unchanged in size.

THE DISTRIBUTION OF INCOME

The most complete set of numbers on the distribution of income is from the Bureau of the Census, which began compiling distribution figures in 1974. Census Bureau figures include money income from all sources except capital gains, earnings up to $299,999, and lump-sum receipts of money from inheritances and insurance settlements. The Census Bureau figures are before-tax income. The distribution of after-tax income is calculated by the Congressional Budget Office and the Committee on Ways and Means of the House of Representatives.

Numbers from the Commerce Department show that since World War II there have been two major changes in how we are cutting up the income pie (table 5-1). Between 1947 and 1970, there was a mild decline in inequality. While the total size of the pie was growing, families in the lower four-fifths got a slightly larger slice of the pie *relative* to those in the top 20 percent. This is another bit of evidence as to why during the first two decades after World War II nearly every family felt good about its economic position. The rising tide of income growth was lifting all boats! Economists measure inequality by a number called the "Gini" coefficient, a measurement technique developed by an Italian economist, C. Gini, shortly before World War I. A decline in this number means less inequality; an increase, more inequality. Between 1947 and 1970, the Gini index dropped by 6.1 percent, which means that the distribution of income became slightly more equal.

After 1970, this changed, as table 5-1 demonstrates. Between 1970 and 1990, families in the lower three-fifths of the income-distribution scale lost ground, families in the fourth quintal from the bottom held their own, and families in the top 20 percent scored substantial gains. In percentage terms, the share of income

TABLE 5-1 *The Distribution of Money Income Among American Families in Selected Years: 1947–90 (in percent)*

Year	Lowest Fifth	Second Fifth	Third Fifth	Fourth Fifth	Top Fifth	Top 5 Percent
1947	5.0%	11.9%	17.0%	23.1%	43.0%	17.5%
1950	4.5	12.0	17.4	23.4	42.7	17.3
1955	4.8	12.3	17.8	23.7	41.3	16.4
1960	4.8	12.3	17.8	24.0	41.3	15.9
1965	5.2	12.2	17.8	23.9	40.9	15.5
1970	5.5	12.2	17.6	23.8	40.9	15.6
1973	5.5	11.9	17.5	24.0	41.1	15.5
1975	5.5	11.8	17.6	24.1	41.1	15.5
1980	5.2	11.5	17.5	24.3	41.5	15.3
1985	4.7	10.9	16.8	24.1	43.5	16.7
1990	4.6	10.8	16.6	23.8	44.3	17.4

SOURCE: Bureau of the Census, Current Population Reports, P-60, no. 162, *Money Income of Households, Families, and Persons in the United States: 1987*, table 12; no. 174, *Money Income of Households, Families, and Persons in the United States: 1990*, table B-5.

going to the top fifth rose by 8.3 percent, the share going to the lower three-fifths fell by 3.7 percent, and the share of the fourth fifth from the bottom was unchanged. Families at the very top of the income pyramid—the upper 5 percent—saw their share of total money income jump from 15.6 percent in 1970 to 17.4 percent in 1990, an 11.5-percent gain in their *relative* position. As noted in chapter 2, in the 1970s and 1980s the size of the total pie—the nation's total output—grew more slowly than it did from 1947 to 1990.

Between 1970 and 1990, the Gini index rose by 12.1 percent, indicating a substantial increase in inequality. In short, what we had in the 1970s and 1980s was a time when the pie grew more slowly, but when families at the top got *relatively* bigger slices of the pie. The rising tide was lifting the yachts, but not the rest of the boats.

Actual dollar income received by families offers a more vivid picture of the growing gap between families at the top and families at the bottom. In 1970, the average income of a family in the bottom fifth was $10,176 (in dollars measured in 1990 purchasing power). This income was only 13.3 percent as high as the average income of $76,544 for a family in the top fifth of the income scale. It was only 8.7 percent as high as the average income of $116,555 enjoyed by a family in the top 5 percent.

By 1990, twenty years later, the income of a family in the lowest fifth had shrunk by 3.4 percent to $9,833. This was but 10.4 percent of the average income of $94,404 for a family in the highest fifth. Families in the "fortunate fifth" enjoyed a 23.3-percent gain in income over this period. By 1990, the income of families in the lowest fifth had slipped downward to only 6.6 percent of the average income of $148,124 for families in the favored top 5 percent. These families saw their incomes leap upward by 27.1 percent between 1970 and 1990.

There is yet another way to look at how the slicing of the income pie has changed since 1970. In the latter year, there were 2.6 million families in the top 5 percent. The total income received by these families ($304.3 billion) was equal to 88.3 percent of the total income received by 40 percent of the families at the bottom ($344.7 billion). By 1990, however, the total income received by the 3.3 million families in the top 5 percent was $491.2 billion, which was larger by 12.9 percent than the total income of $434.9 billion going to the bottom 40 percent of American families.[6]

TAXES AND THE DISTRIBUTION OF INCOME

What about taxes? Don't they make the distribution of income somewhat less equal? Isn't the federal tax system *progressive*, designed to lessen inequality by taking more from the rich than the poor? This is how many people think that, in principle, the federal tax system works. Reality is different.

The major source for after-tax income numbers is the *Green Book*, a massive compendium on federal taxes and spending published in the spring of each year by the Committee on Ways and Means of the U.S. House of Representatives.[7] There are also important differences between the *Green Book* measures of family income and those used by the Census Bureau. The major ones are that the *Green Book* figures contain an adjustment for family size, and define families to include single persons living alone, who are *not* included in the Census Bureau definition of a family. Both Census Bureau and *Green Book* numbers are essential for getting a complete picture of how income is distributed in America.

Before-tax figures from the *Green Book* show a greater concentration of income at the top—the upper 20, 5, and 1 percent—both in 1977 and 1989—than do Census Bureau numbers. According to the Census Bureau, the top 5 percent of families received 15.7 percent of total family income in 1977, and 17.9 percent in 1989. For these same years, the *Green Book* numbers show the top 5 percent of families getting 20.1 percent of income in 1977 and 26.0 percent in 1989. Why the difference? One reason is that the *Green Book* includes income from capital gains, which is highly concentrated among wealthy families. It also counts specific earnings of more than $299,999, whereas in the Census Bureau calculations an individual or a family with an income of more than $299,999 is recorded as earning only $299,999, not what is actually earned. (Table 5-2 gives the details.)

Two findings emerge from an examination of the *after-tax* income distribution data found in the *Green Book*. The first is that the distribution of after-tax income is slightly more equal than the distribution of before-tax income. For example, in 1989, the upper 20 percent of families (as defined by the *Green Book*) got 51.7 percent of before-tax income. After taxes, they got 49.7 percent, a 3.9-percent drop in their relative share. For the lowest 20 percent of families, income shares in 1989 changed from 3.7 percent of before-tax income to 4.4 percent of after-tax income, a relative gain of 18.9 percent. This is the way a progressive tax system is supposed to work, but, as the next section will show, it results more from the spending policies than the tax policies of the federal government.

Of greater significance is a second finding, which shows that, overall, *after-tax* income was more concentrated in 1989 than it was in 1977. When you compare after-tax incomes over the period 1977–89, there were significant percentage *declines* in the share of income going to the bottom four-fifths of families in America, and significant, even spectacular *increases* in the relative size of the income pie going to families at the top. Whereas families in the lower four-fifths lost ground between 1977 and 1989, families in the top fifth increased their share of after-tax income from 44.0 to 49.7 percent, a 12.9-percent gain in their relative share. For the top 1 percent of families, the gain in the relative size of their piece of the after-tax income pie was a dazzling 69.9 percent (table 5-2).

Again the question is, why has this happened? How can the numbers show, on the one hand, that the tax system works the

TABLE 5-2 Before- and After-Tax Income Shares for Families: 1977 and 1989 (in percent)

Year	Lowest Fifth	Second Fifth	Third Fifth	Fourth Fifth	Top Fifth	Top 5%	Top 1%
Before-Tax Income							
1977	4.9%	10.6%	15.7%	22.5%	46.6%	20.1%	8.7%
1989	3.7	9.3	14.6	21.4	51.7	26.0	13.0
Percent Change in Relative Share: 1989/1977							
	−24.5	−12.3	−7.0	−4.9	10.9	29.4	49.4
After-Tax Income							
1977	5.7%	11.6%	16.3%	22.8%	44.0%	18.5%	7.3
1989	4.4	10.1	15.2	21.6	49.7	24.7	12.4
Percent Change in Relative Shares: 1989/1977							
	−22.8	−12.9	−6.7	−5.3	12.9	33.5	69.9

SOURCE: U.S. House of Representatives, Committee on Ways and Means, Green Book (Washington, D.C.: U.S Government Printing Office, 1992), pp. 1519, 1520.

way a progressive system is supposed to work, and that after-tax income is getting more unequal? One part of the answer lies in faster growth in income from property—interest, dividends, rents—in the 1980s than in income from work. Much more important, however, is the effect of the 1977, 1981, 1983, and 1986 changes in personal and corporate income and Social Security tax rates. These changes eroded progression in federal personal and corporate income taxes, but increased the regressive effect of Social Security (payroll) and federal excise (sales) taxes.

What counts for any family is the "effective" rate of taxation—the percent of the family's income actually paid in taxes. Between 1977 and 1992, the effective rate for all federal taxes combined declined for the lowest fifth of families, increased for the second, third, and fourth quintals (fifths), and dropped for families in the top fifth. For families at the very top—the 5-percent and 1-percent levels—the drop in effective rates was large—7.5 percent and 17.5 percent respectively.[8]

These changes in effective tax rates led to extremely large income gains for families at the top, as shown in table 5-4. According to the House Ways and Means Committee, tax savings in 1992 for families in the upper-1-percent income bracket totaled $41,886, a result of the drop in the effective tax rate for these families from 35.5 percent in 1977 to 29.3 percent in 1992 (table 5-3). In contrast, a family in the lowest fifth gained but $57 from these changes in tax rate. Families between the lowest fifth and the top fifth paid more in taxes on their 1992 incomes than they would have paid at the overall effective tax rates in effect in 1977.[9]

The reason for the extraordinarily large gains in income for the superrich between 1977 and 1992 compared with all other income groups is three major tax changes. First, there was a decline in the effective rate of the personal income tax for families in the top 1 percent, from 25.2 percent to 21.2 percent, a greater proportional change than for any other income group. Second,

TABLE 5-3 *Effective Tax Rate for Families for All Federal Taxes (in percent)*

	1977	1992*
Lowest Fifth	9.3%	8.6%
Second Fifth	15.4	15.6
Third Fifth	19.5	19.7
Fourth Fifth	21.8	22.2
Top Fifth	27.2	26.8
Top 10%	28.8	27.7
Top 5%	30.6	28.3
Top 1%	35.5	29.3

*Estimated.
SOURCE: U.S. House of Representatives, Committee on Ways and Means, *Green Book* (Washington, D.C.: U.S. Government Printing Office, 1991), p. 1299.

since 1977, Social Security taxes rose from 6.5 to 8.9 percent of family income, an increase felt heavily by low- and middle-income families, but having little impact upon family incomes at the very top. Finally, corporate taxes dropped between 1977 and 1992 from 3.9 to 2.3 percent of family income, a change of major benefit to the top 1 percent of families, because ownership of stock is heavily concentrated in this group. The federal government taxes corporate profits much less heavily now than in 1977.[10]

In sum, numbers from the best sources confirm what anecdotal evidence in the press and newsmagazines shows—the rich really have been getting richer, much richer. If what has happened recently to the distribution of income is seen as a horse race, it was one with a reverse handicap. The most disadvantaged entrants—the poorest families—started the race farthest behind, and ended even farther back than when they started. A factor that might have evened the odds—taxes—didn't help.

TABLE 5-4 *Net Increases or Decreases in Federal Taxes Between 1977 and 1992 (in dollars and in percent)*

Income Group	1992 Income	1977 Tax Rate	Tax*	1992 Tax Rate	Tax*	Difference
Bottom Fifth	$ 8,132	9.3%	$ 756	8.6%	$ 699	$ -57
Second Fifth	20,094	15.4	3,094	15.6	3,135	41
Third Fifth	31,970	19.5	6,234	19.7	6,298	64
Fourth Fifth	47,692	21.8	10,397	22.2	10,588	191
Top Fifth	112,652	27.2	30,641	26.8	30,191	-450
Top 5%	230,936	30.6	70,666	28.3	65,355	-5,311
Top 1%	675,589	35.5	239,834	29.3	197,948	-41,886

*1977 and 1992 effective tax rates are applied to estimated 1992 income by income class.

SOURCE: Updated data supplied by Committee on Ways and Means, House of Representatives, Washington, D.C.

HOW THE FEDERAL
GOVERNMENT CHANGES INEQUALITY

If the federal government, through its tax policies, has not made the slices of the income pie much more equal, one might legitimately ask whether Washington does *anything* of consequence to lessen inequality. The answer is yes. Government makes a difference—a big difference—but this is primarily because of income that the federal government transfers to lower-income families than because of the income it taxes away from families at the top. Federal spending that provides income directly to individuals or families is called "transfer spending," of which Social Security, welfare checks, and unemployment compensation are probably the best-known examples. These are cash transfers, but transfers also can be in noncash form, as with Medicare or Medicaid benefits.

In 1988, the Bureau of the Census undertook the most complete study ever done of the impact of *both* taxes and transfers on the distribution of income to American households.[11] What the study shows is the distribution of income by fifths—the usual format for distribution studies—to American households for three key measures of income, as seen in table 5-5. The first of these three is money income generated in the private sector, labeled "market income." The second is market income *minus* all federal and state income taxes and Social Security taxes. This is called "after-tax income." The third and most crucial measure is after-tax income *plus* all federal cash and noncash benefits, defined as "net income." This last measure shows the combined effect of income and Social Security taxes and transfer payments on market income. The main purpose of the Census Bureau study is to show the average dollar value of each of these three types of income received by households in each quintal (fifth), and also show the share of the total income of each type received by households in that quintal.[12] A word of caution. These numbers are for 1986 only—they are a "snapshot" picture for a particular

TABLE 5-5 *Income Distribution by Households: 1986 (in dollars and in percent)*

Income by Definition	Lowest Fifth	Second Fifth	Third Fifth	Fourth Fifth	Top Fifth
Average Income in Dollars					
Market Income	$1,563	$11,734	$23,391	$37,064	$81,813
After-Tax Income	1,445	10,749	20,218	31,149	64,352
Net Income	6,805	15,258	23,186	33,213	66,107
Net Change	$5,242	$ 3,524	−$ 205	−$ 3,851	−$15,706
Distribution of Income in Percent					
Market Income	1.0%	7.6%	15.1%	23.9%	52.5%
After-Tax Income	1.1	8.4	15.8	24.4	50.3
Net Income	4.7	10.6	16.0	23.0	45.7
Net Change*	3.7%	3.0%	0.9%	−0.9%	−6.8%

*In percentage points.
Source: Bureau of the Census, Current Population Reports, ser. P-60, no. 164-RD-1, *Measuring the Effect of Benefits and Taxes on Income and Poverty: 1986*, December 1988, pp. 18, 19, table 2.

time. Thus, no generalization is possible about how the picture has changed over time.

Two major conclusions can be derived from this landmark Census Bureau study.

First, if we could wave a magic wand and get government entirely out of the business of influencing the distribution of

income—something that many conservatives would like to do—
the relative sizes of the pieces of the income pie would be far
more unequal than they are now! In 1986, market-determined
income was fifty-two times greater for households in the "fortunate fifth" than for those in the bottom 20 percent. The income
that an average household in the lowest fifth drew from the market in 1986 was $1,563; that of a household in the top 20 per-
cent, $81,813.[13] If unrest is growing over the current distribution,
imagine what might happen if *all* income were distributed on the
basis of the "impersonal market forces" beloved by many economists.

Second, the study shows clearly that the major way in which
the federal government has a major impact on the distribution
of income is by transferring income to households and families,
not by taxing them. The distribution of income after taxes is not
much changed from the distribution of income before taxes
(remember, the taxes involved are federal and state income taxes
and Social Security taxes, which account for the bulk of taxes
collected at both the federal and the state levels). Income after
taxes for households in the top fifth of the income scale is still
enormously larger than income in the lowest fifth—44.5 times
larger, in fact.[14]

What really makes a difference—a big difference—in how
the income pie is sliced is the transfer of income in both cash
and noncash form by the federal government to persons and families. After both taxes and transfers are taken into account, net
income for households in the top fifth is only 9.7 times greater
than the income of households in the bottom fifth. In dollars,
the average income for households in the lowest fifth was $6,805,
in contrast to the average of $66,107 in the top fifth. Overall,
the combined effect of taxes and transfers increased household
incomes at the bottom by $5,242 and decreased those at the top
by $15,706 (table 5-5). The lesson in this is that transfers may
be a much more effective—and probably more popular—route to

reducing inequality than taxes. As I will show later, the implications of this for effective tax reform are far-reaching.

THE DISTRIBUTION OF WEALTH

The Federal Reserve and its chairman, Alan Greenspan, are often in the news, but usually what the "Fed" says pertains to arcane topics like the discount or federal-funds interest rates and other monetary minutiae found on the financial pages. Not so in April 1992, when a report co-authored by a senior economist in the Fed and a mathematical statistician from the Internal Revenue Service made front pages across the nation. "Fed Gives New Evidence of 80's Gains by Richest" was a headline typical of the way the story played in many newspapers.[15]

The report itself is complex and technical, not the stuff for light bedtime reading. Still, the basic findings of the Fed researchers are clear as a bell. Between 1983 and 1989—the best of the Reagan years—the share of household net worth owned by the top 1 percent of households jumped from 31.5 percent to 37.0 percent, a 17.5-percent increase in their comparative position. The share of net worth owned by the next 9 percent below the 1 percent at the very top dropped by 11.1 percent, from 35.1 percent to 31.2 percent. Ownership of net worth by the remaining 90 percent of households fell from 33.4 percent to 31.8 percent, a relative decline of 4.8 percent.[16] Net worth is the estimated value of financial assets owned by households, including equity in homes, plus automobiles, minus total indebtedness. Thus, the sharp increase in the share of income going to families at the top is more than matched by an even sharper increase in the share of net wealth owned by an even smaller number of families—the 1 percent at the very top! These findings from the banker-dominated Federal Reserve System lend enormous weight to the argument that the 1980s saw especially lopsided growth in the disparities in both income and wealth between people at the pinnacle of income and wealth and the rest of the population.

The 1989 figure showing that the top 1 percent of households owned 37.0 percent of the nation's financial net worth is not reassuring. In 1929, the comparable figure was 36.3, a mere 0.7 of a percentage point below the new peak for wealth concentration in the United States. This percentage—the share of net wealth owned by families at the very top of the income-and-wealth pyramid—is not especially stable. Given the degree of concentration in the ownership of common stock (see below), the top 1 percent's share of total wealth is influenced strongly by fluctuating values in share prices on the nation's stock exchanges.

After the Great Crash of 1929, the percentage declined to a low of 20.8 in 1949, primarily because of the impact of New Deal legislation and wartime tax rates. Since 1949, the trend in the share of net wealth owned by the top 1 percent of families has been climbing back to the levels of the 1920s. In the aftermath of the 1929 crash, Marriner Eccles, chairman of the Federal Reserve during most of the New Deal era, speculated that the depression may have been caused by the "giant suction pump" of maldistribution, the result of policies that pulled more and more income into fewer hands.[17] Is such a suction pump at work today?

Remember the Gini coefficient, the number that tells us whether the distribution of income is getting more or less unequal? Gini numbers are also computed for the distribution of wealth—that is, net worth. Between 1983 and 1989, the Gini coefficient for the distribution of wealth rose by 2.1 percent, indicating more inequality in the distribution of wealth. Of more significance is the actual size of the Gini number for both income and wealth. In 1983, the Gini number for income distribution was .414; the number for wealth distribution was .777. By 1989, the Gini number for income distribution had risen to .428, and for wealth distribution to .793. The higher the number, the greater the amount of inequality in the distribution of both income and wealth. The fact that in 1983 and 1989, and in other years as well, the Gini number was much higher for wealth than for income tells us that the distribution of wealth is much more unequal than the distribution of income.

Inequality in income and inequality in wealth usually move together. In 1977, the top 1 percent of households got 7.3 percent of the income, whereas in 1983 the top 1 percent owned 31.5 percent of the nation's financial wealth. By 1988, the top 1 percent had increased their income share to 12.8 percent, and their share of net worth to 37.0 percent. Income and wealth interact strongly with each other. The greater one's share of income, the easier it is to increase one's share of wealth, and the greater one's share of wealth, the higher will be one's share of income. Once the ownership of wealth reaches a kind of "critical mass"—a level at which the income generated by wealth begins to exceed what any single person or family can consume or use—the "magic" of compound interest can ensure the accumulation of wealth practically without limit! There is no guarantee, of course, that such a process will continue through succeeding generations. Although most members of the Vanderbilt family attending a reunion in Nashville, Tennessee, in 1991 were from the upper middle class, the critical mass of wealth accumulated by their ancestor Cornelius had long since dissipated. Stories in the popular press about the squandering of inherited wealth show there is some truth in the popular saying "From shirtsleeves to shirtsleeves in three generations." Nonetheless, the concentration of wealth continues to increase.

Information on the ownership and distribution of wealth is much more sketchy than information on the distribution of income. There is no government agency like the Census Bureau responsible for collecting and publishing periodically figures on the amount of wealth owned by American families. What we do know, sketchy as it is, comes from a handful of classic academic studies, or occasional reports from the Federal Reserve System, based upon periodic surveys of consumer finances.[18] Perhaps it is as William Greider suggests, that our political leaders fear that the "hard facts of who owned capital might excite class jealousies or raise questions about the system for which they had no answers."[19]

What we know about the distribution of wealth shows not only that net wealth in the United States is highly concentrated, but also that the vast majority of American families and households own little wealth. According to information in the 1992 *Green Book*, 66.5 percent of the wealth owned by families in the lower 90 percent of families was real estate, and of this the overwhelming proportion (85.8 percent) was equity in the family home. Money in checking and savings accounts, CDs, and money-market funds accounted for the next-largest form of family wealth (13.3 percent), followed by automobiles (6.8 percent). Families in the lower 90 percent had only 3.4 percent of their financial assets in stocks and bonds. The notion that stock ownership is widespread in America—an idea once touted as "people's capitalism"—is largely false.[20]

Aside from equity in homes and the cash value of life-insurance policies, most of the common forms in which financial wealth is held are even more concentrated than total net worth. For example, in 1989 the top 1 percent of families owned 49.4 percent of common stocks and 78.9 percent of bonds, public and private. The lower 90 percent owned only 14.6 percent of stocks and even less of bonds, 6.5 percent. Of business assets, 61.9 percent were owned by the top 1 percent, and another 29.1 percent by the next 9 percent of families, leaving only 9.0 percent owned by the lower 90 percent of families. The latter owned 46.2 percent of real estate, but, as already noted, the bulk of this was equity in owner-occupied homes. The lower 90 percent of families owned only 20 percent of nonresidential real estate. As for life insurance, 60.5 percent of the cash value of policies is owned by the lower 90 percent of families. The latter fact is not particularly significant, since the cash value of life-insurance policies accounted for only 1.4 percent of financial wealth in 1989.[21]

WHY IS THE DIVISION OF
INCOME AND WEALTH SO UNEQUAL?

The question why the distribution of income and wealth is so unequal is one for which the economists have never had a satisfactory answer. This does not mean that they have nothing to say on the subject—they have had, and continue to have, much to say about how society cuts up its income and wealth pies. Unlike most other topics in economics, what is lacking is a basic *theory*, an agreed-upon explanation of *why* income and wealth are distributed in the way that they are. There is no general economic principle that explains why unfettered market forces deliver more than half the income to one-fifth the nation's families, or why the top 1 percent of families own 37 percent of the nation's financial net worth. As a distinguished Dutch economist has said, "Not a single theory has so far succeeded in sorting out how the high incomes come about."[22] Textbooks in economics describe why different individuals command different wages, but you will search them in vain for a set of principles that *explains* why market forces produce such unequal outcomes. No modern-day Keynes has appeared on the scene to do for income-and-wealth distribution what the real-life Keynes did for output and employment in the 1930s—give the profession and the public a general theory that explained the ups and downs of the economy.

One reason, perhaps, is that it is not often in the United States that the basic issue of who gets what and why is at the forefront of public concern. Society's changing climate of opinion strongly influences economics, in spite of its claim to objectivity as a science. From the 1930s through the 1960s, economists, like the public generally, tended to look with favor on government, seeing it as a means to make life less harsh for families on the lower rungs of the economic ladder. Lyndon Johnson's Great Society and War on Poverty were the high points for the faith that the national government, when properly motivated and managed, could make a real difference in the well-being of the individual and the individual's family. The bitter divisions that erupted over the Vietnam War and the near-runaway inflation of the early 1970s destroyed much of this confidence in government—in the public generally, and among economists in particular. For the last two decades, the climate of opinion among mainstream economists has largely mirrored the antigovernment, antitax, and promarket views of the voting public that put the Reagan and Bush administrations in power.

The strongly proactivist Clinton administration is led by a president the *Los Angeles Times* described as a "policy wonk." This phrase, the *Times* hastened to add, was meant as a compliment, because it describes a person deeply immersed in the issues. If success comes to the Clinton administration, it is reasonably certain that professional economic opinion will swing back to a less promarket stance. What is less certain, though, is whether the reaction against the excesses of the 1980s will lead in the 1990s to any searching examination by Americans and their political leaders, including the Clinton administration, into the painful and politically explosive questions involving the terms on which the "market" delivers income to persons at different levels in our society. Americans are curiously ambivalent about the rich in our midst, at times envious and at other times openly admiring. The surge of Texas billionaire Ross Perot in the spring of 1992 to popularity as an independent presidential candidate testifies to this. As a recent cover story on the rich in the *U.S. News & World Report* also pointed out, not only do most Americans "admire and respect the rich," but many believe that the rich earned their incomes. Public-opinion polls, the article went on to say, show strong hostility to the idea that government ought to play a role in equalizing incomes. Besides, the belief that through hard work one can become rich remains strong, although this aspect of the American Dream has been badly battered by the economic stagnation of the last two decades.[23]

Conservative politicians like Presidents Reagan and Bush

skillfully exploited this ambivalence, deflecting the anger and frustration of the middle class away from the rich and toward government itself as the source of their economic difficulties. In an era of near-stagnant real incomes for four-fifths of America's families, it has been comparatively easy for skilled wordsmiths to picture government as the villain, taxing the hard-pressed middle class to lavish benefits on the poor, many of whom are black and "undeserving." It is instructive that, in the aftermath of the Los Angeles riots in the spring of 1992, the first instinct of the White House was to blame the Great Society programs of the 1960s. President Bush, through his spokesmen, subsequently backed off from this extreme position, but not until he had made his point. The strategy was that of a defense lawyer who makes a point to a jury even though he knows it will be stricken from the record.

The tactic of creating an implicit alliance between the rich and the middle class based upon the fear of crime, a fading empathy for the poor, and antitax and antigovernment rhetoric has been a major means by which those at the top—the "fortunate fifth"—have dominated the political process for the last twenty years. In the spring of 1992, there was some evidence that this ploy would not be so successful in the 1992 presidential election as it had been in previous contests, although the Democrats did not go so far as to make income-and-wealth distribution a major issue in the campaign. What did happen was that newspapers and newsmagazines increasingly carried stories—often on the front page or as cover stories—about the growing gap in income and wealth between those at the top and at the bottom.

Statements by MIT economist Paul Krugman to the effect that some 60 percent of the income growth between 1977 and 1989 went to the upper 1 percent of families stirred up a hornet's nest of controversy, involving then presidential candidate Bill Clinton, conservative economists from the staff of the congressional Joint Economic Committee, *The New York Times, The Wall Street Journal,* and even the director of the Congressional Budget Office.[24] The increasing publicity given to reports on income-and-wealth distribution—ranging from arguments over the meaning of the CBO numbers on income distribution to the dry findings of the Federal Reserve System on the growing concentration of wealth—touched a sensitive nerve among conservatives. Conservative think tanks such as the Center for the Study of American Business at Washington University, the Heritage Foundation, and the Hudson Institute mounted aggressive counterattacks, designed to show that Census and other figures on income distribution, including the Fed's findings, drastically overstated the gains in income and wealth made by the top during the 1980s at the expense of the rest of the population.[25] Whether these developments foreshadow enough of a rise in public consciousness concerning income-and-wealth distribution to generate serious discussion of this "buried fault line of American politics" remains to be seen. If there is to be any such serious *political* discussion, the Clinton administration will have to lead the way. At this writing, there is no clear indication that President Clinton and his administration will venture into this sticky territory. What does seem certain is that the smoldering discontent that lies behind the numbers—the Los Angeles riots were described by some observers as a class conflict as much as a racial conflict—cannot be kept off the political agenda indefinitely.

This brings the discussion back to the key question raised in this section: Why *is* the division of income and wealth so unequal? What do we really know, both historically and more recently, about the causes of this inequality? It seems that, as far as we can peer into antiquity, income and wealth have been unequally distributed. It is also true that writers, philosophers, and religious leaders rarely have had much good to say about the rich, although throughout most of human history there has been little certainty about how much wealth or income is too much, or what, if anything, should be done about it.[26]

Historically, the picture is somewhat clearer when we turn to the United States. It is also paradoxical. In the beginning, both income and wealth were more equally distributed in the American colonies than in Europe, primarily because America lacked a feudal past with its hereditary aristocracy and rigid structure of rights, wealth, and social responsibilities. The paradox is that, three centuries after America's colonial beginnings, wealth and income are more unequally distributed in the "New World" than in most of the nations in Europe. The truth is that colonial America was far less egalitarian than commonly supposed. Early colonies in Virginia and Massachusetts attempted to build societies based upon an equal distribution of the products of labor, but these experiments did not last. By the end of the colonial era (1776), the top 10 percent of the population owned about 40 percent of colonial wealth, a distribution not so unequal as today, but far from egalitarian.[27] From the nation's independence in 1776 until World War I, the trend was toward increasing inequality in the distribution of income and wealth.

Here we encounter another paradox. It was the war and the way it was financed—not peacetime policies—that temporarily halted the trend toward greater inequality. World War I was financed by a combination of income and profit taxes and the creation of new money through borrowing. Because the federal income tax was new, techniques of tax avoidance now commonplace had not been invented. Thus, wartime tax policy effectively reduced incomes at the top. Money creation raised prices, but the wartime-induced demand for labor raised wages even faster. Also, prices climbed more rapidly than did the yields on corporate bonds and stocks, as well as stock prices.[28] Between 1914 and 1919, the combination of progressive income taxation, money creation, and inflation brought a redistribution of income from the *rentier* class to wage-earners.

This changed after 1919. Wartime tax rates ended, real wage gains slowed, and the great bull market of the 1920s exploded. The result was a return to the trend toward greater inequality in the distribution of income and wealth. In 1922, the top 1 percent of families held 31.6 percent of the nation's net worth; by 1929, this figure had climbed to 36.3 percent, the highest degree of concentration recorded before the most recent figure of 37.0 percent in 1989![29]

The Great Depression, New Deal legislation, and financing during World War II combined to set in motion forces that led to another period of reduced inequality in the distribution of both income and wealth. The collapse of stock-market prices was a major cause of the decline in the share of net worth owned by the top 1 percent of families. Their share of net worth fell from 36.3 percent in 1929, to 28.3 percent in 1933, and still further, to a low of 20.8 percent, in 1949. The Dow-Jones price index for thirty key industrial stocks did not regain its 1929 level until twenty-five years later in 1954.[30]

The financing of World War II was largely a repeat performance of World War I, and the effects upon the distribution of income were similar. The decline in income inequality was not so large as some may think, but it was measurable. Between 1935–36 and 1946, the share of the top fifth of families dropped from 51.7 percent of total personal income to 46.1 percent, while the share of the top 5 percent of families declined from 26.5 to 21.3 percent.[31] New Deal legislation such as the 1935 Social Security Act had some effect in bringing about this change, but most came because of the war. As noted earlier, in the first quarter-century after the end of World War II, the trend toward less inequality in the distribution of income continued. The reason was the steady growth in output, low inflation, and near-full employment that characterized the Age of Keynes (1945–70).

It was a different story for the distribution of wealth. After a low point of concentration of the ownership of wealth among the top 1 percent of families was reached in 1949 (20.8 percent), the trend toward greater equality in the ownership of wealth ended. By 1972, the share of net worth held by the top 1 percent of families had climbed back to 27.7 percent. Again, the stock market was undoubtedly the major reason for this change in the economic fortunes of the top 1 percent of American families. Between 1954 and 1969, the Dow-Jones average for industrials more than doubled in value.[32] The concentration of wealth continued to rise, reaching a new peak of 37.0 percent in 1989.

When we look at the swing, over the last two decades, toward greater inequality in income and wealth, we have not only good factual knowledge about what happened, but also some understanding of the specific causes of changes in income-and-wealth distribution—the "buried fault line" of American politics. These causes fall into two categories: (1) policy actions by the federal government, and (2) market developments that reflect some fundamental changes in the American economy, especially in its relationship to the world economy.

In the realm of economic policy, two broad developments help explain what happened, one highly visible and well known, and the second much less apparent, but much more extensive in its economic impact. The first is the highly publicized "Reagan Revolution" of the 1980s, which drew its intellectual substance from journalists like George Gilder and Jude Wanniski and the economist Arthur Laffer.[33] Ronald Reagan sought simultaneously to roll back the size of the federal government, shift spending from social to military priorities, and stimulate growth in the private sector. The chosen policy instruments were massive reductions in the federal income tax, a reorientation of the federal budget away from social spending and toward military spending, and deregulation—getting government "off our backs"— a policy shift that had begun under President Carter. "Supply-side" economics was the name given to the bundle of policy initiatives that the Reagan administration believed would launch the economy on an era of unprecedented prosperity.

Mr. Reagan's "revolution" did not reduce the size of the federal government, although the president's soothing, avuncular manner perhaps persuaded the public otherwise. As measured by spending as a percent of the nation's output, the size of the federal government was greater when Reagan left office than when he assumed the presidency. What "Reaganomics" did through the 1981 Economic Recovery Tax Act was shift in a major way the tax burden at the federal level from families at the top to families further down the income scale. The 1981 tax cuts, in combination with the exploding deficits and the gargantuan federal debt, played a major role in reversing the trend toward more equality in the distribution of income. In contrast to Keynes, who once suggested the "euthanasia of the rentier," Reaganomics strengthened the claims of the *rentier* class for a share of society's income. Since 1980, interest income has grown faster than any other kind of income. Supply-side economics failed totally to deliver on its promise that the tax cuts would stimulate the economy's growth sufficiently to balance the budget within three years. Instead, as is well known, the federal budget has been out of control since the early 1980s. The debt of the federal government more than quadrupled, to over $4 trillion, between 1980 and 1992.

Far less well known or understood is how a series of tax- and spending-policy changes since the early 1970s has transformed America's welfare state into a mechanism for the transfer of income not just to the poor, but to significant numbers in the middle class, and even to many wealthy. America's welfare state began in 1935, when the Social Security Act set up a system of payroll-financed old-age pensions, a system of unemployment compensation, and a mechanism to deliver income to the "deserving poor"—families with dependent children, the blind, the disabled, and the aged.[34] In the 1960s, the Johnson administration enlarged the welfare state by adding Medicare (health care for persons over sixty-five), Medicaid (health care for the poor), and expanded the Aid to Families with Dependent Children (AFDC) and food stamp programs.

Here we encounter another paradox in the American economy. Presumably, the modern welfare state taxes the more affluent segments of the population to provide benefits for the economically impoverished—the elderly poor, low-income families with children, the unemployed, and others who have lost their sources of income. If this is true, then one might expect that the 1960s expansion of America's welfare state would have brought more—not less—equality in the distribution of income. As noted, beginning in the early 1970s, income inequality became greater, not smaller.

What happened essentially is that, as federal income-transfer spending expanded dramatically in the 1970s, the federal government increasingly channeled the benefits from such spending toward the middle- and even upper income classes. This is the way the big social-spending programs—the so-called entitlement programs—work, especially Social Security and Medicare. Simultaneously, the progressive character of federal income taxes—both personal and corporate—was drastically undercut by an explosion of "tax expenditures." The latter term refers to "loopholes" in the tax system—the exclusion of some income from taxation, the special treatment for other types of income, or the taxing of some income at more favorable rates than other forms of income. The major loopholes in the tax system are heavily skewed toward persons and families in the upper ranges of the income ladder.

America's once modest welfare state was transformed over the past two decades into a three-tiered welfare system, one tier for the rich, one for the middle class, and one for the poor. The tier for the rich works largely through the tax system; the tiers for middle and lower classes, through the transfer of income. In total, the benefits from both taxes and transfers for America's welfare state are skewed much more heavily toward the middle and upper classes than toward the poor.[35] This helps to account for both the persistence and the growth of poverty in America, although transfer spending now equals two-thirds of federal spending.[36]

The second set of causes that helps to explain the recent surge in income and wealth inequality involves developments that largely lie outside the realm of public policy. They work through market forces, directly affecting the income that people get from the market—especially the income they get from their jobs. What has happened can be explained in terms of a broad generalization—the fragmentation of the labor market.

From the end of World War II to the onset of the silent depression in the early 1970s, the wages of American workers at all income levels grew at about the same pace—between 2.5 to 3.0 percent a year. As happened to incomes generally, there was a mild reduction in inequality of earnings during this period. A rising tide was lifting nearly all boats.

Early in the 1970s, this trend abruptly reversed itself. Since then, there has been a growing inequality in income from work, reflecting fragmentation in the job market. What this means, in other words, is that the *rates* at which pay for different kinds of jobs increased began to diverge from one another. No longer were workers marching ahead at about the same pace, so the inequality between pay for different types of work got wider. The growing inequality in the distribution of wage and salary income is an important cause of the increased inequality in income from all sources. Increased wage-and-salary-income inequality is another reason the general level of employment is less important than it used to be as an indicator of the nation's economic health. What counts increasingly in determining the well-being of a worker and his or her family is the *kind* of job held, not just the fact that an individual is employed.

A good indicator of fragmentation in the labor market is what has happened to the number and proportion of full-time workers whose wages don't lift them or their families above the poverty level—the "working poor." Census Bureau data and other studies show that, until the early 1970s, poverty-level jobs declined as a percent of jobs. No longer is this true. Since the early 1970s, the proportion of low-wage or poverty-level jobs in the total wage picture has risen steadily. Between 1979 and 1990, the Census Bureau found that the proportion of full-time, year-round workers whose wages were so low that they could not support a family of four above the poverty line rose from 12 to 18 percent of the work force.[37] Equally devastating is a Senate report documenting that, of the nearly twelve million new jobs "created" between 1979 and 1987, one-half (50.4 percent) paid an annual wage below the poverty level ($11,611 for a family of four in 1987). Only 11.9 percent of these new jobs were high-wage jobs, ones that paid over $46,444.[38]

Why has this happened? The reasons are complex, neither self-evident nor clear with respect to an appropriate remedy. Conservative economists downplay concern, arguing that such numbers are normal, the product of demographic changes (unskilled baby-boomers entering the labor force), or of the economic turbulence that is a part of the economy's continued transition into a service-oriented society. Unfortunately, the numbers are there and have persisted too long to be dismissed, as *Newsweek*'s economic columnist, Robert Samuelson, said, as mostly a "statistical illusion."[39] For nearly two decades, the "Great American Job Machine" has been churning out many jobs that don't pay very well. This may well be one of the toughest problems facing the Clinton administration—not getting the economy to create more jobs, but getting it to create jobs with pay adequate to support a family. With the loss of over two million well-paying manufacturing jobs since 1973, this will not be easy. The full dimensions of this complex issue are explored in chapter 9.

Among economists there is, sad to say, no agreement on the precise reasons for the fragmentation in the labor market. This not only reflects the complexity of the problem, but underscores the difficulty of finding a solution. Nonetheless, economists most directly interested in this development suggest causes that fall into three broad categories.

First, there is "corporate restructuring," a euphemistic phrase to describe the elimination of jobs by America's big corporations. In response to falling profit rates after the mid-1960s, the slowing of productivity growth, and intense foreign competition, American corporations began a ruthless elimination of thousands of middle-level (white-collar) and production-line (blue-collar) jobs, moved many operations to low-wage areas abroad, and whenever possible substituted part-time and contract workers for full-time employees. In late 1992, alongside the "good" news about the recovery from the 1990–91 recession, IBM, one of the bluest of America's "blue-chip" corporations, said it would cut another twenty-five thousand jobs in 1993. A weakened labor movement, hobbled in the 1980s and early 1990s by a hostile administration in Washington, was largely helpless in opposing the "deindustrialization" of America's work force. Ironically, while workers were being squeezed by corporate America's "lean-and-mean" campaign, corporate executives were being amply rewarded, irrespective of the economic performance of the firms they led. In 1974, a typical chief executive officer (CEO) in manufacturing earned thirty-five times the pay of an average worker, but by 1990 the average earnings (excluding perquisites and fringe benefits) of a CEO had climbed to 120 times the pay of an average worker in manufacturing, and 150 times the pay of workers in both manufacturing and services. In contrast, in Japan, America's leading competitor in the international economy, the differential between the earnings of CEOs and average workers is under twenty.[40]

A second set of causes lies in far-reaching developments in the global economy. Robert Reich, who taught at the John F. Kennedy School of Government at Harvard University before becoming secretary of labor in the Clinton administration, and Lester Thurow, dean of the Sloan School of Management at MIT, say that the splintering of America's labor market should be traced to an integrated global economy, one in which the United States plays an ever-enlarging role.[41] America's labor market is being split along global lines because earnings in different kinds of work are determined increasingly by international competition, not by competition within our national borders. Routine production work—the kind found not only in manufacturing but in a multitude of data-processing and other service industries—can and is performed almost anywhere around the globe. So routine workers in advanced economies like the United States find themselves in competition with low-paid workers in Third World nations. Such competition has exerted enormous downward pressure on the wages of the unskilled and the less educated during the last two decades. It is only the approximate 20 percent of highly educated workers at the top whose stock in trade, according to Reich, is skill in the manipulation of information—the key resource of the modern economy—who are doing well in the new and intensely competitive global economy that is shaping all our lives.

Third, there is the matter of demographics and education. This is a more broadly-based category than the other two, reflecting developments in both the domestic and international economies. Contrary to the views of some conservative economists, the entry of the baby-boom generation into the labor force was not a major factor in fragmentation in the labor market. More new workers entered the labor force during the Carter years (2.7 million per year) than in either the Reagan years (1.8 million per year) or the Ford years (2.3 million per year).[42] The major way in which demographic change affected the rise of low-wage jobs was through the increasing entry of women into the labor force. In spite of some gains in recent years, wages for women average approximately 60 percent of the wages of men. The fact that more women are working at lower wages than men, plus the sharp increase in families headed by women—the "feminization of poverty"—has been one of the major causes for wage polarization in the last two decades. Between 1973 and 1990, the number of single-parent families headed by women rose 65.5 percent, in contrast to an increase of 20.5 percent in all families, and only 11.4 percent in married-couple families.[43] Finally, and as noted in detail in chapter 4, a part of the polarization in wages stems from changing educational requirements linked to different types of work. The wage gap that has opened up for different educational levels has not resulted primarily from higher returns for college graduates compared with high-school and grammar-school graduates. It stems from the disappearance of low-level jobs that don't require much skill, especially in manufacturing, and a relative decline in the wages of low-skill jobs that remain.

WHERE IS THE ECONOMY HEADING?

At this point in our story several observations are appropriate. The distribution of both income and wealth in America is now more unequal than at any time since the end of World War II. What does this portend for the future? Since there is such a striking parallel between the 1920s and the 1980s, the temptation is strong to see the current—and growing—inequality in the distribution of income and wealth as leading to another spectacular "great crash" on the model of 1929. The fact that the concentration of wealth among the top 1 percent of families has surpassed the 1929 ratio offers support to those who fear another 1929 debacle is waiting in the wings.

There are reasons, however, why this is not likely to happen. Though the distribution of income is less equal than at any time since the end of World War II, it is still not so lopsided as it was in 1929. Then the top fifth received 54.4 percent of family income, in contrast to 44.3 percent in 1990.[44] In the 1920s, as America was entering the age of mass production and mass consumption, the growing concentration of income at the top made it less and less possible for the four-fifths of families below the top to consume the goods that were turned out in ever-increasing numbers.

The situation is different today. The top 40 percent of the income pyramid now get 68.1 percent of family income, enough to keep the entire economy moving upward, though the bottom 60 percent of families are struggling—and will continue to struggle—to stay afloat economically. Unless public awareness and anger over the income-and-wealth-distribution problem worsens enough to create serious political and social unrest, the economy could continue indefinitely in the sluggish situation characteristic of the silent depression.

A more ominous development for the viability and cohesiveness of American society is already under way. The "fortunate fifth" and their allies and followers in the fourth quintal from the bottom are buying their way out of the failures of society that confront 60 percent or more of the nation's population—poor schools, decaying cities, crumbling sewer and water systems, crime-threatened neighborhoods, and inadequate public transportation, both within and between major population centers. Charles Murray, conservative social critic and author of *Losing Ground: American Social Policy,* fears that a new American caste system is taking shape, one based upon the Latin American "model," in which the 10 to 20 percent at the top seek "to preserve the mansions on the hills above the slums."[45] A critical question is whether the economic and political power of the contented majority of Galbraith's "culture of contentment" has become so great that America's drift into the caste system, feared by Professor Murray, is irreversible. Beyond jobs, beyond the deficit and the debt, this could prove to be the most difficult of all the challenges facing the Clinton administration.

CHAPTER 6

•

•

•

•

... While Life at the Bottom Goes On

On the front page of the May 24, 1992, Sunday edition of the *Kansas City Star*, a color photo shows Pamela Cox and three of her four preschool children crossing a street near a park where the family slept under the trees during most of the summer in 1991. Pamela Cox and her small brood are a part of what *Star* writer Toni Wood described as Kansas City's "unseen world," the thousands of homeless women and children "who drift through Kansas City like unanchored vessels, from a shelter to Grandma's house to a dreadful apartment and back to a shelter. They scramble not just for a place to sleep, but for food, diapers, rides on the city buses. . . ."[1]

Kansas City, where homeless women and their children now outnumber homeless men, is a microcosm of the latest dimension of poverty in America—women and their children wandering the streets and alleyways of America's great cities in search of shelter and food. How many are there? No one really knows, although estimates of homeless children alone have ranged as high as 1.5 million in a year's time.[2] This is but one of the many faces of poverty that continues to mock the American Dream as the nation nears the twenty-first century.

POVERTY IN AMERICA

In 1962, Michael Harrington published a remarkable little book, *The Other America: Poverty in the United States.*[3] Until Harrington's book appeared, the general assumption was that there wasn't much poverty in America. Whatever poverty existed came mainly from: (1) a loss of income because of unemployment caused by a recession or depression; (2) inadequate income after retirement; or (3) income lost because of the premature death or disablement of the family breadwinner from disease or accident. The old-age, survivors', and disability provisions of the Social Security Act—the crown jewel of America's welfare state—were supposed to eliminate poverty caused by any or all of these events. Other forms of poverty were believed to be isolated and residual, easily dealt with by the public-assistance provisions of the Social Security Act—aid to people who are blind, disabled, or to dependent children.

Harrington showed that this was wrong. Not only was poverty far more widespread than anyone suspected in the affluent America of the 1950s, but it was largely invisible to the great majority of Americans. *The Other America* led President Kennedy to direct Walter Heller, chairman of his Council of Economic Advisers, to plan a full-scale assault on poverty for the president's second term. Because of the assassination, this never happened. Nevertheless, the plans drafted by Professor Heller and the council became the basis for President Johnson's War on Poverty, a major thrust of the bundle of Great Society legislation passed after Johnson's landslide election victory in 1964.

Contrary to the conventional wisdom, President Johnson's "war" on poverty did not fail—actually, it was more like a small skirmish than a war. What failed was an original plan that was never implemented.[4] The reason was Vietnam, which after 1965 took most of the money that might have gone into the battle against poverty if the nation had not gotten bogged down in the hopeless misadventure in Southeast Asia. Although the War on Poverty as such was a casualty of the Vietnam War, the Great Society's major additions to America's welfare state survived. These include broadened coverage for Social Security, an enlarged food-stamp program, expanded assistance for families with dependent children, a revamped scheme for aid to the aged, blind, and disabled, now called Supplemental Security Income (SSI), plus Medicare and Medicaid. It is through these programs that the federal government continues to struggle against poverty, even though no administration since Johnson has put a formal attack on poverty at the top of its legislative agenda.

The experience of the Johnson years, the disillusionment with the antipoverty struggle that surfaced in the 1970s, the counter-assault of the Reagan administration on America's welfare state, and the resurgence of poverty in the 1980s underscore two points, both of which are highly relevant to the nation's current situation. First, poverty is far more deeply rooted in American society, more intractable, and its causes are far less understood than was thought in the halcyon mid-1960s, when all things economic seemed possible. Second, and as Michael Harrington pointed out in 1984 in *The New American Poverty*, there is no such thing as poverty; there are *poverties*.[5] This is a key lesson. Poverty is not monolithic, but something with many faces, many dimensions. The poverty of the 1990s is not the same as the poverty of the 1960s, just as the poverty of the 1960s was not the same as the poverty of the Great Depression, nor the poverty of the 1930s the same as that of the nineteenth century. The experience of the last thirty years also shows that finding a solution to the nation's *poverties* involves politics as much as economics. Because poverty is a moving, changing target, solutions are difficult and elusive, which makes the topic a tempting one for political demagoguery. There is always political mileage in attacking spending on the "poor," even though federal spending that directly benefits poor people (AFDC, food stamps, and Medicare) is only one-fourth as large as the social-insurance programs that are not targeted specifically at the poor, particularly Social Security, Medicare, and unemployment compensation.

WHO ARE THE POOR IN AMERICA?

In 1963, Mollie Orshansky, a statistician in the Social Security Administration, invented the first official definition of poverty. Using information from the U.S. Department of Agriculture showing that a family of four normally spent about one-third of its income for food, Ms. Orshansky multiplied by three the cost of a minimal, nutritionally adequate diet for a four-person family. This yielded a "poverty threshold" for a family of four. This standard was adopted by the president's Council of Economic Advisers in its 1964 report and, with only minor adjustments, is still used to measure poverty in the United States. Each year, the poverty line is adjusted only for inflation. In 1959, the first year for which figures exist, the poverty threshold for a family of four was $2,973. In 1992, the projected threshold was $14,464.[6] The income used in defining the poverty level is money income from all private and public sources.

As with productivity growth, real wages for workers, and family incomes, 1973 was a watershed year for poverty in America. Between 1959 and 1973, the number of persons officially classified as "poor" in America dropped from 39.5 million (22.4 percent of the nation's population) to 22.9 million (11.1 percent of the population), a 42.0-percent decline. After 1973, the trend toward fewer poor reversed itself. By 1990, the number of poor people had climbed to 33.6 million (13.5 percent of the population). The increase in the number of people in poverty between 1973 and 1990 was 46.7 percent. Among the years since the federal government has been measuring poverty, 1973 was the low point for the percent of the nation's total population below the poverty line. The poverty ratio rose to 15.2 percent in 1983, in the aftermath of the 1981–82 recession, and averaged 13.5 percent between then and 1990.[7]

Who are the people behind these numbers? The Census Bureau breaks down the overall rate into specific rates for seven major subgroups: children, the aged, single persons, persons in single-parent families headed by women, blacks, Hispanics, and whites. This covers the spectrum of America's poor from the perspective of what sociologists call "demographic subgroups."

For all persons and for all categories, poverty rates declined between 1959 and 1973. After that, the picture is mixed. For the aged and single persons, poverty continued to decline after 1973, but for all other groups, the rates rose through the 1981–82 recession, and then declined slightly or leveled off. Except for the aged and single persons, there is now more poverty for persons in all the other subgroups than in 1973, the most successful year in the struggle against poverty in the United States. (Table 6-1 shows poverty rates for persons in each subgroup for selected years from 1959 through 1990.)

There is overlap between the different categories listed above, so any ranking of the different categories by the extent of poverty found among them is tricky. Nevertheless, it is worth noting that in 1990 persons living in families headed by females had the highest poverty rate (37.2 percent), followed by blacks (31.9 percent), Hispanics (28.1 percent) single persons (20.7 percent), children (20.6 percent), the aged (12.2 percent), and whites (10.7 percent). These rankings are not much changed from 1959, although in that year blacks ranked highest, followed by female-headed families, single persons, the aged, children, and whites. Of all these demographic groups, the most progress in poverty reduction has been among the aged, a fact in accord with comments made in chapter 4 about what has happened to different kinds of families over the course of the silent depression.

Percentage figures (poverty rates) give a broad picture of what has happened in the United States since the government began to compile poverty numbers in the 1960s. We also need to look

TABLE 6-1 *Poverty Rates for Persons in Selected Years for Selected Subgroups (in percent)*

Poverty Category	1959	1965	1970	1973	1975	1980	1982	1985	1990
All Persons	22.4%	17.3%	12.6%	11.1%	12.3%	13.0%	15.0%	14.0%	13.5%
Children	27.3	21.0	15.1	14.4	17.1	18.3	21.9	20.7	20.6
Aged*	35.2	NA	24.6	16.3	15.3	15.7	14.6	12.6	12.2
Singles	46.1	39.8	32.9	25.6	25.1	22.9	23.1	21.5	20.7
Single-Parent†	49.4	39.8	38.1	37.5	37.5	36.7	40.6	37.6	37.2
Blacks	55.1	41.8	33.5	31.4	31.3	32.5	35.6	31.3	31.9
Hispanics	NA	NA	NA	21.9	26.9	25.7	29.9	29.0	28.1
Whites	18.1	13.3	9.9	8.4	9.7	10.2	12.0	11.4	10.7

*Over sixty-five years of age.
†Persons living in single-parent families headed by females.
SOURCE: Bureau of the Census, Current Population Reports, ser. P-60, no. 175, *Poverty in the United States: 1990*, pp. 16–18, table 2.

at a breakdown in terms of the categories just described of the total number of people in poverty in any given year. Again, it is a question of who are the people behind the numbers. The most shocking statistic is that, ever since the government began counting poor people in 1959, the largest number and largest percent of people in poverty have been children. Table 6-2 shows that in 1959, 44.4 percent of the 39.5 million people living below the poverty line were children. Thirty-one years later, 40 percent of the 33.6 million persons in poverty were children. In every year since 1959, the highest percentage of persons living in poverty have been children. Are our children becoming an endangered species?

The number of children in poverty is disproportionate to their numbers in the nation's total population. In 1990, children accounted for 26.2 percent of the total population, but 40.0 percent of persons living in poverty. The 13.4 million children in poverty equal 20.6 percent of the 65.0 million children in the nation's population in 1990. Thus, almost one child out of every five was living in poverty in America in 1990. The second-largest number is persons living in families headed by women, which, of course, usually includes children, and in which most of the time no husband or father is present. Linked together is the "feminization of poverty" and the plight of America's children, the topic for the next section. From 1959 through 1990, children averaged 41.4 percent of the poor, and persons in families headed by women constituted 31.2 percent of all persons living in poverty. (See table 6-2.)

Contrary to impressions one might gain from news photos and headlines, the largest number of poor people are not black, but white. In 1990, white persons accounted for 66.5 percent of all poor, blacks 29.3 percent, and other races 4.2 percent. This is only logical, since the overwhelming proportion of Americans are white. In 1990, whites made up 83.9 percent of the total population, blacks 12.4 percent, and other nonwhites 3.7 percent. Blacks and other nonwhite races are disproportionately

TABLE 6-2 Persons in Selected Subgroups as a Percent of Total Persons in Poverty in Selected Years (in percent)

Poverty Category	1959	1965	1970	1973	1975	1980	1982	1985	1990
Children	44.4%	44.2%	41.1%	42.0%	42.9%	39.4%	39.7%	39.3%	40.0%
Aged*	13.9	NA	18.9	14.6	12.8	13.2	10.9	10.4	10.9
Singles	12.4	14.5	20.0	20.3	19.7	21.3	18.8	20.3	22.2
Single-Parent†	17.7	22.7	29.5	35.6	34.2	34.6	34.0	35.1	37.5
Blacks	25.1	NA	29.7	32.2	29.2	29.3	28.2	27.0	29.3
Hispanics	NA	NA	NA	10.3	11.6	11.9	12.5	15.8	17.9
Whites	72.1	67.8	68.8	65.9	68.7	67.3	68.4	69.1	66.5

*Over sixty-five years of age.

†Persons living in single-parent families headed by females.

SOURCES: Bureau of the Census, Current Population Reports, ser. P-60, no. 175, Poverty in the United States: 1990, p. 16, table 2; U.S. House of Representatives, Committee on Ways and Means, Green Book (Washington, D.C.: U.S. Government Printing Office, 1992), p. 1274.

represented in the poverty statistics. Black persons averaged 29.2 percent of persons living in poverty between 1959 and 1990, which is more than twice their overall share of the population. In 1990, almost one out of every three black persons was poor. Other nonwhites—Native Americans, Hispanics, and Orientals—constituted 12.3 percent of the poverty population in 1990, 22.7 percent of the total population.

Since 1973, the Bureau of the Census has tabulated detailed poverty statistics on Hispanics. Since that time, the poverty rate among Hispanics has increased—from 21.9 percent in 1973 to 28.1 percent in 1960—as has their share of the total number of persons in poverty, going from 10.3 percent in 1973 to 17.9 percent in 1990. Immigration—legal and illegal—of large numbers of often desperately poor Hispanics from Mexico and Central American countries is responsible for these trends.

WOMEN AND CHILDREN LAST

As *Newsday* columnist Robert Reno asked, "What country has more poor children than Somalia has population, immunizes a lower percentage of its infants than China . . . has higher rates of infant mortality and subnormal birth rates than most of Europe . . . ?"[8] It is wealthy America, where children are the nation's largest single group in poverty. This is the way it was in 1959, and this is the way it is today. America prides itself on having the world's highest living standard, but when it comes to how we treat children, we don't stack up very well compared with many advanced countries. One recent study shows that the percentage of children in poverty in America is 3.8 times the average in Australia, Canada, and five West European countries (West Germany, Sweden, the United Kingdom, Netherlands, and France). Outside the United States, Canada had the highest poverty rate for children (9.3 percent), and Sweden the lowest (0.8 percent).[9]

Since 1959, poverty among the elderly has been cut by

two-thirds, from 28.5 percent in 1965 to 12.2 percent in 1990. For children, substantial progress took place between 1959 and 1973, when their poverty rate dropped from 27.3 percent to 14.4 percent, a 47.3-percent decline. After 1973, progress came to a halt and the poverty rate for children rose steadily, reaching a post-1973 high of 22.3 percent in 1982, and then dropping slightly to the 1990 rate of 20.6 percent.[10] In 1990, 40.0 percent of all persons in poverty were children (table 6-2). Poverty among children today is about where it was a quarter-century ago. In one of the richest nations on earth, poverty among children persists year after year. Why?

The glib—and widely accepted—answer is to blame "welfare," and the deviant, antisocial behavior that it is supposed to spawn. "Welfare," as Michael Harrington points out, is a "bad" word, its recipients presumably lazy and dedicated to cheating society.[11] Perhaps the most widely repeated welfare cliché in our society involves unmarried welfare mothers who become pregnant in order to avoid work and increase their income from AFDC. The widespread and popular belief that welfare rewards chronic dependency, laziness, and illegitimacy led many states, during the tough times of the 1990–91 recession, to tie welfare benefits to working, staying in school, or not having more children. Poor people are an easy target for a demagogic war on welfare: poor children can't vote, and often the adult poor don't vote. The real reasons for the plight of children in America are more complicated, involving both the "feminization of poverty" and the ever-present issue of race. The term "feminization of poverty" originated in the 1980s as a headline-catching phrase to describe what was happening to poverty in the United States and the structure of the American family. Consider these numbers. In 1990, there were 33.6 million persons living below the poverty line. Of these, 75.0 percent (25.2 million) lived in families, but 50.0 percent of all poor persons in families (12.6 million) were living in families headed by women! This is the statistical meaning of the "feminization of poverty." Poverty is heavily concentrated in female-headed families. This situation has worsened since 1973. In that year, the percentage of persons living in families headed by women was 44.7 percent of all those living in poor families.[12]

Consider some additional numbers. Between 1960 and 1990, the number of children living with their mothers in single-parent families increased from 8.0 percent of all families with children to 21.6 percent of all families with children. This was a 170.0 percent increase in the *relative* importance of single-parent families headed by women, compared with traditional, two-parent families. The latter dropped from 87.7 percent of all families with children in 1973 to 72.5 percent in 1990, a 17.3-percent *relative* decline. The most important change in the structure of the American family during the years of the silent depression is the growing proportion of the nation's children who live in single-parent families headed by the mother.[13]

Finally, there are these facts. The percentage of single-parent families headed by women grew by 67.7 percent between 1973 and 1990, whereas the percentage of married-couple families with children declined by 2.2 percent during the same period. The poverty *rate* among single-parent families headed by women remains shockingly high, changing little over the last seventeen years. In 1973, it was 43.2 percent; in 1990, 44.5 percent. In contrast, for married-couple families with children, the poverty rate in 1974 was only 6.0 percent, and just slightly higher, at 7.8 percent, in 1990.[14] Statistically speaking, the odds are five to six times greater that a child in a single-parent family will be poor, as compared with a child in a two-parent family.

In these numbers we have in a nutshell a major explanation for the high level of poverty that persists among the children of America. It is rooted *primarily* in the continued breakdown of the traditional two-parent family, *plus* the persistence of serious poverty among families with children headed by women. This raises three questions: (1) What accounts for the decline in the relative importance of the traditional two-parent family in

America? (2) Why are single parent families—especially families headed by women—so poor? (3) What role does race play in the poverty picture for children and women?

THE GROWTH OF THE
SINGLE-PARENT FAMILY

There is no single or simple explanation for the growth of the single-parent family over the last two decades. Some observers attribute this development to far-reaching changes in attitudes, patterns of behavior, and life styles, many of which began to take shape in the social turbulence of the last half of the 1960s. Among the possible causes that can be reduced to numbers and measurement, three are of particular interest. They are the massive increase in the number of women who work, especially mothers of small children; the sharp deterioration in the real earnings of men; and the growth of spending for "welfare," the politically popular explanation for the relative decline in the importance of the traditional two-parent family.

One of the great post–World War II transformations in American society is the increase in the number of women who work outside the home. Working wives and mothers are now commonplace, although this was not the norm as recently as the mid-1960s. It was thereafter that the proportion of women— especially women with children—in the labor force began to increase sharply. In 1960, only 20.2 percent of women with children under age six and only 30.4 percent of all women with children under eighteen were at work. Even among women without children, only 35.0 percent worked in 1960. By 1991, however, the percentages for working women were: 58.4 for women with children under six, 74.4 for women with children between six and seventeen, and 52.0 for women without children.[15] These numbers reflect an enormous, radical change in the role of women in our society. But do they explain why single-parent families have grown so rapidly since the 1960s? Not really. What they do is indicate a rough correlation between the rise of women in the labor force and the increase in single-parent families. We know that more women—women with children and women without children, women who are married, and women who are divorced or separated—are working, but we are unsure whether this is a cause or an effect of the increase in single-parent families. It is probably both.

As with the increase of women in the work force, the numbers show that earnings for men worsened significantly between 1973 and 1990. According to the Census Bureau, the median income (measured in dollars of constant purchasing power) for all males fifteen years and older rose by 81.4 percent between 1947 and 1973. From 1974 through 1990, though, the real (constant-dollar) median income for males fell by 14.4 percent. The story is different for women. Their median income (in constant dollars) increased by 38.1 percent from 1947 to 1973, and by another 22.3 percent from 1974 to 1990. Here is further evidence that working wives and mothers kept family incomes from actually falling after the onset of the silent depression in 1973. The downside to this is that median income for women in 1990 was only 49.6 percent of median income for men, even though there was an improvement over the 1973 figure of 34.7 percent and 45.6 percent in 1947. Women lost ground relative to men between 1947 and 1973, ground they more than regained between 1974 and 1990 because their incomes rose while those of men fell.[16]

What do these numbers mean? Though they don't give a clear-cut answer to the question why single-parent families have grown so rapidly, they have a bearing on the matter. The worsening income situation for men after 1973—which was especially pronounced for younger men—strained existing marriages, and slowed family formation. In 1990, the divorce rate was 80.8 percent higher than in 1950, and the marriage rate had fallen off by 11.7 percent.[17] The increasing extent and ease with which women entered the work force was also a factor. The ability to make a living on their own made it easier for women to resolve a strained marriage through divorce.

Clearly, the most controversial question centering on the single-parent family—especially single-parent families headed by women—is that of welfare. In the public's mind, AFDC and to a lesser extent food stamps are synonymous with "welfare," a word that, when linked to the phrase "the welfare system," has become a pejorative term. As already noted, the public views "welfare" as a major—if not the major—cause of the growth of single-parent families. There is a certain logic to this, because the growth of public assistance means that women with children can turn to the state for support instead of depending upon a man. Reality, however, doesn't support such a proposition.

Consider these facts. Over the thirty years 1960–90, the number of children living with their mothers in single-parent families increased by 172.5 percent, from 5.1 million to 13.9 million. Yet, during this same period, the real value of the combined total AFDC and food-stamp benefits received by welfare families rose by only 3.8 percent. Only during the 1960s was there a significant increase in the real value of AFDC and food-stamp benefits. After that, it was all downhill. From 1970 through 1991, the median monthly AFDC benefit (in 1991 dollars) for a family of four (a mother and three children) with no income dropped from $777 to $435, a 44-percent decline! The severity of this cut in a welfare family's real income was mitigated somewhat by adjustments in the value of food stamps to reflect inflation. Even so, from 1972 through 1991, the combined real value of AFDC and food-stamp benefits dropped by 27 percent. While this was happening, the number of children living in single-parent families with their mothers increased by 86.2 percent.[18]

It is difficult to see in these figures any economic incentive encouraging women of any age to form single-parent households or have more children simply to get more AFDC money from the government. What is particularly shocking, though, is the drastic increase in births to unmarried mothers, a development that is difficult to link to welfare benefits. In the 1980s, when the real value of AFDC and food-stamp benefits were being cut by 9.7 percent, the number of births to unwed mothers jumped by an astonishing 64.3 percent! Interestingly, the age group with the greatest percentage increase in out-of-wedlock births was for women between thirty-five and thirty-nine—from 13,187 in 1980 to 39,030 in 1990, a 196.0-percent increase. The total births in this group were only 3.6 percent of all births to unmarried mothers. One can wonder, though, whether life was imitating Murphy Brown in the popular TV sitcom, or whether Murphy Brown was imitating life.

In 1989, the largest number and percentage of out-of-wedlock births were to women in the twenty-to-twenty-four age group (378,122 and 34.6 percent of all such births), followed by the fifteen-to-nineteen age group (337,268 and 30.7 percent of all births to unmarried women). Together, women from fifteen to twenty-four account for 65.3 percent of all unwedded births. As might be expected, women under twenty-four have the highest rate of out-of-wedlock births per thousand women, but since 1980 the rate of increase in births for women in this group has been below the rate of increase for women in all higher age groups. Murphy Brown's cohort had the greatest increase, 64.9 percent.[19]

Black women at all age levels have the highest rates of out-of-wedlock births, but the percentage increase in out-of-wedlock births for black women between 1980 and 1989 was much less than the increase for white women—40.4 percent compared with 85.6 percent. This reflects the fact that in the 1980s the rate of increase in the out-of-wedlock birthrate for black women was lower than the rate for white women.[20]

The rising number of births to unmarried mothers as a percentage of all births is not confined to the United States. Practically all the nations of Western Europe experienced sharp increases in the number of births to unmarried women between 1970 and the mid-1980s.[21] Is the welfare state responsible for this? Some will argue that it is, especially in Europe, where social-welfare programs are more extensively developed than in the United States. This argument, though, is not particularly plausible, because in no Western nation have social-welfare benefits increased enough to account for the more than doubling in the last twenty years of births to unmarried women as a percentage of all live births. As noted earlier, the real value of welfare was dropping over this period in the United States, while stagnant economies in Western Europe precluded any major expansion in welfare spending. Changing social values affecting women, children, and the role and nature of the family have been more important than economics in accounting for these developments.

WHY ARE SINGLE-PARENT FAMILIES SO POOR?

Of all the questions related to poverty, this is undoubtedly the easiest to answer. In the single-parent family headed by a woman, there is only one person to support the family. The situation is made more difficult by the fact that, on the average, the wages or earnings of women are less than those of men. Thus, the single-parent family headed by a woman has a dual handicap.

But there are further complications. Absent fathers contribute far less to the support of their children than do fathers in married-couple families. One recent study showed that absent fathers contributed through alimony or child support to their families only 3.8 percent of the earnings of a father in husband-and-wife families! On the average, only 27 percent of poor female-headed families received alimony or child support in *any* amount.[22] Single mothers who work usually earn more than mothers who work in two-parent families, but this is primarily because married mothers work only part-time.[23]

Contrary to the popular view, mothers in single-parent poor families work, although income from work is not the major source of income for the family. Public assistance (AFDC, SSI, food stamps, and housing aid) provides 59.4 percent of the income for poor single-parent families headed by women. Work provides 27.8 percent of the family's income, and the rest (12.8 percent) comes from a variety of other sources, including alimony and child support (5.9 percent). The overall average of mothers who get some income from work in single-parent poor families is 50.6 percent, as compared with 95.6 percent of working women who head nonpoor families with children.[24]

How much do single mothers in poor families work? According to the Bureau of the Census, 46.2 percent of single mothers worked in 1990, but only 8.4 percent of them worked full-time. Family responsibilities were the main reason why mothers did not work full-time (56.9 percent), or did not work at all (71.4 percent). Only 5.4 percent of mothers who did not work at all and 4.9 percent of mothers who worked part-time gave lack of jobs as a reason for their status. Most of the women who do not work at all are poorly educated—a majority are high-school dropouts—and more than one-third have over two children.[25]

A fundamental problem for the mother who heads a single-person family is that the welfare system is so structured that it does not make economic sense for many mothers to work. For example, a 1989 study showed that a mother with two children who worked full-time at a job that paid 50 percent more than the minimum wage would take home (after deducting taxes and the costs of child care) only about $1,500 more than what she would receive from welfare and food stamps.[26] Her effective wage rate was 75 cents an hour. The dilemma facing many mothers with children is either to work full-time or to collect welfare. In the circumstances just described, the sensible economic decision for a single mother concerned with her children's welfare is to choose AFDC, food stamps, and Medicaid, rather than full-time work. Yet in no state are welfare benefits great enough to lift a family out of poverty, and many single-parent families in which the mother works full-time remain poor. Only single-parent families in which the mother has a good education and substantial work experience have much chance of staying out of poverty. If the nation had adopted President Nixon's proposed Family Assistance Plan (FAP) in 1969, the situation might be entirely different today. The FAP was based upon Milton Friedman's idea of a "negative income tax," a mechanism designed to provide a minimum income to a family, but also to ensure that it was more advantageous for family members to work than not to work, if work were available. To solve the problem of poverty in America—especially poverty in single-parent families headed by a woman—a modernized version of the negative income tax will have to be used.

RACE AND CHILDREN IN POVERTY

As with almost every other facet of life in modern America, race enters strongly into the problem of poverty among the nation's children. Though it is not true that most of the nation's poor children are black or Hispanic, it is true that the forces that have brought about changes in the American family, and brought poverty to so many single-parent families, have affected children in minority families much more strongly than children in white families. For example, among black people, 54.8 percent of children under eighteen lived in 1990 in a single-parent family, compared with only 19.2 percent of white children. In 1990, there were 13.5 million children under eighteen living in families in which the mother was the only parent. Of these, 8.3 million children were white (61.5 percent), and 5.1 million children were black (37.8 percent).[27] The proportion of black children who are poor far outweighs the overall proportion of black people in the nation's total population.

One factor that weighs heavily upon the extent of poverty among minority children (mostly black) is location. Poverty in the United States is primarily, though not wholly, an urban development. Of the 33.6 million people living below the poverty line in 1990 in the United States, 72.9 percent were in metropolitan areas, which the Census Bureau defines as cities with populations of at least fifty thousand, or urbanized areas of a hundred thousand persons. The Census Bureau also defines a "poverty area" as any tract, township, or district in which 20 percent or more of the population is below the poverty line. All persons living in a poverty area are not poor, but the poverty rate in such areas is typically far above the average for the nation as a whole. As one would expect, most poverty areas are in metropolitan areas (64.9 percent), and, within metropolitan areas, the overwhelming majority of poverty areas are in the central cities (78.8 percent). (A central city is the largest city in any metropolitan area.) The poverty rate in 1990 for persons living in poverty areas in central cities was 38.4 percent, as compared with the overall average for the nation in 1990 of 13.5 percent: the incidence of poverty in America's central cities is nearly three times greater than in the nation generally.[28]

To understand how these general findings on poverty and location are linked to poverty for white and minority children, we must look at the distribution of children in terms of where they live—metropolitan areas, nonmetropolitan areas, inside the central cities, in poverty areas—and the poverty rates for children living in poverty areas (table 6-3). The United States is an urbanized nation as measured by where the nation's children live. More than three-quarters of white, black, and Hispanic children live in metropolitan areas. It is also clear from the Census Bureau figures that the nation's suburbs are predominantly white, and the inner cities predominantly black and Hispanic. A far greater proportion of black children live in poverty areas than do white children—71.7 percent versus 12.3 percent—and the incidence of poverty for black children living in poverty areas is much greater than for white children—71.1 percent versus 32.6 percent. For Hispanic children, the distinctions with white children are not quite so severe. Numbers from the University of Michigan study of family incomes over time (chapter 3) show that the

TABLE 6-3 *The Distribution of Child Population in Metropolitan Areas, Central Cities, Suburbs, Nonmetropolitan Areas, and Poverty Areas: 1988 (in percent)*

| | Percent of Children | | |
Living Area	White	Black	Hispanic
Metropolitan Area	75.3%	81.5%	91.6%
Central Cities	25.0	56.3	53.9
Suburbs	50.3	25.2	37.8
Nonmetropolitan Areas	24.7	18.5	8.4
Poverty Areas	12.3	52.7	40.6
Poverty Rate*	32.6%	71.1%	57.5%

*Poverty rate for children living in poverty areas.
SOURCE: U.S. House of Representatives, Committee on Ways and Means, *Green Book* (Washington, D.C.: U.S. Government Printing Office, 1992), pp. 1171, 1172.

overwhelming majority of white children (73 percent) will escape poverty, but only a small minority of black children (22 percent) will avoid poverty during childhood.[29] For children as for adults, poverty in America remains very much a matter of the color of one's skin. The nasty fact is that poverty among children in America cannot be separated from race in America.

FEDERAL SPENDING ON THE ELDERLY AND ON CHILDREN

One of the most widely repeated clichés is that "you can't solve problems by throwing money at them." The cliché is trotted out most frequently in conjunction with federal spending, especially federal spending on social programs. The facts belie the notion. Since the 1960s, one of the major achievements of America's Social Security system has been the near elimination of poverty in elderly families as the twentieth century is coming to a close. There is no guarantee that this success will be permanent, since the system faces enormous demands when the first of the baby-boomers begin to retire early in the next century. Nonetheless, "throwing money" at the aged through Social Security, Medicare, and other income-support programs lifted large numbers of people sixty-five years of age and older out of poverty.

At the other end of the age spectrum, one of the least successful attainments of America since the 1960s is the failure to eliminate poverty among children. Why the difference? No single thing accounts for it, but surely a factor of major importance has been the difference in the amount of money spent by the federal government on the elderly (persons over sixty-five) and on children (persons under eighteen).

Unfortunately, the federal government does not keep its books in a way that classifies its expenditures by age of beneficiary. Recently, the Congressional Budget Office (CBO) tabulated for the House Ways and Means Committee figures that estimated for 1990 and projected for 1995 the proportion of all federal outlays going to the elderly people and to children. The numbers are instructive, if not startling. In 1990, 28.3 percent of *all* federal spending was for the elderly; in the same year, 5.2 percent was for the benefit of children. By 1995, the percentage of federal spending going to elderly persons is expected to increase to 33.9 percent, and the percentage going to children to 7.1 percent. In dollars in 1990 purchasing power, the amount spent by the federal government in 1990 per aged person was $11,350; the amount spent per child was $1,260. On a per-person basis, the federal government spent nine times more on aged people than on children. In 1995, the CBO estimates, federal spending on a per-person basis for the elderly will be $12,940, and for children $1,730, resulting in a slight decline in the overall ratio of federal per-person outlays both for the elderly and for children.[30]

Is this a fair comparison—the amounts that the federal government spends upon the elderly versus the amounts spent upon children? Obviously, children and the aged have different needs, but there is enough similarity in the purposes for which the federal money was being spent to justify a comparison. Except for federal spending for education (less than 10 percent of federal money spent to benefit children in 1990), federal spending for both aged adults and for children was for income support, housing assistance, and health care, types of spending that have a direct impact upon poverty. Ever since the birth of the nation's welfare state in the 1930s, Americans have looked primarily to the federal government, not state and local governments, for the redress of poverty. From this perspective, far more has been done—and is still being done—at the federal level to eliminate poverty among the elderly than among children.

Behind the foregoing comparison lies a problem of enormous economic and philosophical dimensions. What is not well understood, either by the public or by politicians, is that practically *all* social spending—including spending for such well-known and popular programs as Social Security and Medicare—is what economists call "transfer spending." This means that the government collects money through taxation—or obtains money by borrowing against future revenues—and then "transfers" this money through social programs to specific individuals and families. Basically, the working and taxpaying population pays for all transfers. In the United States over the years reviewed, we as a people have used the federal government as the means to transfer a significantly larger portion of the income produced annually to people who are aged than to children.

Spokespersons for the aged, especially the American Association of Retired Persons (AARP), argue that this is not so, that Social Security and Medicare are insurance programs in which beneficiaries (the aged) have paid for what they get by Social Security taxes deducted during their working lives. Though this is only partly true—most of the aged receive more from the Social

Security system in benefits than what they paid into the system as taxes while working (table 6-4)—the contributory aspect (Social Security taxes), universal coverage, and non–means-tested character of the Social Security system accounts for its popularity. From a philosophical perspective, through Social Security the nation has established a system in which specific taxes are used to prevent or reduce poverty once people are no longer working. The benefits in such a program become "entitlements"—that is, benefits to which people have a claim by virtue of law and prior financial contributions.

What we have not been able to do as a nation is devise a system of transfer spending aimed at reducing poverty among children that is as effective and popular as Social Security. The vast differences between what the federal government spends on reducing poverty among the aged and what it spends to reduce poverty among children suggests that as a nation we are far more interested in investing in the past (the elderly) than in the future (children). Perhaps this is too harsh a judgment, and perhaps, too, it is a false choice. An implicit, underlying factor accounting for these differences is that the elderly people may not have anyone able to take care of them, which is less often true for children. In any event, the United States is rich enough to do both—most West European nations do better in this respect than we do. What is needed is greater awareness of the transfer character of most social spending. Without such understanding, it will be difficult to gain public support for new forms of transfer spending designed to reduce or eliminate poverty among children. A system of family allowances for children, such as exists in our neighbor Canada and most West European states, is one possible solution. This would establish a system of entitlements for children, which eventually would probably become as popular as Social Security.

TABLE 6-4 *Payback Times for Social Security * (in years)*

	Earnings		
	Minimum Earner	Average Earner	Maximum Earner
	Employee Taxes Only		
Male:			
Social Security	3.0	4.2	5.3
Social Security and HI†	2.8	4.2	5.8
Social Security, HI, and SMI‡	2.5	3.8	5.4
Female:			
Social Security	3.0	4.2	5.3
Social Security and HI†	2.9	4.3	5.9
Social Security, HI, and SMI‡	2.6	4.0	5.5
	Combined Employee and Employer Taxes		
Male:			
Social Security	6.4	8.9	11.4
Social Security and HI†	5.8	8.8	12.2
Social Security, HI, and SMI‡	5.1	7.9	11.0
Female:			
Social Security	6.4	8.9	11.4
Social Security and HI†	5.9	8.9	12.3
Social Security, HI, and SMI‡	5.3	8.1	11.2

*Number of years it takes for benefits received to equal taxes paid into the Social Security system.

†Hospital insurance.

‡Supplemental Medical Insurance.

SOURCE: U.S. House of Representatives, Committee on Ways and Means, *Green Book* (Washington, D.C.: U.S. Government Printing Office, 1992), p. 1267.

THE WORKING POOR

Who are the "working poor"? There is no precise definition for them, although generally they are persons in households or families where one or more members work full- or part-time during the year, yet the family's income is below the poverty line. They are often "invisible," are far more numerous than many people think, and rarely fit the popular stereotypes that see the poor as either "shiftless, black urban males unable to hold jobs, or inner city mothers on welfare whose sole work experience is the repeated bearing and raising of illegitimate children."[31] Historically, the fate of the working poor is tied closely to the overall performance of the economy, their numbers falling during good times and rising during bad times. This pattern changed during the 1980s. By 1990, the number of poor people who worked full time (two million) was 55.8 percent higher than in 1978, even though the unemployment rate in 1990 was 5.5 percent, as compared with the 1978 rate of 6.1 percent.[32] Along with other forms of poverty, the number of working poor grew substantially in the 1980s. The existence of the working poor is another major explanation for poverty among children in America, because about 40 percent of America's children in poverty live in two-parent families, and many of these families, of course, are among the working poor.

Since the working poor are a heterogeneous group, and since, too, there is considerable overlap when the poor are classified in other ways—by sex, race, or age, for example—there is no single way to measure the number of persons who fall into this category. The Census Bureau in its annual surveys of poverty in the United States estimates, out of the total number of persons in poverty, how many are fifteen years of age and over, and of this number it further estimates how many worked at all during the year, and how many worked full-time during the year. The Census Bureau figures show that, contrary to what many may think, a significant proportion of poor people work. For example, for the thirteen-year period from 1978 through 1990, Census Bureau figures reveal that, on average, 40.3 percent of all poor persons over fifteen years of age worked at least some of the time during the year, and 8.8 percent worked full-time the year around.[33] Recent figures show even higher percentages for work among poor families with children. In 1990, for example, 63.2 percent of all poor families with children had someone who worked during the year, and 27 percent of all poor families with children had the equivalent of one or more persons working full-time during the entire year.[34]

In the spring of 1992, the Census Bureau released a new report on the number of workers with low earnings in the American economy. This report, whose publication was delayed for several months by the Bush administration, showed a sharp increase between 1979 and 1990 in the number (and percent) of full-time workers whose earnings and wages fell below the poverty level for a family of four.[35] To get a better statistical picture of the working poor, this report developed and used the concept of a year-round, full-time attachment to the labor force as its basic measurement category. In short, the report's definition includes in the full-time labor force every person sixteen years or older who either worked a normal amount of time for at least fifty weeks out of the year, or wanted to work a normal amount of time. The report then calculated for selected years since 1964 the number and percent of workers with a full-time attachment to the labor force whose earnings (before taxes) fell below the poverty level for a family of four (table 6-5).

The findings in this Census Bureau report reflect the same basic split in the trend lines for the numbers before and after the early 1970s as is found in nearly all the other data examined in this book. Between 1964 and 1974, the percent of all workers, male workers, and female workers whose earnings were below the poverty level for a family of four fell sharply, from 24.1 to 12.0 percent for all workers, from 16.5 to 7.4 percent for male workers, and from 45.2 to 22.1 percent for female workers. After

TABLE 6-5   *Percent of Year-round Workers with Annual Earnings Below the Poverty Level, Selected Years, 1964–90 (in percent)*

	1964	1969	1974	1979	1984	1990
All Workers	24.1%	14.4%	12.0%	12.1%	14.6%	18.0%
Male Workers	16.5	8.8	7.4	7.7	10.5	13.9
Female Workers	45.2	27.6	22.1	20.4	21.3	24.3

SOURCE: Bureau of the Census, *Current Population Reports*, ser. P-60, no. 178, *Workers with Low Earnings: 1964 to 1990*, p. 3, table B.

1974 and through 1990, these percentages rose, to 18.0 percent for all workers, to 13.9 percent for male workers, and to 24.3 percent for female workers. In 1990, the threshold for low annual earnings was $12,195, which is the annual income for a person working forty hours per week, fifty weeks per year, at an hourly wage of $6.10.[36]

Numbers in this Census Bureau report also show in yet another way how disadvantaged female workers are in the marketplace. In 1964, for example, for every male worker with annual earnings below the poverty level there were 2.7 female workers. Because earnings for women rose faster than earnings for men after 1970, by 1990 the ratio had dropped to 1.7 female workers with earnings below the poverty level for each male worker in this situation. This is improvement, but it also shows that, even below the poverty level, earnings for females lag behind earnings for males.

The total number of year-round, full-time workers with earnings below the poverty level in 1990 was 14.4 million, of which 6.7 million were men and 7.7 were women. If you add the number of workers with earnings below poverty level to the actual number of unemployed in 1990 (6.9 million), the combined total represents 16.0 percent of all persons seeking full-time work during the year, a figure much higher than the nominal unemployment rate of 6.6 percent in 1990.[37]

If the findings from this special Census Bureau report are factored into the Census Bureau numbers on poverty in 1990, the picture of poverty in America becomes much grimmer. In 1990, there were 33.8 million persons living below the "official" Census Bureau poverty threshold. If we subtract from this figure the 2.0 million poor people who worked full-time, the poverty figure is then 31.5 million persons living below the poverty level who work less than full-time (or not at all). Add to this figure the 14.4 million workers from the 1992 Census Bureau report on workers with low earnings, and the total of persons who were living below the poverty line in 1990 becomes 45.9 million, or 18.5 percent of the nation's population—not 13.5 percent, as officially reported by the Census Bureau.

In their book, *The Forgotten Americans,* John E. Schwarz, political-science professor at the University of Arizona, and Thomas J. Volgy, mayor of Tucson, Arizona, from 1987 to 1991, estimate the number of working poor in the United States by an alternative measure of the poverty threshold.[38] Instead of using the basic Census Bureau definition of the poverty threshold— $13,359 for a family of four in 1990—as a benchmark, they develop a "self-sufficiency" threshold, defined as an economy budget that would allow a family of four (two adults and two children) to purchase the minimum but essential items for food, housing, clothing, transportation, and medical and personal incidental expenses, and to pay expected federal and state taxes. Their self-sufficiency threshold for 1990 was $20,658, which is 154.6 percent of the Census Bureau poverty threshold. Public opinion surveys, Schwarz and Volgy assert, show that Americans consistently report that a family of four needs from 140 to 160 percent of the official poverty level in order to live.[39]

On the basis of their self-sufficiency threshold, and using figures from the Census Bureau's annual survey of income for families, households, and persons, they calculate the population of working poor in the United States. These "forgotten Americans" are employed full-time the entire year, usually receive no welfare assistance (AFDC, food stamps, or Medicaid), and live below the self-sufficiency threshold. How many are there, according to the Schwarz-Volgy standard? In 1989, a year when the nation was at the peak of the longest peacetime expansion it had ever known, they numbered 24 million family members, of whom 6 million were full-time workers.[40] If we modify again the official poverty statistic (33.5 million minus 2.0 million working full-time), and add to the figure the Schwarz-Volgy estimate of 24.0 million for the working poor and their families living below a self-sufficiency budget, the adjusted poverty total for the nation is 55.5 million persons, or 22.6 percent of the nation's population of 246.0 million in 1989. What this figure means, they point out, is that poverty in America is just about as widespread as it was in 1959, the first year for which the government calculated a poverty index.

As with poverty in general, there is no single explanation for the existence of the working poor. Most people who find themselves among the working poor are there either because, for a variety of reasons, they simply cannot find a full-time job that pays above poverty-level wages, or because their family situation pushes them below the poverty level. The latter is most likely to happen to single-parent families headed by women.

Consider the following. Bob is a construction worker, married with two children, and his wife does not work. In 1987, he earned $5.25 an hour, but because of the intermittent nature of construction work, his yearly wage income was only $9,555. That year, the poverty threshold for a family of four was $11,611, so Bob found himself among the working poor, with an income $2,056 short of the amount needed to lift his family out of poverty. Bob's situation was perhaps temporary, depending upon the development of his own skills as a construction worker plus the cyclical fortunes of the industry. In 1991, the average annual earnings of construction workers were significantly above the poverty level.

Barbara is in a different situation. She is a single mother with two children, a minimal education, and no special skills. So she worked for a cleaning service, earning the minimum wage of $3.35 an hour (1987). Her total income for a full year's work, except for two weeks without pay when her children were sick, came to $6,700, an amount $2,355 short of the poverty-threshold income for a family of three in 1987. Barbara's prospects for ever getting out of the working poor are slim. For her, AFDC plus food stamps would clearly be a better economic deal, but she chooses to work. Why? Is it because of the work ethic that is so strongly ingrained in many Americans? Perhaps.

Jane is a single woman, living alone, working in a cafeteria four hours a day at $3.75 an hour. Her annual earnings were $3,750 before taxes, which was $2,031 below the poverty level for a single person in 1987. Jane wanted to work full-time, but could not find a full-time job. In October 1992, there were 6.2 million people working part-time who wanted to work full-time but were unable to do so because of the depressed state of the economy.[41]

Although the circumstances that thrust individuals and families into the ranks of the working poor vary, there are several common threads running through their lives. First, existing tax and welfare programs rarely help them, although their numbers are sizable. Because so often they are "invisible," policy-makers have not taken much notice of them. Second, a common element in the lives of almost all of the working poor is the absence of health insurance, something that many Americans take for granted. A large proportion of the estimated thirty-five to thirty-seven million Americans without any health insurance are among the working poor. Third, as reporters from *U.S. News & World Report* discovered while doing an in-depth story on the working poor, their poverty is not of the grinding Third World variety. What so often they lack are the commonplace amenities enjoyed by the vast majority of Americans—vacations, meals out, leisure time, movies, baby-sitters, music lessons for their children, toys for the children except at Christmas.[42] Fourth, the families of the working poor are not especially large—less than 25 percent have more than three children—and a majority of the heads of families have a high-school education. Finally, a strong work ethic, determination to make life better for their children, and a strong religious faith are common to many of working poor people.

POVERTY AND THE BLACK COMMUNITY

When rioting exploded in Los Angeles in 1992 following the verdict in the Rodney King case, the nation's attention was focused once again on black poverty, racism, and the links between the two. Twenty-four years after the 1968 President's Commission on Civil Disorders—the Kerner Report—warned that the nation was heading toward two societies, separate and unequal, the findings of the commission, which went largely unheeded, were more relevant than ever.

Though it is true that there has been substantial economic progress for some black people—in 1988, 12.6 percent of black families had incomes over $50,000 (in 1988 dollars), compared with 7.1 percent in 1973[43]—the overall mood of America's black community has turned increasingly toward despair and hopelessness. In the aftermath of the Los Angeles riot, *Newsweek* cited in roll-call fashion the following grim statistics.[44] They need little comment.

The infant mortality rate for black Americans is 17.7 per thousand births, more than double the rate for white Americans, and higher than the rate for Malaysia.

Black children are three times more likely than white children to live in a single-parent household, and 43.2 percent of all black children live in poverty (the 1990 Census figures put this percentage at 44.8).

Black people now account for 28.8 percent of all AIDS cases in the United States. Black women constitute 52 percent of women with the disease, and black children represent 53 percent of all pediatric AIDS cases.

In 1989, 23 percent of all black men aged twenty to twenty-nine were either in prison, on probation, or on parole.

Homicide is now the leading cause of death for black American males between the ages of fifteen and thirty-four. Nearly one-half of all U.S. murder victims are black people.

The latter shocking number was analyzed in detail in one of several articles that explored gunshot deaths from both murder and suicide as a major medical problem in America in the June 10, 1992, issue of the *Journal of the American Medical Association* (*JAMA*).[45] In a signed editorial, Dr. C. Everett Koop, former surgeon-general of the United States, and Dr. George D. Lundberg, editor of *JAMA*, described violence in America—especially handgun violence—as a "public health emergency." No segment of American society is more at risk in this emergency than the black community.

Black Americans are 12.4 percent of America's population, but their 1990 poverty rate was 31.9 percent, roughly three times the rate of white Americans (10.7 percent). Put differently, slightly more than one out of every three black Americans lives in poverty, whereas only one out of every ten white Americans lives in poverty. As noted earlier, poverty in America is not primarily a black problem when viewed in terms of the total number of poor, black and white. Of the 33.6 million Americans listed as poor by the Census Bureau in 1990, 9.8 million (or 29.2 percent) were black. However, if the problem is viewed from the perspective of the *proportion* of any group found to be poor, then poverty in America is primarily a black problem. A group of which one-third of the members are in poverty is in far more serious trouble than a group that has only one-tenth of its members in poverty.

If we look at poverty from the perspective of where the poor people live, we see yet another dimension to the problem of black poverty in America. It then becomes mixed up with the decaying inner cities in this country. From a geographical perspective, as mentioned above, poverty in America is primarily an urban matter.

The Census Bureau uses four basic categories to describe where people live: (1) metropolitan areas; (2) central cities within metropolitan areas; (3) suburbs; and (4) rural areas. Data compiled annually by the Census Bureau show not just the total number and percent of the nation's population and families living in each of these geographic areas, but number and percentage living in poverty.

Technically, a "metropolitan area" is defined as a geographic area "with a large population nucleus, together with adjacent communities which have a high degree of economic and social integration with that nucleus."[46] In plain English, as noted earlier, a metropolitan area consists of any city with a population of at least fifty thousand and its surrounding suburbs. Chicago with all of its suburbs is a metropolitan area. Also as noted before, the largest city in each metropolitan area is always designated as the "central city." But the "central city" is not the same as the "inner city," the phrase so commonly used on television and the press to describe the central area of America's great cities, where poverty, crime, and decay are most rampant. The inner city consists of places within the city where the poverty rate exceeds 20 percent, called "poverty areas" by the Census Bureau.

What do Census Bureau numbers tell us about where Americans live? Overwhelmingly (76.5 percent), American families (white, black, and Hispanic) now live in metropolitan areas; of the families living in metropolitan areas, two-thirds live outside the central city of any particular metropolitan area. America basically has become a suburban society in terms of family living, but this generalization applies primarily to white families, nearly 70 percent of whom live in the suburbs (table 6-6).

The reverse is the case for black and Hispanic families. In 1990, 82.7 percent of all black families lived in metropolitan areas, and of these, two-thirds (67.7 percent) lived in central cities. For Hispanic families, the figures are 92.6 percent in metropolitan areas, and 55.5 percent in central cities.[47] Behind these latter numbers lies a growing animosity between blacks and Hispanics, as cultural and economic conflicts arise between the two groups in America's crowded central cities. The 1992 Los

TABLE 6-6 *The Location of All Families and Poor Families in America: 1990 (in percent)*

| | Percent of Families | |
Category	In Poverty	All Families
All Families	100.0%	100.0%
In Metro Areas	71.4	76.5
In Central Cities	58.9	36.7
In Suburbs	41.1	63.3
In Rural Areas	28.6	23.5
White Families	100.0%	100.0%
In Metro Areas	67.9	75.2
In Central Cities	48.1	31.8
In Suburbs	51.9	68.2
In Rural Areas	32.1	24.8
Black Families	100.0%	100.0%
In Metro Areas	77.8	82.7
In Central Cities	77.5	67.7
In Suburbs	22.5	32.3
In Rural Areas	22.2	17.3

SOURCE: Bureau of the Census, Current Population Reports, ser. P-60, no. 175, *Poverty in the United States: 1990*, p. 151, table 21.

Angeles riots, according to one Los Angeles writer, were a "black vs. brown" conflict as much as a black-white clash.[48] Increasingly, America is dividing geographically along racial lines—mostly white suburbs and black and Hispanic central cities. The suburbs are not all lily-white; about one-third of all black families live outside the central cities. Middle-class blacks as well as whites have been a part of the post–World War II flight from the cities, although their numbers are far smaller than those of whites.

Finally, there is the geography of poverty (table 6-6). Figures from the Census Bureau show that poverty among families is heavily concentrated in metropolitan areas, 71.4 percent compared with 28.6 percent in rural areas. Most of the latter is found in the small towns of the Midwest and the South, and among subsistence farmers in the South. For the general population, nearly 60 percent of poor families in metropolitan areas are found in central cities; for blacks, the comparable percentage is 77.5; for Hispanics, 65.9. For white poor families, slightly more (51.9 percent) live outside the central city than in the central city (48.1 percent). More poor white families (32.1 percent) live in rural areas than do black families (22.2 percent).[49] Thus, poverty in the central cities is heavily concentrated among black and Hispanic families, and the incidence of poverty in the suburbs and in rural areas is greatest among white families.

THE BLACK UNDERCLASS

For most Americans, the kind of poverty among black people that is best known—and most feared—is the poverty of the "underclass"—the poverty of black ghettos in the inner cities. The Los Angeles riots were but a reflection, as *Newsweek* described it, of "a complex social crisis that is shaking Black America. It is a crisis of the inner city. . . . Its causes—poverty, crime, drugs and the disintegration of family and community—are obvious to everyone and its severity is beyond dispute."[50] This does not mean that all poor black people are a part of the underclass—far from it. But it underscores the fact that the impact and consequences of the hard-core poverty found in America's inner cities extend far beyond the lives of persons trapped in the underclass. To solve the problems of the black underclass—if they are solvable—will take us a long way toward solving the overall problem of poverty.

The contemporary meaning of the term "underclass" stems largely from a series of articles by Ken Auletta in *The New Yorker* in 1981. In these articles, later published as a book entitled *The Underclass,* Auletta focused on the hard-core jobless minority of the population who are poor, white and black, who see themselves excluded from society, reject commonly accepted values, and "suffer from *behavior* as well as *income* deficiencies."[51] Included in Auletta's version of the underclass are the *passive poor,* usually long-term welfare recipients; the *street criminals,* who terrorize the inner cities; the *hustlers,* who may not be poor but make their living from illegal activity in the underground economy; and the *traumatized* "drunks, drifters, homeless shopping bag ladies, and released mental patients who frequently roam or collapse on city streets."[52] It is the violent street criminals, the gang members like those from the notorious Bloods and Crips in Los Angeles, who are seen by the public as the real—and feared—underclass.

In his 1982 book, Auletta reported that, although no one really knows the true size of the "underclass," estimates place it at 20–30 percent of the number of persons in poverty. If we accept these estimates, the underclass in 1990 totaled between 6.7 and 10.1 million persons, or between 3.6 and 5.4 percent of the nation's population. Unfortunately, the precise number of street criminals is not known, although their impact on public feeling and the fear they create far outweighs their relatively small proportion in the overall picture of the nation's underclass. In New York City, for example, a tiny handful of violent criminals has destroyed Central Park as a safe place to stroll at night.

By far the most analytical account and explanation of the emergence of the *black* underclass is found in *The Truly Disadvan-*

taged, a study that appeared in 1987, written by William Julius Wilson, a sociologist at the University of Chicago.[53] Like Auletta, Wilson identifies the underclass as a heterogeneous group "of inner city families and individuals whose behavior contrasts sharply with that of mainstream America."[54] However, Wilson's analysis differs from most other studies in two major ways.

First, he makes it clear that the emergence of violence-ridden black ghettos in the nation's inner cities is a recent development. In the 1940s, 1950s, and even into the 1960s, lower-class, working-class, and middle-class black families mostly lived in the same community, sending their children to the same schools, shopping in the same stores, and having black lawyers, doctors, teachers, and other professionals in the community. This is no longer true, as middle-class black persons—especially black professionals—flee the inner city to better neighborhoods or the suburbs. Ironically, the civil-rights legislation of the 1960s, which ended the legal barriers that kept *all* black persons in segregated enclaves in the city, helped make possible the exodus of middle-class blacks from the inner city. As Wilson points out, the population remaining in the inner city is thus deprived of the role models and stabilizing influence offered by successful middle-class businessmen and professionals. Today the inner-city ghettos are populated almost entirely by the most disadvantaged segments of the black urban community.

Second, Wilson, a black person who does not readily fit either the usual liberal or conservative stereotypes, does not regard racism as the primary cause for the emergence of a violent black underclass in America's inner cities. It is true, he says, that *historic* discrimination helped create an impoverished black community in the first place, but the real causes for the plight of the black population trapped in inner-city ghettos are found in recent, far-reaching changes in the economy. Urban minorities—and especially inner-city blacks—have been particularly vulnerable to the "shift from goods-producing to service-producing industries, the increasing polarization of the labor market into low-wage and high-wage sectors, innovations in technology, and the relocation of manufacturing out of the central cities."[55] Thus, the flight of both middle-class black people and low-skill but well-paying manufacturing jobs has left the inner cities with more and more young blacks without jobs or the hope of a job. In the 1950s, for example, unemployment among teenage blacks averaged 18.9 percent, a figure much too high even then, but in the 1980s, the unemployment rate climbed to an average of 40.3 percent.[56] If we take into account the difficulty of securing an actual unemployment figure in ghetto areas, the real rate of unemployment for black youth is probably closer to 60 percent!

Wilson's real message is that *class* differences, exacerbated but not caused by race, are at the root of the violence, the despair, and hopelessness of the underclass in the inner city. Far-reaching changes in the structure of the economy—changes that are both a cause and a consequence of the silent depression—have sharpened the differences between classes in America, especially for black people who live near the bottom of the economic ladder.

What is called for, in Wilson's view, is a shift away from "group-specific" to universal programs of reform. By "group-specific," Wilson means programs targeted at specific groups such as poor people, welfare mothers, black teenagers, and others. The difficulty with the group-specific approach is that it arouses strong resentment among those who do not benefit, especially blue-collar workers who see themselves paying for programs to help the "undeserving poor" but reaping little or no benefit for themselves. What is needed are comprehensive policies aimed at the general population, including meaningful full employment and job training that works. As *Los Angeles Times* columnist Roger Wilkins wrote shortly after the Los Angeles riots, "The main thing needed to connect the poor people of Los Angeles to the economic and political life of the country are jobs. . . . The most useful explanation for the suffering poor people endure and the behavior they exhibit is that too few jobs of any kind are available to them."[57]

Wilkins is partly right. A long period of sustained full employment, one that brought the unemployment rate down to 3 or 4 percent, would go far toward ending the silent depression. But employment by itself is no longer enough. What is needed, as chapter 9 will show, are programs that create higher-wage jobs, a challenge that so far the nation's policy-makers have not over-come.

HOMELESSNESS IN AMERICA

Finally, there is the newest strain of poverty to plague America—homelessness. Like the black underclass of the inner city, homelessness is a recent development; homeless people are not even mentioned as one of the categories of the poor population in the 1964 *Economic Report of the President,* the document that launched Lyndon Johnson's War on Poverty.

Drugs and alcohol, family violence, broken marriages, lost jobs, lack of affordable housing, even fear of homeless shelters by homeless people—these are the circumstances that pushed increasing numbers of Americans into the streets during the 1980s. Pamela Cox, in Kansas City, was pushed onto the streets by drugs for a year; sometimes she and her four children lived in the public parks, and at other times she wandered alone while the children stayed with her mother. Ultimately, with the help of dedicated staff at the City Union Mission Family Shelter in Kansas City, she began the painful task of putting her life back in order.[58] For another Kansas City resident, forty-four-year-old Lynn Shepard, it was a series of losses—her brother killed in a car accident, the breakup of her marriage, the loss of a sales job at which she had earned handsome commissions, the temporary loss of her voice—which led her, in eighteen months, from a comfortable middle-class life in a townhouse, to a homeless shelter, to a hospital psychiatric ward, and, finally, to a new job and the hope of starting over.[59] Once the "homeless" in America consisted mainly of the relatively few alcoholics and derelicts who populated the "skid rows" found in most large American cities, or a few hoboes wandering across the land. No longer. Now the people wandering the streets are not always technically "homeless"—without any roof over their heads—but they are uprooted, cast adrift in a society where there is no place for them. Aside from the docile "bag ladies," the new breed of uprooted are younger, angry, and more prone to violence than those of an earlier era. Many are young workers, often from minorities, unable to find a place in the emerging high-tech economy of the 1980s and 1990s; others are former mental patients, dumped onto the streets as a result of the misguided and maladroit "deinstitutionalization" movement of the 1960s and 1970s.[60] As the silent depression unfolded during the Reagan era, the ranks of homeless persons continued to grow. Women and children are now the fastest-growing category of the homeless, as the stories from the *Kansas City Star* attest.

How many homeless persons are there in America? As with the black underground, no exact figures exist to answer this question. Since no government agency systematically collects statistics on homeless people, available estimates come primarily from private sources. The Urban Institute, drawing upon several different sources, estimated that in the late 1980s the number of homeless in America ranged from 560,000 to 680,000. The National Alliance to End Homelessness estimated that, on any given night in 1987, 735,000 Americans were homeless, of which 100,000 were children.[61] As noted earlier, the Children's Defense Fund estimates that as many as 1.5 million children are homeless at some time during any single year. Pamela Cox's children fit the latter statistics, for, even though their mother was on the streets for an entire year, they were not, spending most of the year with Pamela's mother.

We do not have precise numbers on the total of people who are homeless in America, but much is known about their general characteristics. In spite of the rapid growth of homelessness among women and children in recent years, the overwhelming majority of homeless are still men. The Urban Institute's 1989 study, *America's Homeless*, found that 81 percent of homeless people are male, and 54 percent are nonwhite. Forty-eight percent have not graduated from high school, as compared with 19 percent for all adults; 15 percent of the homeless are children; the average monthly income for a homeless person is $135, less than one-third the poverty level; one-fifth have a reported history of mental hospitalization, and one-third have been patients in an alcohol-or-drug-treatment center; the median length of homelessness for homeless persons was ten months, although households with children are homeless for shorter periods; and homeless persons have been jobless longer than they have been homeless. Somewhat surprisingly, few if any of the services offered to the homeless—primarily shelters and soup kitchens—receive any federal support other than surplus food; most of their support is from the United Way, churches, and business firms. Homeless people are eligible for government benefits such as food stamps, AFDC benefits, and public assistance such as SSI, but few of single homeless persons take advantage of these benefits. In 1989, only 15 percent of homeless single persons got food stamps, and only 10 percent got any general assistance.[62]

CAN POVERTY BE CURED?

America's checkered record in coping with poverty since Michael Harrington first discovered the nation's hidden poverty in 1963 might lead one to conclude that, as the Bible says, "the poor always ye have with you." Perhaps. The fact of the matter is, however, that, save for Lyndon Johnson's brief but ill-fated War on Poverty in the late 1960s, ending poverty in America has not been high on the agenda of *any* administration since then. Poverty, as this chapter has shown, is something with many faces, so it is unlikely that any administration, including President

Clinton's, will give its elimination the same priority it had before the Johnson administration sank into the morass of Vietnam. Much of the nation's poverty can be reduced if not eliminated; this, however, will come not from a "war on poverty" as such, but as a consequence of actions taken to end the silent depression, actions discussed fully in chapters 8, 9, and 10.

CHAPTER 7

Getting from There to Here

Twenty years of the silent depression have left America with a legacy of a shrinking middle class, lost jobs, destroyed dreams, growing class divisions and antagonisms, and fear in the hearts of many young persons that they will never achieve the economic standard of life enjoyed by their parents. This raises two central questions. First, how did the nation get into this fix, this two-decade-long period of subpar economic performance? Second, what can be done to get us out of the silent depression, to get the nation back to a more normal path of growth and prosperity? This chapter answers the first question; the remaining chapters propose cures for the silent depression.

PRODUCTIVITY ONCE AGAIN

Nothing useful can be said about either the causes or the cures for the silent depression without understanding the nature and the importance of productivity. The most important *single* fact about the American economy is the productivity slowdown since 1973. If one had to point to a single cause for the silent depression, this would be it—the slowdown in productivity growth. Yet productivity as such was hardly mentioned by either candidate in the bitterly fought 1992 presidential campaign, even though both candidates no doubt had productivity in the back of their minds when they spoke of the need for economic growth. Why was such a crucial topic ignored? The simplest explanation is that productivity is a technical subject of the sort that political handlers advise their candidates to avoid at all costs.

"Productivity" has not always been a word avoided by our political leaders. In the Marshall Plan era, when America led the world to a rapid and awesome recovery from the ravages of World War II, productivity was the economic gospel that our leaders took to the rest of the world. America's defeated enemies, Germany and Japan, took this message to heart, placing productivity growth at center stage in their recovery and growth plans, which led them to the forefront of the world economy. As America struggles to escape from stagnation, understanding how crucial productivity growth is to our economic well-being is necessary for all citizens.

Productivity is not an esoteric, difficult-to-understand concept. It is nothing more than an average—a measure of how much output a worker produces during a particular period of time. The Bureau of Labor Statistics uses an hour as its standard unit of measurement, but productivity can just as easily be measured on an annual basis. For example, in 1990 an employed person in America produced $35,249 worth of goods and services, measured in 1982 prices. Forty-two years earlier (in 1948), an employed person produced $19,017 worth of goods and services, also measured in 1982 prices.[1] Over this period, the average productivity of an employed person increased by 85.4 percent.

These figures were obtained by dividing the nation's output (the gross domestic product) in a given year by the number of people at work in the same year. Productivity is a simple, numerical average. It tells us how effective labor is in producing goods and services in a particular year. It is *not* just a measure of the skill of labor. Productivity measures *everything*—the actual skill and education of the labor force, the kind of machines and tools being used in production, the technology at work, the effectiveness of management—that contributes to the ability of labor, in combination with all other resources, to produce the goods and services that determine our living standards.

No great mystery attaches to the key sources of productivity growth. They are essentially three. The first is economists' "capital goods"—the tools, machines, and buildings available to workers. Providing the work force with more and better machines, tools, and buildings—with more capital, in other words—is essential to increasing productivity. Second, there is that mysterious thing called "technology," the catchall term that describes the application of scientific knowledge to the task of producing goods and services. Technology does not exist in the abstract. To be useful, technology must become a part of either physical capital or the skill and training of labor—or both. For example, the shift from the manual to the electric typewriter and then to the word processor reflects a changing technology which has become a part of increasingly complicated and sophisticated machines. Finally, there is the actual skill of the worker. An illiterate person cannot use even a typewriter, let alone a personal computer and word processor. Education and training—sometimes called "human capital investment"—are also necessary if productivity is to improve.

What about savings? For years, the American public has been told that our fundamental problem is that we are not saving enough—that Germany and Japan, our chief global competitors—save far more than we do, and thus are forging ahead in productivity growth. At best, this is a half-truth. Until the 1980s, there was little change in the overall rate of savings in America by business firms and people. It is more important to understand that the role of savings in promoting investment in new capital and new technology is essentially *permissive*. It is not fundamental, which is to say that, while savings are necessary for investment, they do not *determine* investment. What really counts is the expectation of business leaders that investing in new equipment and new structures will be profitable. If there is the prospect of profit, the money and savings necessary to carry out the investments can be found.

WHY HAS PRODUCTIVITY GROWTH SLOWED?

Volumes have been written about America's productivity crisis and puzzle.[2] Like the concept itself, however, the explanations for the slowdown in productivity growth are not nearly so mysterious or unfathomable as many suspect. The sources of productivity growth discussed above tell us where to look. Three major long-term developments account for our sagging rate of productivity growth. They are, first, "military Keynesianism"; second, the decline in public investment in the nation's infrastructure of highways, mass-transit systems, airports, electrical, gas, and water facilities, and sewage systems; and, third, the failure of the private economy to invest adequately in the quantity of equipment available for every worker in the labor force.

Military Keynesianism

The colorful phrase "military Keynesianism," was coined by a British economist, the late Joan Robinson, in an address to American economists in 1971. She used this phrase to describe how military spending in the era of the Cold War had become a major—if not *the* major—force in the American economy. She attached the adjective "Keynesian" to the growth of military spending in the Cold War era because in Keynesian economics one of the key ideas is that government spending for goods and services is a major determinant of the economy's overall level of output and employment. For the more than four decades of the Cold War, military spending propped up the economy.

Military Keynesianism is President Dwight Eisenhower's nightmare come true—the domination of the American economy by the military-industrial complex. Since 1947, slightly more than 75 percent of the goods and services purchased by the federal government were for military purposes.[3] This 75-percent figure does not apply to the total of federal-government spending, for that total includes transfer spending as well as the purchase of goods and services. Economists measure the output of the public sector by the goods and services that governments (federal, state, and local) purchase in the marketplace. A society that for nearly half a century has devoted three-fourths of the output of its national government to military purposes is a society dominated by military Keynesianism.

The crucial question is, how has military Keynesianism affected both productivity and general economic growth? The answer lies in the way in which the military-industrial complex that President Eisenhower warned against evolved during the Cold War. Spending for modern weaponry created what Ann Markusen and Joel Yudken of Rutgers University described in 1992 as an "aerospace-communications-electronic complex (ACE)."[4] These three industries, plus those that supply ships, ordnance, and tanks, have been the prime beneficiaries of the more than $4.5 trillion spent on defense in the forty-seven years since the end of World War II.[5] How much is $4.5 trillion? It is $95.7 billion a year, $262.2 million a day, $10.9 million an hour, $181,666 a minute, or $3,028 a second!

What few people realize is that America has had a closet industrial policy—one carried out through Pentagon spending for weapons.[6] As Markusen and Yudken note, "For a good forty years, the aerospace-communications-electronics complex (ACE) has benefitted from every advantage attributed to industrial policy elsewhere—government fostering of research and development, public capital for plant construction and modernization, guaranteed markets for products, bailouts for firms in troubled periods, training funds for employee development, trade protection, export promotion, and economic adjustment for displaced workers and communities."[7]

America's closet industrial policy has been a phenomenal success for the industries that benefited most from Pentagon spending—aerospace, communications, and electronics. The big firms of the ACE complex prospered, offered well-paying jobs to thousands of white- and blue-collar workers, and became competitive in world markets. Unfortunately, much of the prosperity enjoyed by the ACE complex, especially during the boom years of the Reagan arms buildup, came at the expense of the rest of America's industrial base, including the industries producing capital goods—the goods producers need to improve their efficiency. During the great military buildup from 1979 through the mid-1980s, the ACE-complex industries increased significantly their share of manufacturing output, while nearly all of those manufacturing industries outside of the ACE complex saw their share of manufacturing decline. Many of the latter industries— iron and steel, machine tools, chemicals, motor vehicles, consumer electronics, and wearing apparel, to name but a few—lost significant parts of both their American and overseas markets to foreign producers.[8] In the meantime, America's leading competitors, Germany and Japan, pushed their resources, including engineering and scientific talent, into making consumer goods, displacing American leadership both at home and abroad in a long list of consumer industries—automobiles, television sets, cameras, sewing machines, tape recorders, bicycles, calculating machines, and many more.[9]

For a time, it was possible to ignore the adverse effects of the drain of resources into military activity because of the stimulus to growth provided by military spending, the belief that military programs yielded favorable "spinoffs" for commercial development, and the high-wage jobs associated with industries belonging to the ACE complex. In the mid-1980s, these reasons began to fade, even before the end of the Cold War. In the matter of spinoffs, for example, the early years of the Cold War saw many direct and spectacular spinoffs from the military to the civilian economy—jet aircraft, microchips, satellites, and computers come quickly to mind—but this is no longer true. Military technology, according to one critic, has become so increasingly esoteric and "baroque" that hardly any spinoffs for the civilian economy still exist.[10] For example, the very high-speed integrated circuits needed for the kind of electronic wizardry displayed during the Desert Storm offensive are only marginally useful to the commercial producers of semiconductors. The technology that produced Stealth airplanes is of little use in commercial aviation. It is also true that the fiscal stimulus from military spending is long gone, more than offset by the deflationary consequences of interest payments on the gargantuan federal debt, which basically came into existence because of the military buildup during the Reagan years. With the Cold War over, military spending is no longer a dependable source of jobs—by the end of 1991, an estimated fifty thousand jobs had been lost in the aircraft industry alone.[11]

America's closet industrial policy has thrown up barriers between the military and the civilian way of doing business, another adverse consequence of this development.[12] Not only is the ACE complex dominated by a relative handful of very large firms—the top twenty-five corporations have 50 percent of prime military contracts—but often these firms depend upon the Pentagon for 50 percent or more of their sales.[13] Defense firms (or the defense divisions of large firms operating in both civilian and military markets) become so accustomed to *maximizing* their costs in a market dominated by a single buyer—the Pentagon—that they cannot survive in the more competitive atmosphere of the civilian economy. In the *Alice in Wonderland* world of Pentagon capitalism, profits increase perversely with costs. During previous military "build-down" periods, especially after Vietnam, there were few success stories among the big military contractors that tried to convert to civilian production. Consequently, military-dependent producers often chose to "hunker down," determined to wait out the build-down, confident that sooner or later there would be a revival of defense spending.

America's Decaying Infrastructure

On April 13, 1992, an ancient freight tunnel running under the Chicago River suddenly ruptured, allowing millions of gallons of dirty water to gush through the network of utility tunnels that lie beneath Chicago's Loop, the city's central business district. The irony in Chicago's invisible, underground flood, whose costs ultimately will run into the billions, is that the original leak in the century-old system of underground tunnels could have been fixed for an estimated $10,000. Bureaucratic procrastination and budgetary penny-pinching delayed necessary repairs until it was too late.

Chicago's invisible spring flood of 1992 symbolizes a much larger problem—the continued neglect of a deteriorating infrastructure, not only in Chicago but nearly everywhere else in the nation. The dismal state of America's stock of public capital has been described as the nation's "third deficit," equal in economic size and seriousness to the chronic federal and trade deficits. This third deficit is a major cause of the nation's long-term stagnation and the slowdown in the rate of productivity growth, key elements in the silent depression.

The word "infrastructure" describes the basic supply of public facilities such as streets and highways, bridges, airports, mass-transit systems, water-supply and sewage systems, and electrical- and gas-distribution networks that is necessary before almost any activity can take place. Some writers include in the definition not just these basic facilities, but also educational structures and hospitals, as well as conservation and development facilities, such as dams, canals, and irrigation systems. Some, like electrical-power and natural-gas grids, are privately supplied, but overwhelmingly the infrastructure results from public investment. What is usually referred to as the core infrastructure—highways, sewer systems, and water-supply systems—is nearly 100 percent supplied through public investment. It is the massive, nation-wide neglect of public investment in infrastructure in the last two decades that is the source of America's third deficit.

Without an adequate and well-maintained public infrastructure, the efficient and profitable production and distribution of goods and services by the private sector either cannot take place or is severely handicapped. Highways are a case in point. Congestion on overloaded and undermaintained highways causes delays that the U.S. Department of Transportation estimates will total nearly four billion hours by 2005 if improvements to the nation's interstate highway system are not undertaken. Gasoline wasted by cars and trucks stuck in idle or slow-moving traffic now equals three billion gallons, almost 4 percent of the total gasoline consumed annually. The cost of this waste is estimated at $9 billion. The Federal Aviation Administration estimates that air-travel delays cost the airlines $1.8 billion in additional operating expenses, and travelers $3.2 billion in time lost.[14]

It is one of the curiosities of modern economics that the analysis of the role played by physical capital in the functioning and performance of the economy is limited almost entirely to *private* capital. Yet the private production and distribution of goods and services would be almost physically impossible without a basic network of public capital—roads, airports, water and sewage systems, and other facilities. Only recently have economists undertaken any serious research in this area. Their research provides numerical underpinnings for the intuitive argument that output, profits, and productivity in the private economy are significantly dependent upon the economy's willingness to invest in public capital.

There are three key questions needing answers. First, how important is public capital with respect to the nation's overall stock of physical capital? Second, what is the precise *numerical* link between a dollar invested in public capital and the rate of growth in productivity? The answer to this question will tell us how much of a gain in productivity we can expect by increasing the *rate* of investment in public capital. Third, how large and how serious is the decline in investment in the nation's infrastructure? The evidence of decline is all about us—the Chicago underground flood, bridges that fall down, dams that burst, street, highway, and airline congestion—but numbers as well as anecdotal evidence are needed to measure the magnitude of the economy's third deficit. There are several ways to approach this.

In 1947, public, nonmilitary physical capital was equal to 32.3 percent of the nation's total stock of physical capital. By 1970, this percentage had climbed to 35.0, but it declined thereafter. By 1990, the public share of the nation's total stock of physical capital had fallen to 29.3 percent. On the average since 1947, public capital has accounted for roughly $1.00 out of every $3.00 of the economy's stock of physical capital in the post–World War II era. The *rate* at which the nation invested in its stock of nonmilitary public capital rose from 3.4 percent of GNP in the early 1950s to a peak of 3.9 percent in the late 1960s, and then fell to a low of 2.2 percent in the latter half of the 1980s.[15] The decline in the investment rate for public capital in the 1970s and 1980s explains why there has also been since 1970 a drop in the public share of the nation's total stock of physical capital.

This brings up the second question: what is the exact relationship between investment in public capital and productivity growth? Extensive recent economic research on this vital question shows that there is an extremely close correlation between the rate of growth in public capital and the rate of growth in labor productivity, a relationship that exists not only for the United States, but for the other so-called G-7 countries—Japan, France, Germany, the U.K., Italy, and Canada—as well.[16] Economist David Alan Aschauer, a leader in public-capital research, found that, between 1950 and 1970, when the nation's stock of public capital grew at a 4.1-percent annual rate, productivity was growing at an average annual rate of 2.0 percent. From 1971 through 1985, however, the average annual rate of growth of public capital dropped to 1.6 percent, while productivity growth slumped to 0.8 percent (table 7-1). Aschauer argues that nearly 60 percent of the drop-off in the annual rate of growth in productivity is explained by the downturn in spending for public investment in the 1970s and 1980s.[17] Aschauer also found that, among the G-7 nations, Japan had, over the period 1973–85, both the highest rate of investment in public capital and the highest rate of productivity growth, whereas the United States had the lowest figures for both rates. Aschauer's work has not gone unchallenged by critics within the economics profession, but to date it has weathered this scrutiny successfully.[18]

What do these numbers mean with respect to public policy? Obviously, they point to the need for more investment in public capital as one way to reverse the decline in the rate of growth for productivity. How much of an increase is needed in this form of investment? Aschauer says his research indicates that a 1-percent increase in the size of the nation's core infrastructure will increase the national output by 0.24 percent.[19]

Aschauer's figure (0.24 of a percentage point) points the way to an answer for part of the third question posed above: how serious are the effects of the drop in the rate of investment in public capital? If the stock of public investment had increased at the same rate after 1973 as it did between 1950 and 1970 (4.1 percent), output per employed worker in 1990 would have been

TABLE 7-1 *Average Annual Rates of Growth for Productivity and Nonmilitary Public Capital: 1950–85 (in percent)*

Rate of Growth of:	1950–70	1971–85	1950–85
Productivity	2.0%	0.8%	1.5%
Public Capital	4.1	1.6	3.0

SOURCE: *Chicago Fed Letter*, Federal Reserve Bank of Chicago, no. 13, September 1988.

$39,833, as compared with the actual output of $35,249 (both figures are in 1982 dollars). On the average, each worker in 1990 would have produced 13.0 percent more goods and services than was actually produced.

Consider further what this means. The dollar difference between the actual and the potential figures for worker productivity is $4,584, which is the annual output lost per employed worker because of the nation's productivity slowdown. Multiply this figure by the number of persons actually at work in 1990— 117.9 million—and we get $540.5 billion, which is output forever lost because of insufficient investment in public capital during the 1970s and 1980s! On a per-person basis, there would have been an average of $2,149 *more* goods and services available to meet both private and public needs in the economy.[20] Without knowing how the additional infrastructure spending was financed—from current tax revenue or by additional borrowing—the precise amount of additional revenue $540.5 billion more in output would have brought into the federal treasury cannot be determined. One can be certain, though, that revenues would have been higher and the deficit lower if the $540.5 billion of potential output had been reality. A high price has been paid for the nation's neglect of its public capital!

Another useful way to get a measure of the magnitude of the third deficit is to compare the quantity of public capital per employed worker for the periods before and after 1973. Between 1947 and 1973, nonmilitary public capital per employed worker grew at an average annual rate of 1.7 percent. This led to a 68.1-percent increase in the dollar amount of nonmilitary public capital available per employed worker: from $17,425 in 1947 to $29,295 in 1973 (measured in constant 1987 dollars). After 1973, however, nonmilitary public capital per employed worker grew at the nearly invisible pace of .09 percent annually. Thus, by 1990, the dollar amount of nonmilitary public capital per employed worker was only $29,726, a mere 1.5 percent greater than the 1973 figure.

Now for another "what-if" figure. *If* public capital per worker had grown after 1973 at the same annual rate of 1.7 percent, the 1990 figure would have been $37,773, an amount $8,047 greater than the actual 1990 quantity of $29,726. Thus, in 1990, the nation's shortfall in public capital per worker was $8,047.

How large overall is the shortfall? In 1990, the total stock of nonmilitary public capital (federal plus state and local governments) was $3,498.4 billion, up by 40.3 percent from the 1973 figure. Between 1974 and 1990, the stock of nonmilitary public capital grew at an average annual rate of 2.0 percent, in contrast to a 3.4-percent average annual rate of growth between 1947 and 1973. If the nation's stock of nonmilitary public capital had grown at the same rate *after* 1973, it would total $4,408.4 billion. Thus, the overall shortfall in the nation's stock of nonmilitary public capital is $910.0 billion, almost $1 trillion.

By comparison, the outstanding debt of the federal government in 1990 was $2,844.0 billion (also in 1987 dollars), and the cumulative trade deficit measured in 1987 dollars for the United States from 1973 through 1991 was $914.7 billion. In 1990, the current market value of foreign-owned assets in the United States exceeded the market value of American assets abroad by $319.4 billion (in 1987 dollars). Most experts agree that this "net-asset position" is the best measure available of the size of the nation's second deficit.[21] Of America's three "deficits"—federal government, trade, and infrastructure—that of the federal government is greatest, the infrastructure second, and trade smallest. On a per-person basis, the federal debt is $11,309, the shortfall in public-capital infrastructure is $3,618, and the nation's international deficit is $1,270. This ranking is by numerical size. By far the most significant "deficit" is that of the infrastructure. The reason is because of its impact upon productivity—the strong correlation between the nation's failure to invest adequately in its infrastructure and the slowdown in productivity growth. Until productivity growth gets back onto its long-term historic track, most, if not all, of the many problems the nation faces will elude solution. Yet the infrastructure deficit is the least known and receives the least attention in the press and from the nation's policy-makers.

There is one other aspect of the public-investment problem that needs to be mentioned. Among economists (and some politicians and policy-makers), there is a long-standing and unresolved controversy over the effect of federal deficits upon investment in real capital—equipment and structures—by private business firms in the economy's private sector. This is known as the "crowding-out" thesis; it is argued that borrowing by the federal government reduces overall the amount of saving available, and thereby "crowds out" a certain amount of private investment because of insufficient savings. Crowding out rests upon the belief that the existence or nonexistence of savings is a primary determinant of spending for new capital. As noted earlier, however, the expectation of profit is far more important than the availability of savings.

If we move beyond the financial side of the federal deficit to the use of borrowed money by the public sector to buy real capital—roads, airports, sewage and water systems, for example—a different picture emerges. Good public facilities enhance the profit prospects for private firms. Better airports and better roads make it possible for firms like Federal Express or United Parcel to use their own physical capital (planes and trucks) more efficiently. Public capital can boost the return on private capital. So, instead of crowding out private investment, it is possible that public borrowing invested in real assets may crowd in private investment. This is not just an intuitive judgment. Aschauer in his research has found that, over a period of four to five years, for every dollar of investment in public capital, private investment will increase by about 45 cents.[22] This is a crucial finding, helping to explain why a part of the productivity problem is linked to a decline in the rate of private investment.

The Slowdown in Private Investment

It is no accident that the slowdown in the rate of growth of nonmilitary public capital has had a parallel in the private economy—a slowdown in the rate of growth of private capital (table 7-2). As just noted, the two are closely linked, so much so that it is not an exaggeration to say that the real source of America's productivity problem is insufficient investment in both the private and the public sectors. Rather than seeing the public and private sectors as rival claimants for scarce resources, as the crowding-out controversy suggests, public and private capital should be seen as complementing each other. Commercial airlines invest in private capital in the form of better airplanes; the public, through government, invests in airports and air-traffic control systems. Private trucks run on public highways; private factories could not operate without publicly supplied roads and water. Without a sustaining structure of public capital—including schools—most private production would come to a halt.

TABLE 7-2 *Average Annual Rates of Growth in the Stock of Capital per Worker in the United States: 1947–90 (in percent)*

Rate of Growth for:	1947–73	1974–90
Private Economy		
Fixed Capital per Worker*	1.5%	1.4%
Equipment per Worker	3.3	1.9
Structures per Worker	0.5	1.1
Public Economy		
Nonmilitary Capital per Worker	1.7	0.09
Total Private and Public Capital per Worker	1.6	0.3

*Excludes residential structures.
SOURCE: U.S. Department of Commerce, *Survey of Current Business*, January 1992.

Table 7-3 *Private Capital per Worker: 1947, 1973, and 1990*

Type of Capital	1947	1973	1990
Total per Worker	$36,481	$56,348	$71,748
Equipment per Worker	10,835	25,254	34,514
Buildings per Worker	25,644	31,094	37,233

Source: U.S. Department of Commerce, *Survey of Current Business*, January 1992.

What counts for productivity is the quality of the tools, the machines, and the buildings used by labor in the production of goods and services. A look at the numbers since 1973 (tables 7-3, 7-4) reveals that the nation has been *oversupplied* with buildings—vacant office space and the overbuilding of shopping malls across the country attest to this—and *undersupplied* with the tools and machines workers need to do their jobs. Redundancy of

Table 7-4 *Comparison of Potential and Actual Public and Private Capital per Worker in 1990 (in 1987 dollars)*

Type of Capital	Potential	Actual	Shortfall
Public Nonmilitary Capital per Worker	$37,773	$29,726	$8,047
Total Private Capital per Worker	73,061	71,748	1,321
Equipment per Worker	44,073	34,514	9,559
Buildings per Worker	34,072	37,233	−3,151

Source: Table 7-2; U.S. Department of Commerce, *Survey of Current Business*, January 1992.

buildings and a shortage of equipment in the economy's private sector are important reasons for the productivity slowdown.

Why has this happened? What caused investment in buildings to grow faster than necessary, while investment in equipment and tools faltered? One reason was the extension of the investment tax credit in 1981 to business structures as well as equipment, a move that helped stimulate the office-building and shopping-mall boom of the 1980s.[23] More important in explaining the overall decline in the rate of growth in private capital per worker are sagging profit rates in the post-1973 period. In general, after tax profits, whether measured as a fraction of the national income, as a percentage of stockholders' equity, or per dollar of sales, tended to be lower in most years after 1973 than during the pre-1973 period.[24] A major lesson from Keynes's classic work, *The General Theory of Employment, Interest, and Money*, is that the expectation of profit leads businesspeople to spend for new equipment and structures. It is not surprising, therefore, that profit rates sagged in the 1970s and 1980s, given the economy's subnormal performance during these years. Under such conditions, business spending for new capital goods will not be robust.

GLOBAL ECONOMICS AND AMERICA'S DEINDUSTRIALIZATION

In 1955, Mollie James went to work for 95 cents an hour at the Paterson, New Jersey, plant of Universal Manufacturing Company, a firm that made electrical components for fluorescent lights. Thirty-four years later, when Mollie was fifty-eight years old and earning $7.91 an hour, she came to work one morning only to learn that the plant was being shut down. After a lifetime of struggling to reach the lower fringes of middle-class life, Mollie found herself being thrust back toward poverty.

Three years before Mollie's plant closed down, Universal Manufacturing Company had been acquired by MagneTek, Inc., of Los Angeles, a firm created in 1984 by the Spectrum Group, a Los Angeles investment company. With the help of Michael Milken, former junk-bond king for the Drexel Burnham Lambert investment underwriter, MagneTek acquired the millions of dollars needed to buy out Universal Manufacturing and other companies.[25] Shortly after MagneTek closed down the Paterson plant, leaving five hundred people without jobs, the company reached full production in a new plant in Matamoros, Mexico, a border town across the Rio Grande from Brownsville, Texas. Mollie James's counterpart in MagneTek Mexican plant earns $1.45 an hour!

The tale of Mollie James and the shut-down of the manufacturing plant where she worked for so many years is a story in miniature of two separate though closely related economic developments that have generated intense fear and controversy everywhere in the United States. The first involves the increasing, pell-mell involvement of the United States with the powerful, highly competitive forces loose on the stage of the world economy, forces that seem beyond the control of any one nation, even a powerful nation like the United States. The second concerns the loss of well-paying, secure jobs in manufacturing, a development sometimes described by the pejorative term "deindustrialization," and other times described by the more hopeful-sounding phrase "a postindustrial society."

Two sets of facts concerning these developments seem beyond dispute.

The first centers on the magnitude of America's economic linkages to the rest of the world. One useful way to measure the "internationalization" of an economy is to calculate the sum of what it exports and imports as a proportion of its total domestic production, what economists call the gross domestic product (GDP). In the 1950s, exports plus imports were less than 10 percent of the GDP for the United States; now they exceed 20 percent, which means more than one-fifth of all U.S. economic activity is tied into the global economy.[26] The sum of exports plus imports calculated as a percent of American manufacturing output has jumped much more dramatically, rising within the last two decades from 20 to 80 percent!

These numbers are a big part of the reason for the controversy that surrounds trade and America's role in the global economy. The recently negotiated North American Free Trade Agreement is a case in point. It was strongly pushed by the Bush administration, is supported by the Clinton administration and a majority in the Congress, but opposed by many trade-union leaders and ordinary workers, who fear it will lead to the "export" of more American jobs to Mexico. Although academic economists argue that the benefits of freer trade in the form of lower prices and more economic growth outweigh the effect of job losses, many workers remain unconvinced. Allen McAmis is among the latter, since he was laid off from his $13-an-hour job in February 1992 at the Greenville, Tennessee, plant of North American Philips Corporation. The job was moved to Juarez, Mexico, where it pays $2 an hour.[27] Academic economists and supporters of free-trade principles may argue that McAmis's real productivity did not justify his $13-an-hour pay rate. But for McAmis and millions of other American workers like him, the impact of trade on jobs in America is not an academic matter.

The second set of facts involves the continued, relentless decline in employment in manufacturing in the American economy. This ranks as a major cause of the deterioration in the American worker's real weekly wage that has characterized the silent depression. Between 1947 and 1990, manufacturing employment in the United States not only dropped *relative* to employment in the rest of the economy, but since 1980 it has dropped in an *absolute amount*. In 1947, 35.3 percent of the nation's work force—more than one-third—were employed in manufacturing—in making things. By 1991, this percentage had fallen to 16.9, a 52.1-percent decline in the proportion of the work force employed in manufacturing. Up until 1980, the absolute—that is, total—number of workers in manufacturing continued to increase, even though their relative share overall had dropped. But since 1980, an estimated 2.5 million jobs in manufacturing have been lost permanently.[28] By the end of 1992—and for the first time in American history—more people were employed by governments (18.7 million) than in manufacturing (18.1 million).

Manufacturing employment typically has provided good jobs with high wages for workers with few skills and little education. Economic globalization has sent many of these jobs to low-wage countries, leaving factory workers to scramble for low-paying service jobs.[29] What is to be done?

First, American workers need a better grounding in basic educational skills—more mathematics, more knowledge of basic science, more reading and writing ability, and more computer literacy. Within corporate America, means must be found to encourage firms to switch from a low-wage strategy, which often leads them to move production plants overseas to low-wage countries, to a higher-skills strategy for their employees, designed to enable them to compete in the global economy. Some firms are attempting this—Motorola and Levi Strauss & Co., for example—but public policies should be devised to make it more widespread.

For most nations, free trade is normally superior to protectionism, but two caveats are in order. As most economists readily admit, the benefits from free trade are long-term in character. With respect to the economic long run, it may not be, as Keynes once quipped, that "in the long run we are all dead," but it can easily stretch over five to ten years, if not longer. For people like Mollie James and Allen McAmis, it is the short run that matters. They need help now, not in the distant future.

Second, it is important that ways be found to ensure that the benefits from trade and America's involvement in the global economy don't go only to those at the top of the income pyramid. This is a task for public policy, not something that can be left to the free play of market forces. Retraining and relocation assistance can be part of the answer, but not necessarily the whole answer. Workers displaced by *major* changes in trade policy—ratification of the NAFTA will be a major change in trade policy—may be too old to benefit from retraining, or may have such deep ties to a community that relocation is not practical.

The question of America's deindustrialization is more critical—and more controversial. Granted that the loss of manufacturing jobs is real, some observers deny that this means that a process of deindustrialization is under way in the American economy. Critics of the deindustrialization argument, like Robert Lawrence of the Brookings Institution, say that such a view is misleading. The crucial statistic is manufacturing's share of the nation's total output. Manufacturing measured as a percent of output has hardly changed since 1947. From 1947 through 1988, manufacturing output averaged 21.4 percent of the nation's total production of goods and services. This percentage shows the nation is not deindustrializing.[30] Furthermore, the fact that the economy produces about the same proportion of manufactured commodities with a smaller proportion of workers is a plus—it means the productivity of workers in manufacturing has been improving.

Though all of the foregoing is true, it does not put the problem to rest. "Deindustrialization" may be the wrong word for describing what is taking place in the industrial sector of the American economy, especially when developments are viewed in the context of the transnational economy to which America increasingly is tied economically. What has been happening is a slow and insidious erosion of America's capacity to make things and compete in world markets. There is solid evidence in support of this view, in spite of the presumed stability of manufacturing's share in total output. In addition to the loss of jobs in manufacturing already mentioned, there was a sharp drop in the rate of growth in the sales of manufactured goods after 1973. Between 1948 and 1973, the sale of manufactured goods (measured in constant 1982 dollars) grew at an average annual rate of 4.1 percent. After 1973—between 1974 and 1990—the average growth rate dropped to 1.7 percent, a 59-percent decline.[31]

Even more serious is what has been happening to investment in equipment in American manufacturing—the process of providing American workers with the tools they need to compete internationally. The pattern is a familiar one. Between 1947 and 1973, the stock of equipment capital in the manufacturing sector grew at an annual average rate of 4.2 percent. From 1973 to 1990, however, this rate dropped to 1.8 percent, a 57.1-percent decline.[32] These numbers would not be so serious if during these years the American consumer's appetite for manufactured goods had declined to the same degree as the fall-off in the sales for domestically manufactured goods or investment in equipment in the manufacturing sector. This did not happen. America's balance of trade in manufactured goods turned sharply negative during the 1980s. During these same years, America's major competitors in the international economy—Japan and Germany—were increasing their trade balances in manufacturing.[33]

There is some comfort to be found in America's presumed superiority in the manufacture and export of high-technology goods—especially aircraft and parts, computers, and agricultural chemicals. In these areas, America has maintained or increased its share of world trade since 1965. However, a substantial part of these exports have been military goods. The picture is much less favorable for many other high-technology commodities— professional and scientific instruments, electrical equipment, optical and medical instruments, drugs and medicines, synthetic and plastic materials, and industrial chemicals. For these goods, America's share of world markets has been eroding since the mid-1960s.[34] What some observers find especially troublesome in this picture is the possibility that America, though not lacking in the knowledge to produce high-technology goods, lacks the skill— or the will—to apply such knowledge to the production of less esoteric commodities—like shoes and textiles—spreading, thereby, the best of technology throughout the manufacturing economy.[35] The Germans and the Japanese have proved they can do this.

Why does manufacturing matter? Isn't the loss of manufacturing jobs simply part of a long-term, normal economic process of growth, one in which the economy moves from agriculture, then to industry, and, ultimately, to knowledge-based services as the dominant form of economic activity? This idea was advanced more than half a century ago by the distinguished British economist Colin Clark in his classic work, *The Conditions of Economic Progress*.[36] The contemporary version of Clark's stages-of-development process sees the ultimate outcome as a high-wage, high-income postindustrial society based upon services, especially those of a symbolic-analytical nature, as found in Reich's analysis (see note 29).

Unfortunately, there are two flaws in this scenario. The first concerns what has actually been happening to workers displaced from jobs in manufacturing as the economy presumably moves toward a postindustrial society. To the extent that displaced manufacturing workers do find jobs elsewhere, most of their new jobs will be somewhere within the broad array of activities loosely classified as services. However, the jobs they have moved into are not necessarily found among the knowledge-based services, where high incomes are the norm. Between 1979 and 1988, the number of jobs in the American economy grew by nearly seventeen million, but slightly more than one-half of these jobs paid an annual wage below the poverty level. Only 12 percent paid a wage that could reasonably be considered high—over $46,000.[37]

The second flaw is more fundamental, arising out of a challenge to the basic idea that economic progress involves a continuing, though at times turbulent, process of shifting workers from lower-valued to higher-valued production—from agriculture to industry to services. In 1929, for example, 21.2 percent of the American work force was employed in agriculture; by 1991, this figure had dropped to 2.5 percent. The movement of workers away from low-paying jobs on the farm to better-paid jobs in industry and in services is seen as normal. What is missing in this analysis is an awareness of strong and important *linkages* that exist between many types of goods production and service activities. Because of these linkages, well-paying service jobs won't continue to exist if the production of goods giving rise to the services disappear.

This argument is developed fully by Stephen S. Cohen and John Zysman, professors at the University of California, Berkeley, in their book, *Manufacturing Matters: The Myth of the Post-Industrial Economy.*[38] The more conventional stage-of-development process fails to distinguish between two kinds of transitions—a complete shift out of production, as happened when MagneTek moved a manufacturing plant to Mexico, and a shift of labor out of a particular type of production because of productivity changes.

Cohen and Zysman illustrate the difference between these two types of transitions by discussing what has happened to American agriculture. Between 1929 and 1991, there was a colossal increase in the output of American agriculture, even though the quantity of labor used in the direct production of farm products dropped in spectacular fashion. Direct labor on the farm was replaced by machines, education, and new technologies, which led to an enormous increase in the productivity of the direct labor that remained in agriculture. Between 1947 and 1990, for example, farm output per hour of farm work increased 7.9 times![39] This is but part of the picture, because the farmer remaining on the farm is only "the point man in a long, elaborate chain of specialists [in agriculture]—most of whom don't often set foot on the farm—all of whom are vital to its successful operation and directly depend upon it."[40]

Workers in activities as diverse as crop dusting, food processing, or large-animal veterinary medicine not only are employed in agriculture, but have their jobs because of the complicated chain of linkages between agricultural commodities and the services now necessary to produce them. Consider, Cohen and Zysman ask, what would have happened to jobs in America if, instead of merely shifting workers out of agricultural production, American agricultural production overall had been shifted "off-shore"—that is, transferred to foreign sources. They estimate that at least three to six million jobs are tied tightly to agricultural production, jobs that would not exist if the whole of agricultural production had moved offshore as happened with the Greenville, Tennessee, manufacturing plant of the North American Philips Corporation.[41]

The argument that the California professors develop in detail in their book is *not* an argument for protection, for saving all of American jobs from the impact of foreign competition. They assert that the time-honored practice of classifying economic activity and collecting employment, output, and profit data in terms of agriculture, industry, and services has lost much of its usefulness for economic analysis. That is, unless we know more about specific *linkages* that exist between manufacturing and services, it is not easy to tell whether a shift away from manufacturing to service-based jobs represents economic progress. For example, many activities—like selling insurance, hairdressing, dry cleaning, delivering pizzas, etc.—have no strong direct links to manufacturing. This is not to downplay the indirect effect that manufacturing has on such activities through the multiplier effect of manufacturing on total demand and on wage rates across the economy. The demand for pizzas in Detroit will go up when more automobile workers have jobs, for instance.

Cohen and Zysman have a more subtle linkage in mind. They say that much more specific evidence is needed on service-sector jobs that are tightly linked to manufacturing, in the same way that crop-duster pilots and large-animal veterinarians are linked to agriculture. The services they are concerned with are such that, if the jobs in manufacturing are lost to foreign suppliers, the services jobs also will be lost. To illustrate, if the whole of America's agricultural production had moved offshore, there would be no more jobs for crop dusters. Among tightly linked "upstream" services, as Cohen and Zysman describe them, are design and engineering services for products, accounting, inventory, and payroll services, financing and insuring within the manufacturing process, repair and maintenance of plant and machinery, training and recruiting for manufacturing firms, testing services and labs, industrial-waste disposal, and trucking firms that move semifinished goods from plant to plant within manufacturing.[42]

How great is the problem? A report from the Office of Technology Assessment, cited by Laura D'Andrea Tyson, chair of President Clinton's Council of Economic Advisers, found that 25 percent of the nation's output (GDP) originated in services used as inputs for the goods-producing industries—more than the value added to GDP by the manufacturing sector.[43] Cohen and Zysman estimate that possibly forty million workers now classified as being in services have jobs that depend on the eighteen million workers directly employed in manufacturing (1991).[44] When manufacturing jobs disappear, so do many of the better-paid jobs in services.

There really is no such thing as a postindustrial society. What we are experiencing is not a transition out of industry into services, but a transition from one kind of industrial society into another. Manufacturing matters, but if the nation does not understand this, America's once undisputed leadership in the global economy will slip even further from our grasp. The nation's real wealth and power depend upon its ability to produce the goods that Americans and people all across the globe want and need.

CHAPTER 8

Investing in America

Wendell Willkie ran for president against Franklin D. Roosevelt in 1940 on the slogan, "Only the strong can be free, and only the productive can be strong." Willkie did not win. FDR's popularity was too great, even though the president was running for an unprecedented third term. Yet Willkie's message was true then, and in a modified sense it is true today. Our problem is not to remain free in the face of threats from totalitarian regimes—these threats are gone—but to end the silent depression, to regain America's productiveness, which has been slipping away for the last twenty years.

Our problems are far deeper than the usual cyclical ups and downs. The current recovery, which officially began in March 1991, has been weaker by every economic measure than the nine previous recoveries since October 1945. As *Time* ruefully noted shortly after President Clinton took office, "The most recent economic news is upbeat. There is just one little problem: nobody's hiring."[1] Lawrence A. Hunter, deputy chief economist for the U.S. Chamber of Commerce, warns that the nation is facing a "never-ending recession," which by 1996 could lead "to 9 million fewer jobs than there should be and . . . a cumulative loss of output equal to $8,374 [in 1982 dollars] for every man, woman, and child."[2]

Ending the silent depression is a long-term proposition, not a task to be completed within the confines of one, or perhaps even two presidential terms. Nonetheless, it is a task the nation must begin. The alternative is a continued drift into greater and greater mediocrity, a sad prospect for a nation whose economic strength was the key to victory in World War II, and that led the way in history's most spectatcular recovery from the devastating consequences of that war.

The first order of business is productivity—to restore the growth rate for this crucial number to its historic level, the 2.5-percent annual rate that prevailed from the end of World War II through 1973, not the less-than-1-percent rate that has plagued the American economy since that watershed year. There is no other sustainable source for the real resources needed to resolve our pressing problems: putting an end to falling real wages so living standards for everyone will rise, meeting the growing needs of an aging population, finding resources to revitalize our great cities, ending poverty, and creating jobs for all who want to work. To do what needs to be done, there must be a bigger economic pie, and the time-honored way to enlarge the economic pie is to improve productivity.

How can this be done? The answer today is the same as it has always been. Investment. Investment in equipment and buildings, investment in technology through research, and investment in human beings through education and job training are the time-honored means whereby *any* society improves its ability and efficiency in producing everything that enters into its material standard of life. Investment is not only the key to productivity growth, but the key to jobs and overall growth—they all are of one piece.

Investment requires that a society divert some portion of what it produces each year away from the immediate satisfaction of its wants—that is, from consumption—into enlarging its capacity to produce in the future, by adding to its stock of physical capital, increasing the efficiency of its labor, and improving the skill and effectiveness with which it uses its labor, capital, and other resources to produce the goods and services it wants. The means by which more investment is to be achieved is a complex and controversial question in any society, but there is no escape from the fact that there must be more and better investment if productivity is to be improved.

There are two basic facets to the nation's investment problem.

The first involves the need for a massive program of public investment to modernize and rebuild the nation's infrastructure. On the global scene, the economies that have been the most successful in international markets, and which have had the highest rates of productivity growth, are the economies that have the highest levels of investment in infrastructures. Normally, the term "infrastructure" refers to tangible kinds of physical capital developed by the public sector—roads, ports, airports, dams, water and sewage systems, and other such structures. When broadened, the concept includes investment in human capital—education plus the training and retraining of workers to upgrade the work force.

The second facet of the investment problem centers on the private sector and the need for a major increase in the stock of equipment. As noted in chapter 7, the shortfall in private capital per worker in the American economy is in tools (equipment)—not buildings. What is needed to revitalize productivity growth is a spurt in investment in tools, not in more office buildings and retail space (shopping centers). Misguided tax policies in the 1980s left the nation awash in these two categories of capital.

INVESTMENT IN THE INFRASTRUCTURE

Infrastructure investment must be a top priority for the remainder of this century, if not longer. Three tough questions must be answered if the nation is to undertake successfully a program of infrastructure investment. First, how big should such a program be? What, in other words, is its dollar cost? Second, at a time when the Congressional Budget Office forecasts that the federal deficit may reach over $350 billion (in current dollars) by 1998, can the federal government afford to undertake such a program? With deficits of this magnitude, where will the federal government get the money? Finally, how can such a program be organized efficiently, avoiding the pork-barrel and logrolling politics that is too often characteristic of federal spending for public works.

How Much Infrastructure Investment?

The key to the first question is the estimate of the nation's overall shortage of public capital. Calculations in chapter 7 showed that by 1990 the total shortage of *nonmilitary* capital had reached $910.0 billion—an amount equal to $3,618 for each man, woman, and child in the nation. This is a large figure, but not one of insurmountable magnitude. Felix Rohatyn, the distinguished New York investment banker, suggested recently that the federal government commit itself to spending up to $1 trillion over the next ten to fifteen years to supplement state- and local-government infrastructure spending.[3] If the approximately $1 trillion for infrastructure spending were spread over the next ten years, that would entail an outlay of $100 billion per year by the federal government, a figure twice the $50-billion-per-year spending over four years that President Clinton recommended in his campaign document *Putting People First.*[4]

Is a $100-billion-per-year figure for federal infrastructure-investment spending an unreasonable target, a pie-in-the-sky statistic? Not really. A hundred billion dollars is only 1.7 percent of the 1992 GDP of $5,950.7 billion (in current dollars). By way of comparison, the proposed $100 billion is significantly smaller than what the federal government expected to spend in fiscal year 1993 on defense ($289.3 billion, or $1,116 per person), or interest on the federal debt ($202.8 billion or $782 per person), money that doesn't build roads, educate Americans, or restore people to health.[5] As a further comparison, public infrastructure spending averaged 3.5 percent of the national output between 1950 and 1975, then dropped to 2.2 percent from 1975 through 1987. Since 1973, the ratio of public infrastructure investment to the national output (GDP) has been much lower in the United States than in the other G-7 countries.[6]

The $100-billion figure posed in the preceding paragraphs must be interpreted with care. It is in the nature of a target, not a specific dollar amount that can or should be spent immediately by the federal government for infrastructure investment. What really counts is the proportion (or share) of the national output that is invested in public capital. As a percent of the nation's output (GDP), the $100 billion defines the magnitude of the effort that will be required for at least a decade to make good the deficiency in public capital experienced by the economy since the early 1970s. From a long-term planning or target perspective, 1.5 to 2.0 percent of the national output is the additional infrastructure investment that is needed to make up for this deficiency. The public-policy objective should be to raise the level of public infrastructure investment as a percent of the national output back at least to the 3.5-percent average of the 1950 to 1975 period. Investment spending of this magnitude must be phased in gradually and with great care, especially since the actual spending will be done at the state and local level, even though the financing comes from Washington. Just 15.5 percent of the total stock of nonmilitary public capital (equipment and structures) is owned by the federal government.[7]

Where Is the Money Coming From?

This brings us to the second critical question: how can we pay for a federal program of the magnitude just sketched out? Given federal deficits of $300 billion or more stretching into the future as far as the eye can see, and given, too, the current antipathy of Americans to new taxation, there is only one major and immediate source for the financial and real resources needed. This is the military budget. Even with the Cold War over, and Desert Storm a fading memory, military spending in 1993 was expected to total $283.8 billion (in current dollars), compared to the Reagan-Bush peak for military outlays of $323.8 billion in 1991. The fiscal-1993 budget (the last Bush budget) projected current-dollar military outlays at $300.7 billion in 1998, just $5.8 billion less than Bush's projected military spending for 1993. Overall, former President Bush's projections for military spending during the five years 1994–98 averaged only $16.4 billion less than the annual average for military spending during his administration (1989–92).[8]

The picture changed when the Clinton administration took office. In the budget for fiscal year 1994, the president proposed cutting $156.9 billion from the Bush projections.[9] Over the 1994-through-1998 period, President Clinton's projections would average $47.5 billion per year less than was spent annually on the military during the Bush years.

If both the Bush and Clinton projections for 1994–98 are converted to constant 1992 dollars, neither represents a major scaling down in the size of the military budget appropriate to the ending of the Cold War. In constant 1992 dollars, the Bush projections average 98.9 percent of the annual average spending on the military during the forty years of the Cold War (1950–89). Even after cutting back the Bush figures, President Clinton's projections for 1994–98 are, on the average, 88.6 percent of Cold War spending. In current dollars, the Clinton projections result in $19.6 billion savings by 1998 over the probable level of military spending in 1993, an amount that falls far short of the estimated $100 billion needed annually to repair and rebuild the nation's infrastructure.[10] The Soviet Union has disintegrated, the Cold War is over, but the Pentagon may succeed in maintaining what is essentially a Cold War budget.

In 1992, the Congressional Budget Office (CBO) published an extremely detailed analysis of the spending and revenue options available for cutting the federal deficit. In this document, the CBO suggested that real defense spending could be reduced at a 7-percent annual rate over a five-year period without impairing the nation's ability to defend itself against foreseeable military threats. After noting that the "likelihood of a conventional war between East and West in Europe has virtually disappeared, and with it the need for a corresponding size and structure of U.S. forces," the CBO report went on to suggest that, "Instead of planning to fight a global war centering around a ground war in Europe, the United States can focus on threats posed by individual countries."[11] If the CBO's scenario were followed, military outlays in 1998 would drop to $191.7 billion (in 1992 dollars), an amount 30.4 percent below the 1993 constant-dollar figure of $275.5 billion.

Would the CBO formula for a 7-percent annual reduction in real military spending be enough to produce $100 billion (in current dollars) in savings by 1998 from military spending? Unfortunately, the answer is no. The 7-percent formula will yield annual savings (from the 1993 projections) of only $63 billion by 1998. Following the CBO reduction formula will bring average military spending for 1994 through 1998 to 18.3 percent below the average of the Cold War years.

If the CBO 7-percent formula won't yield an annual post–Cold War "peace dividend" of at least $100 billion (in current dollars), how large a reduction is required in direct military outlays to achieve this goal? It will take a 10.4-percent annual cut in real—that is, inflation-adjusted—direct military spending to achieve this goal by 1998. At this rate of reduction, overall defense

spending for 1994 through 1998 would average 73.6 percent of
the average amount spent during the Cold War years. A genuine
post–Cold War military budget would be in place.

Can this be done? Military spending at a post–Cold War
level represents formidable military power—power more than
sufficient to meet any imaginable defense and foreign-policy needs
in the post–Cold War era. The real question is political. Can
the political will and leadership be found to make this transition,
to end forty years of military Keynesianism and move into a genuine post–Cold War environment? This is yet to be determined.
What the nation needs—and has not yet had—is a searching
discussion, debate, and appraisal of our genuine national interest
and international responsibilities in a world no longer dominated
by the Soviet-American confrontation and the threat of nuclear
annihilation.

David Evans, former Marine Corps officer and military ana-
lyst for the *Chicago Tribune,* notes that General Colin Powell has
suggested a functional three-tier strategy that could become the
basis for the fundamental reorganization of the nation's military
establishment in the post–Cold War era. The first tier should
consist of the nuclear deterrent; the second tier, conventional
forces ready to go anywhere, anytime; the third tier would be
concerned with the need to build from scratch additional conventional forces. Crucial to the third tier would be the nation's
industrial base and the state of readiness of the Selective Service
System.[12] The logic of this proposal suggests a single commander
in charge of each function, which raises some fundamental questions about the continued need for separate military services in
the post–Cold War world. As Evans suggests, we no longer need
separate services, just different branches in one unified military
for naval, air, and ground operations.

Projections even five years into an uncertain future are a risky
business, but they must be made. The value in the numbers just
discussed is to demonstrate that a post–Cold War peace dividend
of more than $100 billion is both reasonable and possible.

However, it cannot be achieved either quickly or easily. Realistically, it probably cannot be achieved before the end of the decade. This is not wholly a cause for dismay, though. Much more than money is involved in transforming military spending into investment in the nation's infrastructure. Behind the billions of dollars now being spent annually for military purposes lie the talents and energies of millions of people—engineers, scientists, business executives, and skilled workers and soldiers. This reservoir of human talent must not be wasted or lost—as may happen if major cuts in military spending are made without adequate attention's being given to the enormous difficulties involved in the transition from more than forty years of military Keynesianism to a civilian-based economy. Reduced military spending will affect the employment of from two and a half to three million persons, both directly and indirectly, so it is essential that major and careful reconversion planning is necessary if the peace dividend is not to be squandered. Too much is at stake to leave this task to the free play of market forces.

A major move in this direction was made in mid-March 1993, when the Clinton administration unveiled a $19.6-billion projected plan for defense reinvestment-and-conversion spending covering fiscal years 1993 through 1997. For the five years covered by the Clinton plan, $5.2 billion is allocated to worker retraining and community assistance for people and communities hurt by cutbacks in military spending; $4.7 billion for development through the Pentagon of so-called dual-use technologies, technologies that combine military superiority and commercial potential; and, finally, $9.7 billion for investment in new civilian technologies that enhance U.S. competitiveness and offer as well new opportunities for defense workers and firms.[13] For fiscal year 1993, the administration planned to spend $1.7 billion, of which $1.4 billion came from money that Congress appropriated in 1992 for defense conversion, but which the Bush administration did not spend. The amount of money spent subsequent to 1993 for these programs will depend upon future administration budgets and congressional action. Nonetheless, a start has been made toward a serious conversion of military spending to civilian uses.

Needed: A National Development Bank

This leads to the third key question: how can a large-scale infrastructure investment program be organized efficiently, especially to avoid squandering the peace dividend in pork-barrel politics and business-as-usual logrolling? The crux of the problem is to invent a new mechanism for the transfer of funds derived from reductions in military spending and other sources from the federal government back to the states. Because about 85 percent of public capital is created and owned at the state and local levels, the vast majority of decisions on spending for public capital will and should continue to be made at these levels. The major role of the federal government will be to supply the bulk of the funds needed for rebuilding the nation's infrastructure. At the operational level, where public investment decisions are made and construction actually takes place, an infrastructure investment plan will be highly decentralized, allowing extensive local control over investment decisions for airports, roads, bridges, transit systems, sewage-treatment plants, and water-supply systems. This is a desired outcome.

The federal government has a long history of making grants to state and local governments, some earmarked for particular purposes, like highway funding, and others for more general use. In fiscal 1992, for example, federal grants-in-aid (as such assistance is called) to state and local government totaled $169.2 billion ($659 per person), or 11.8 percent of federal spending for all purposes.[14] Transferring money to state and local governments is something that the federal government has been doing successfully on a large scale for a long time.

A more fundamental question is whether these transfers should be in the form of grants-in-aid designated for infrastructure investment, or as federal loans that eventually must be repaid.

The money needed for capital construction projects by private business and many units of government is normally obtained by borrowing—bond issues to finance school construction are commonplace in the American economy. The same principle should apply to a national infrastructure investment program—that is, federal transfers of money to state and local governments should be in the form of loans, not grants. Because of both the magnitude of the money sums involved—perhaps up to $100 billion annually—and the importance of such a program, as well as for other reasons, a new approach is needed.

To develop, implement, and monitor a national plan for infrastructure investment, we must create a new institution, a National Development Bank. A new institution is needed because the problem confronting the nation is not simply reversing the decline in public investment that began in the early 1970s, but also making certain that the future stock of public capital is adequate to the nation's needs. Since public capital equals approximately one-third of the nation's total stock of nonmilitary capital, leaving its supply entirely to the chance and whims of state and local politics is no longer acceptable. A National Development Bank would be able to take the long view, alerting both the public and the Congress to the needs for public capital facing the economy. Critics—especially those of a conservative persuasion—will no doubt denounce the proposed National Development Bank as a liberal plot to impose national planning on the American economy. Such critics are only partly right.

A National Development Bank can be a planning instrument, just like the budget of whatever administration is in power, and the powers inherent in the Federal Reserve System. The American economy is not—and probably never will be—a planned economy in the sense that the defunct Soviet Union was a planned economy. But it is not a rudderless economy, either, drifting solely according to the whims and uncertainties of private markets. Ever since the founding of the republic, Washington has sought to give direction to the economy, in one way or another, even when regimes such as those of Coolidge, Reagan, and Bush embraced the rhetoric of *laissez-faire*. A National Development Bank that focuses its skills and energies on the nation's public-capital needs will be a highly useful complement to the fiscal- and monetary-policy actions that now are the primary means by which Washington seeks to influence and direct the economy's behavior.

How will such a bank operate, and what will be its major functions? The initial task of a National Development Bank will be to receive the savings that result from cutbacks in military spending, and to make certain that these funds are channeled into infrastructure investment.[15] The Pentagon budget is not, however, an inexhaustible source of money—this well will run dry once military spending has been scaled back to a level suitable for the post–Cold War world. In time, therefore, the National Development Bank will have to depend upon either taxes or its own obligations as a source of funds. By issuing investment-rated bonds, the bank could tap into America's private and public pension funds, whose assets are expected to double from $3 to $6 trillion within a decade. Military savings are essentially start-up sources for the bank's funds. Eventually, as loans are repaid, the bank can be expected to become nearly self-sufficient.

The word "nearly" in the foregoing section is chosen deliberately. This is because the loans made through the bank to state and local governments for infrastructure investment should be *interest-free*. Once the funds coming from reduced military spending are exhausted, the bank will incur interest costs if it issues its own obligations to obtain funds for continued lending to state and local governments. These interest costs will have to be covered either by special taxes whose revenues are allocated to the bank, or by the general revenues of the federal government. What this amounts to is a continued subsidy by the federal government of the interest costs for infrastructure investment undertaken by state and local governments. This is not new. The federal government has long been in the business of subsidizing state- and local-government borrowing through the tax-free treatment under the federal income-tax laws of interest on state- and local-government bonds.

The idea of tax-free loans from the federal government to state and local governments also is not new. In 1985, a bill was introduced into the House of Representatives through the Committee on Public Works and Transportation to establish a "National Infrastructure Fund to provide funds for *interest-free* loans to State and local governments for construction and improvement of highways, bridges, water supply and distribution systems, mass transportation facilities and equipment, and wastewater treatment facilities, and for other purposes."[16] Unfortunately, this bill, which provided a twenty-year repayment period for the loans, never made its way out of the Congress. If such a bill had been passed in 1985 and signed by the president, the nation's infrastructure picture would be much brighter today than it is. Since one of the major policy recommendations of this book is the elimination of nearly all exclusions, deductions, or special treatment of income for income-tax purposes (see chapter 10 on tax reform), tax-free loans to state and local governments are justified. This assumes, of course, that there will be continued political consensus that some subsidy is necessary if the nation is to secure an adequate stock of public capital.

There are several other important responsibilities that a National Development Bank should have.

One major task would be development of a capital budget for the federal government, something that is absolutely necessary for implementing successfully a national infrastructure investment program. A capital budget distinguishes between current outlays (salaries and supplies) and long-lasting structures (buildings, dams, roads, etc). Most state and local governments, as well as private business firms, make such a distinction in their budgeting, as do many foreign governments. But not the United States government.

The capital budget should become an integral part of the

system of National Income and Product Accounts, now compiled in great detail and published by U.S. Department of Commerce. Developing a capital budget for a nation as large and complex as the United States will be a difficult task, although in principle there are but three essential components for such a document: (1) estimates of current and projected capital needs and expenditures for the nation; (2) estimates of current and projected operation and maintenance needs and expenditures for the nation's stock of public capital; and (3) a statement of the necessary sources of finance for (1) and (2). The budget should be framed in terms of the capital needs appropriate to each level of government in the nation—federal, state, and local—and presented in as "jargon-free" fashion as possible, so that it is easily understood by citizens and legislators alike. [17]

A second task would be to provide an annual inventory of the nation's entire infrastructure, including an appraisal of the conditions of the infrastructure in each state. In doing this, the bank should also develop an inventory of infrastructure investments that could be started up whenever the economy began to slide into a recession—an inventory of countercyclical public-works projects. Economists have long argued that public-works spending should be used in a countercyclical fashion, increasing during an economic downturn and tapering off when prosperity returns. Historically, the difficulty with this concept is twofold: (1) governments at all levels have not had an inventory of projects that could be easily started in a downturn and turned off in an upturn; and (2) for both political and economic reasons, state and local governments tend to increase public-works spending when times are good and reduce it when prosperity fades, which tends to worsen rather than mitigate the ups and downs of the business cycle. [18]

Finally, the bank would also be charged with responsibility for developing the necessary criteria by which loans are made to the states. This will not be easy, but it must be done if pork-barrel politics are to be avoided and loans are to be channeled to states and regions where the infrastructure needs are the greatest. Developing an allocation formula is a technical and engineering task, but any formula developed must gain both public and congressional support.

INFRASTRUCTURE INVESTMENT AND THE DEFICIT

If a major infrastructure public-investment program were fueled initially by the peace dividend, the question of the deficit would remain. Even if military spending can be diverted into infrastructure investment, should it be done in the face of deficits that are climbing toward more than $350 billion? This raises a fundamental issue: How critical is the federal deficit? Is it so critical that its reduction or its elimination ought to be the nation's number-one priority? Several observations are in order.

First, the deficit as an economic problem is vastly overrated, even though deficit reduction is the top priority for such respected public figures as former Senators Paul Tsongas (Democrat) of Massachusetts and Warren Rudman (Republican) of New Hampshire. They have joined together to try to persuade the public of the overriding importance of deficit reduction. Ross Perot, who drew 20 percent of the popular vote in 1992, made the deficit the chief concern of his campaign.

In contrast to this view, Robert Eisner of Northwestern University has long argued that the federal deficit, *when properly measured,* is far less threatening to the economy's health than the conventional wisdom maintains. In his 1985 book, *How Real Is the Federal Deficit?*, Eisner doesn't say that federal deficits don't matter.[19] They do. But before we can determine how they matter, they have to be measured properly. This means correcting for inflation, eliminating deposit-insurance transactions from the calculations of the deficit because they don't reflect current income and production, deducting estimated federal outlays for nonmilitary capital, and offsetting the federal deficit by the combined

budget surplus of state and local governments.[20] If these adjustments are made, the federal deficit in 1991 turns out to be only
2.3 percent of the GDP, in contrast to the 5.2 percent arrived
at by measuring in the more conventional fashion.[21] A deficit
equal to but 2.3 percent of the GDP is not a serious problem in
a $4.8-trillion (in 1987 prices) economy.

What is a serious problem is the interest on the debt, which
in fiscal 1993 was the third-largest item of federal expenditure,
following Social Security and defense outlays.[22] Interest on the
debt is serious not only because it is a sterile expenditure eating
away at the federal budget, but also because much of it is a transfer of income from taxpayers at large to persons and families in
the upper income ranges. This worsens income inequality.

Even if many people believe that the deficit as conventionally measured is a serious, even a dangerous economic problem,
the best way to cope with it is through a full-employment policy.
The supply-siders who inspired President Reagan's 1981 tax cuts
contended that the economy would eventually grow its way out
of the deficit because of the growth the tax cuts would induce.
This didn't happen, because their analysis rested more upon wishful
thinking than upon factual analysis. The supply-siders weren't
entirely wrong, however. How fast the economy is growing has
an appreciable effect upon federal tax receipts. The St. Louis
Federal Reserve Bank found, for example, that a main reason for
the increase in the federal deficit after 1989 was a sharp slowing
in the rate of growth of federal tax receipts, because the economy's growth slowed.[23] A full-employment approach to reducing
the deficit offers a more rigorous approach to the problem.

The reason for the latter is "Okun's Law," a relationship discovered by the late Arthur Okun, chairman of President Carter's
Council of Economic Advisers. Okun's Law says that, for every
1-percentage-point reduction in the unemployment rate, *real*
(price-adjusted) output will increase between 2 (minimum) and
3 (maximum) percentage points.[24] Applying Okun's Law to CBO
projections of the deficit shows that, if the unemployment rate

is reduced to 4.0 percent by 1997, there will be a modest improvement in the budgetary picture. If nothing is done, the deficit in real terms will average 3.7 percent of GDP between 1993 and 1997. If the minimum gain is achieved through the Okun formula (a 2-percentage-point increase in real GDP for each reduction in the unemployment rate by 1 percentage point), the deficit will average 3.4 percent over the 1993–97 period. A maximum gain from the Okun formula (a 3-percentage-point increase in real GDP for each 1-percentage-point reduction in the unemployment rate) results in an average deficit equal to 3.2 percent of the GDP between 1993 and 1997.[25] These figures tell us, first, that the slick idea that we can easily grow our way out of the deficit is just that—a slick idea with no substance—and, second, that, even as we move toward a full-employment policy that pegs unemployment at no more than 4 percent of the civilian labor force, progress toward reducing the deficit will be painfully slow.

This leaves basically the "austerity" option, the approach favored by former Senators Tsongas and Rudman, investment banker and former Secretary of Commerce Peter G. Peterson, Ross Perot, and others. In their view, the budget crisis is so severe that the American public must accept a period of austerity of undetermined length in which the budget is brought into balance by a combination of painful cuts in expenditures and increases in taxes. The austerity school also believes that growth is being held back by inadequate private investment, the cause of which is insufficient savings, because the federal deficit "crowds out" the private savings that normally would flow into investment. Once the deficit is cut, savings will expand, followed by higher investment and higher growth.

Two comments are in order on the austerity approach. An immediate program to fix the deficit through spending cuts and tax increases is a formula for disaster in an economy that is suffering from the long-term stagnation of the "silent depression." Austerity imposed upon stagnation can only make things worse, not better. This painful lesson was learned in the 1930s, but some of today's leaders seem to have forgotten it entirely. Second, the leaders of the austerity approach presume that the supply of savings is the main determinant of private investment spending, a view that harks back to the classical economists of the nineteenth century. This neglects another important lesson, one taught by Keynes in the 1930s. The prospect of future profits, not the supply of current savings, is the key to high investment spending. In a sluggish economy, profit prospects are poor, so investment spending will lag. If we improve the economy, investment spending will pick up, and the needed savings will follow. This Keynesian lesson—not austerity—is the answer to the budget dilemma!

INFRASTRUCTURE AND TRANSPORTATION POLICY

The principle of federal funding and decentralized administration and implementation at the state- and local-government levels should govern infrastructure investment policy. This makes good sense, because most public capital—buildings, roads, airports, water-supply and sewage systems—is local with respect to both need and use. However, in one area there must be a much broader federal role, not just with respect to financing, but also in terms of actual design and implementation. This is transportation.

The federal government has long been deeply involved in transportation in both a policy and an operational sense. Federal excise—that is, sales—taxes levied on users play a major role in the financing of highway construction and maintenance, the building and improvement of airports and airway-navigation system, harbors, and inland-waterway systems. Trust funds are used to receive money collected under the numerous types of taxes levied on users and held until drawn upon by the federal agencies that administer the programs, such as the Federal Aviation

Agency, the Federal Highway Administration, and other federal departments. Unspent balances of the various transportation trust funds are "invested" in special U.S. Treasury obligations, which means they become part of the Treasury's revenue stream in any year in which they are not spent. At the close of 1992, the unspent balances in the two major transportation trust funds—highways and airports—totaled $25.4 billion ($100 per person).[26]

The federal government's involvement in transportation became even deeper with the 1991 passage of the six-year, $155-billion Intermodal Surface Transportation Efficiency Act (ISTEA)—immediately nicknamed "ice tea"—a bill that has the potential to change fundamentally the nature of surface transportation in the United States. This act does not state directly, as New York Senator Daniel Patrick Moynihan has said, that "it's time to quit pouring concrete," but the bill has the flexibility to allow the states to confront the growing gridlock in road and highway transportation with solutions other than more building and widening of roads. As one observer notes, "For all its complications and limitations, some two-thirds of the Act's $155 billion ($618 per person) *could* secure public transit and shape livable, walkable environments; it *could* alter the way we move and hence use the land."[27]

If the nation is to reverse its domination by the automobile culture that has destroyed downtowns, crippled public mass transit, overbuilt shopping malls, and led to an unhealthy dependence upon Middle Eastern oil, more is required than the flexibility inherent in the 1991 surface-transportation act. The 1991 bill is broadly drawn, stating that it is the policy of the United States "to develop a National Intermodal Transportation System that is economically efficient and environmentally sound, provides the foundation for the Nation to compete in the global economy, and will move people and goods in an energy efficient manner."[28] In this bill are found the guidelines necessary for the integration of all forms of transportation—public and private— into a viable national system.

Implementing the 1991 act requires *explicit* recognition of a basic principle: an element of subsidy is present in all forms of transportation—even walking, if one treads a path carved by others. The subsidy may be internal to one form of transport, as when an airline covers losses on unprofitable routes through profits on better-traveled routes, or external, when a portion of the costs of transport are covered by government. Amtrak, for example, gets a direct subsidy from the federal government. Other forms of transport, like the airlines or the trucks on the highways, are subsidized, although the extent of the subsidy is often concealed because of the complexities of government financial accounts.

The first step in implementing a national transportation policy should be a careful accounting for—and full public disclosure of—the subsidies now present in transportation. After this, a beginning can be made in the integration of all forms of transportation into a coherent whole that efficiently meets the nation's needs. These needs include increasing—not reducing—the choices open to travelers and shippers. They also include making certain that *all* areas of the United States are served by at least a minimum network of public transportation. In many, if not most, of the Great Plains and Western states, the private autombile has become practically the only form of personal transportation. This will have to change. With an aging population, the number of rural residents needing reliable public transportation—for long trips to urban centers for medical attention, for entertainment, and even for shopping—will increase. In the final analysis, transportation, even though most of it is supplied privately, is a public utility which must serve the public good. This principle should not be lost from sight in the design of transportation policies.

In developing policies directed toward a sensible and integrated national transportation system, careful attention must be given to the energy-use and pollution characteristics of various forms of transportation. Studies by the Worldwatch Institute in Washington, D.C. and the Energy Information Administration show that for urban travel, buses, subways, and trolleys use approximately one-eighth as much energy as do private cars. For long trips, buses and trains require but one-tenth the energy of commercial jets. As is well known, private automobiles are a major source of air pollution in large cities, but the high-altitude pollution of jet airplanes is a threat to the earth's protective ozone layers.[29] In the design of transportation policy, energy-efficiency and pollution dangers must be balanced against speed and other considerations in moving people and goods.

In the case of highway transportation, users in principle pay, through gasoline and other motor-vehicle-related taxes, for the cost of highway construction and maintenance. The reality is different. In 1989, user taxes on fuels and motor vehicles, plus income from toll roads, paid for 60 percent of highway financing at federal, state, and local levels. The other 40 percent came from a mixed combination of general-revenue financing, including benefit charges and property taxes, bond financing, and investment income.[30]

Of more immediate interest to the average citizen is the extent to which the automobile owner subsidizes the large trailer-trucks that increasingly dominate the interstate-highway system. In a 1988 highway-cost-allocation study, the secretary of transportation reported to the Congress that "the typical long haul truck operating close to 80,000 pounds does not pay its fair share of the highway costs it occasions."[31] According to the study, user fees paid by the long-haul trucks weighing seventy to eighty thousand tons cover only 81 percent of their highway costs. Who picks up the difference? Other vehicles, especially owners of passenger cars. What is the dollar cost of the hidden subsidy to big trucks? This is not easily determined, but it is possible to arrive at a reasonable estimate of the extent to which large trucks are subsidized by other traffic, including passenger automobiles. The estimate developed here is for the interstate system, which is where most motorists encounter the heavy trailer-trucks. In 1989, federal and state spending for both capital construction (new roads) and maintenance on the nation's over two hundred thousand miles of interstate highway was $13.1 billion. In the same year, travel on the interstate system reached 461.8 million vehicle miles (a vehicle mile is one vehicle traveling one mile).[32] Dividing spending by miles traveled gives a figure of $28.36 per thousand vehicle miles traveled, or VMT, the unit used by highway experts to measure the amount of travel taking place on a highway. In other words, in 1989, for every thousand miles that a vehicle of *any* size or weight traveled on the interstate system, federal and state governments spent $28.36 for new construction and maintenance.

The problem is to allocate these dollar costs between heavy trucks and other types of vehicles using interstate highways. This cannot be done just on the basis of use, because of the vast differences in weight between trucks and other vehicles, particularly passenger cars. But if the 81-percent cost coverage cited earlier for heavy trucks is applied to the $28.36 cost figure, other vehicles each subsidize large truck-trailers in the amount of $5.39 per thousand miles of travel.[33] Thus, an average passenger-car owner traveling ten thousand miles per year subsidizes heavy trucks by approximately $53.90 a year.[34]

The automobile example just discussed illustrates the general problem of both internal and external subsidies in all forms of transportation. Airlines are subsidized because excise taxes levied on airline passengers, aviation fuel, and air freight do not cover the full cost of airport construction and maintenance and the air-traffic-control system operated by the Federal Aviation Agency, without which the private airlines could not fly. From World War I onward, military spending has been the main source of support for the aerospace giants—Boeing, McDonnell Douglas, and Lockheed—which produce most of the civil airliners now in use in the United States.[35] Privately owned barges carry large tonnages of heavy freight on the nation's inland-waterway system, most of which were developed by the Corps of Engineers of the U.S. Army. And as every schoolchild knows, extensive grants of public lands made possible the development of many of America's railroads in the nineteenth century.

Two major parts of the nation's transportation system—highway and air travel—confront increasingly intolerable levels of congestion. On the ground in urban areas, peak-hour traffic on "freeways" is rapidly approaching gridlock, or travel in stop-and-go conditions. Severe congestion exists for 70 percent of peak-hour traffic on urban interstate highways, according to the U.S. Department of Transportation. The money costs stemming from urban-area congestion—time lost, fuel wasted, vehicles damaged—is estimated at $34 billion ($135 per person). "Pouring more concrete" isn't the solution, because the demand for freeway travel has been growing at a rate from 1.9 to 2.8 times the supply of freeway mileage.[36] The old economic law that "supply creates demand" may not hold for the economy generally, but in the world of the automobile use it works perversely—demand for highways is continually outrunning supply! The promise of the automobile has always been one of liberation, of enhancement of personal freedom through mobility. Of course, this is still true much of the time for many uses, but the insistence of Americans on using the automobile on a one-driver-per-car basis to go to and from work in major urban centers is making a mockery of the promise.

The story is much the same for air travel—overcrowded airports, delays and unexpected flight cancellations, cramped airplanes, overworked flight controllers, and overused airways are all part of the picture of growing congestion. Since 1977, passenger boardings for commercial airlines have jumped from 243 million to 455 million in 1989 (an 87-percent increase), and by the end of the century passenger boardings could increase by another 59 percent.[37] Airports in many major cities are strained to capacity, as is the nation's air-traffic-control system. Former Secretary of Transportation Samuel Skinner estimated that the nation needs twenty new airports by the year 2000, but only one (Denver) is now under construction. Airport construction on the scale envisaged by Mr. Skinner is *not* going to happen, not only because of the cost—$3 to $4 billion per airport—but because of the "not-in-my-backyard" syndrome. Nearly everywhere there is growing citizen opposition to the expansion of existing airports, let alone new airport construction.

What is ironic as well as deeply troubling in this picture is that the nation's major airlines are in deep financial trouble. This is true in spite of the boom in air travel. Since 1989, the airlines have lost between $8 billion and $9 billion, more than the combined earnings of *all* airlines since commercial air transportation began in the 1920s.[38] The periodic price wars waged by the airlines bring more passengers, but also add to their financial woes. Of the 176 airlines started since deregulation in 1977, only one is still in existence (America West); the giants—American, United, Delta, and Northwest—now control two-thirds of the market. In the jargon of economics, deregulation has led the industry overall to domination by a four-firm "oligopoly," and to *de facto* monopoly conditions in many markets where the so-called hub-and-spoke system has made one carrier dominant. Yet the industry remains plagued by overcapacity.

The solution for the problems of ground and air transportation lies in one direction—more and better rail transport for people and goods. The demand for rail-passenger transportation is there, as Amtrak's success proves. This success has come in spite of the belief of many economists that such a demand did not exist, and in spite, too, of the fact that the system was designed originally in a way that made failure more likely than success. Someday America may have "supertrains" that will compare favorably with France's TGV or Japan's bullet train, but meanwhile the most cost- and energy-effective investment the United States can make is to upgrade and complete Amtrak's existing rail network (there are significant north-south gaps in this network). Amtrak is seriously short on equipment. Minimal investments now in equipment and roadbed improvements (the roadbeds are mostly owned by the private rail lines) could easily, within a few years, give the United States the world's best long-haul rail-passenger system.

As for highway congestion and urban gridlock, mass-transit rail and bus systems are the way out of the dead end of continued road construction. Experience ranging from the revival of the old-fashioned trolley in San Diego, California, to the success of the Metro system in Washington, D.C., or BART in San Francisco, indicates a strong preference for trains over buses by urban commuters. The 1991 transportation act (ISTEA) opens the door for alternatives to the automobile; it is now up to advocacy groups wanting to end the nation's dependency upon the automobile to put together an effective coalition to wrest enough power away from the institutionalized prohighway forces to bring about a significant change in the way we move people and goods in this nation.[39]

From the perspective of sound public policy, a major objective should be to shift the long-haul transportation of goods away from trailer-trucks on the interstate highways to the railroads. Energy conservation and increased efficiency would result, as well as the saving of billions of dollars annually because of reduced capital outlays and lower maintenance costs for highways. Technological changes during the last decade have been pushing trucking firms and the major railroads in this direction, a trend that public policy should continue to encourage.

The technological innovation most responsible for this development is the "liner train," a train in which containers for freight are double-stacked on flatcars. A single liner train with 280 containers and a two-man crew can carry as much freight as 280 trailer-trucks. The emergence of the container technique for shipping goods, liner trains, and computer control over the movement of trains enables the railroads to compete effectively with trucks in the shipment of many time-sensitive goods such as fresh produce, electronics, clothing, and auto parts. On long hauls between major rail terminals, as from Chicago to Los Angeles, moving cargo by rail is 50 percent more efficient than by road.[40] This fact, plus the defeat in the Congress of legislation allowing triple-trailers nationwide, led trucking giants like J. B. Hunt Co. to move toward becoming true "intermodal" carriers, shipping goods in double-stacked containers across the country, and giving the shipper specialized services at each end. On the nation's major railroads, intermodal transportation is growing at double-digit rates, a development that will hasten the shift of long-haul freight from the interstates to rail. At this stage, the appropriate role for public policy is to encourage this technological and market-driven process, removing barriers to intermodal transportation, while making certain that the consuming public benefits from the lowering of the costs of moving goods. Since the 1991 act created a new Intermodal Department in the Department of Transportation, the machinery is in place for this to happen if the will is there.

An important by-product of the swing toward intermodal transport by the railroads should benefit Amtrak and rail-passenger service in the United States. In contrast to the slow-moving, heavy-bulk trains typical of freight moving by rail in the past, intermodal freight moves on high-speed, high-priority trains, managed by electronics and computers. High-priority, fast passenger trains can be just as easily fitted into such a system as high-priority freight. This technological development should lessen the hostility that existed in the past among the private railroads toward Amtrak, which uses privately owned roadbeds for the overwhelming proportion of its routes. A new generation of railroad officials has begun to realize that freight trains can benefit from the expensive track upgrading necessary for passenger service.[41]

PUBLIC POLICY AND PRIVATE INVESTMENT

This brings us to another crucial question: what should be the role of public policy in promoting private investment? The years of the silent depression led to a serious shortfall in the quantity of tools and equipment available to American workers. The dollar value of this shortfall in constant 1987 dollars is $9,559 per worker. The failure of private investment in equipment to grow adequately from 1973 onward has been a crucial factor in the nation's productivity slowdown. Inadequate investment in equipment and machines is especially devastating to productivity, because this investment provides the cutting edge for the introduction of new technology into the economy.

What can the government do to reverse the trend? Surprisingly, the federal government has very little *direct* control over the decisions of private business to invest or not to invest in buildings and equipment. Since the 1960s, the investment tax credit has been used on and off with both good and bad results as a way of stimulating investment spending. The investment tax credit allows firms to offset some of their income-tax liabilities with a fixed percentage of their investment spending. Introduced by the Kennedy administration, it was initially applied with modest success to investment in equipment. Extending the tax credit during the 1980s to buildings helped create the oversupply of office space that still plagues the economy. Early in 1993, the Clinton administration was considering its use to stimulate private investment. On balance, the results of using the investment tax credit are mixed. An alternative, highly publicized approach is the favorite panacea of former President Bush, an idea somewhat gingerly supported by President Clinton: reduced rates of taxation for capital gains. Little credible evidence exists to show that such a reduction stimulates private investment. In fact, one recent study shows just the opposite—investment spending rose when tax rates for capital gains increased and fell when the rate fell.[42]

It is a mistake to view the manipulation of tax rates by the federal government as a sound way to stimulate private investment. Increasing private investment in equipment is critical to solving the productivity problem, but the best stimulus for business is a healthy rate of economic growth, not the manipulation of tax rates. A central point of the present chapter is that the key role of the federal government in the overall economic picture is to move the economy in this direction by pursuing a full-employment policy coupled to a program of massive investment in public capital.

The foregoing reasoning is clearly in line with what Keynes taught: expected profitability is the key to new investment, and profitability depends upon a full-employment economy. The soundness of this approach is also reflected in another point, underscored in the last chapter—namely, that over a period of several years dollars spent on public capital *stimulate* private investment, rather than crowd it out. Implicit in the foregoing discussion is rejection of a much-discussed idea—America should have an industrial policy through which the federal government picks and aids future winners and withdraws federal support from the losers. It is doubtful whether the government possesses the knowledge to make wise decisions of this nature. The nation's experience with the "closet" industrial policy bound up with military spending does not encourage confidence in such wisdom. If the federal government uses its power and skill to bring the economy to full employment and a satisfactory rate of economic growth, decisions about the volume and direction of private investment spending are best left to market forces. This was the general position that Keynes took. There is nothing in it that prevents the federal government from taking the lead in developing a better climate of cooperation between government, labor, and management, as is the case in some of the nation's strongest international competitors. Government encouragement of a shift away from the adversarial attitude that dominates labor-management relationships in the nation would have favorable effects on productivity growth.

INVESTMENT IN EASTERN
EUROPE AND THE FORMER U.S.S.R.

A retired Chicago businessman, Warren G. Brockmeier, has come up with a novel idea that would stimulate private investment and manufacturing production in the American economy, while simultaneously bringing much-needed economic assistance to the struggling economies of Eastern Europe and the former Soviet Union. Unlike 1948, when America embarked on a bold experiment to help rebuild the war-shattered economies of Western Europe, the Bush administration as well as the Clinton administration to date have shied away from any comparable aid program for the struggling economies of Eastern Europe. The roadblock is our massive public debt, although the ratio of the public debt to our output in 1948 (82.3 percent) was much higher than it now is (67.2 percent in 1991).[43]

What Mr. Brockmeier advocates is a modernized version of the Lend-Lease program invented by Franklin Roosevelt to aid England and Russia before the United States entered the war. Specifically, he proposes that the United States loan or lease industrial, agricultural, transportation, construction, communications, medical, and computer equipment to the nations of Eastern Europe and the former U.S.S.R. for the rebuilding of their economies. The equipment to be sent to these countries would be purchased by a new federal agency, patterned after the Government National Mortgage Association (popularly known as "Ginnie Mae"), which would raise the money by selling bonds to the investing public.[44]

Mr. Brockmeier sees the agency as playing a middleman role between American manufacturers and foreign governments and companies that need the equipment. Once the latter parties had reached a tentative agreement on equipment needs, they would turn to the federal agency, which would actually purchase the required equipment and arrange for its shipment to the appropriate country. The federal agency would have responsibility for making certain that every aspect of a potential lend-lease arrangement met the program's basic objective of sending economic aid to Eastern economies and stimulating the demand for American manufactured goods.

How would the receiving countries pay for the equipment they receive? Unlike the Marshall Plan, the Brockmeier proposal is not a grant program financed by taxes. The recipient countries would be expected to amortize the principal and pay interest on the value of the equipment received through lend-lease arrangements. Since it will be many years, if not decades, before these economies have recovered sufficiently to earn enough hard currencies (American dollars, German marks, Swiss francs, Japanese yen) to make payments, they will have to repay in the dollar equivalent of their own currencies. In this respect, the repayment process could work as the highly successful post–World War II Fulbright program worked. Initially under the Fulbright program, the U.S. government acquired foreign currencies from the sale of war-surplus equipment in Europe and elsewhere. These foreign-currency balances—French francs, German marks, British pounds, and others—were then used to finance living expenses for American students and professors going to the countries involved for study and research. The Brockmeier plan for aiding the nations of Eastern Europe and stimulating demand for the products of American manufacturing would undoubtedly result in the accumulation of nonconvertible ("soft") currencies by the United States on a scale far greater than happened under the Fulbright program. There is no reason, though, why this nation could not use these monies in as productive and imaginative ways in the future, as Fulbright monies were used in the past.

A CONCLUDING
COMMENT UPON INVESTMEN ·

On the cover of *Time* for March 1, 1993, the headline superimposed upon a picture of President Bill Clinton reads: "You

Say You Want A Revolution . . . But are we willing to pay the price?"[45]

The price, as the cover story makes clear, is the president's proposals for higher taxes and less spending to bring the nation's deficit-and-debt problem under control. Another part of the price, one not stressed in the *Time* story, is the necessity to shift the nation's priorities from consumption to investment. The lesson the nation needs to learn anew is that it is only through increased public and private investment both in physical capital and in human beings that we can restore historic growth trends to productivity and the economy. There is no short-cut.

In the 1980s, there was an explosive growth of both public and private debt, but, unfortunately, much of this growth went to finance consumption, private and public. From 1950 through 1980, the combined total of the federal debt and private debt held stable at about 150 percent of the GDP. After 1980, both expanded rapidly, reaching 225 percent of the GDP at the end of 1992. Debt as such is not necessarily bad. How it is used is what counts, both for a nation and for a family. Now the time has come to reverse course. For the rest of this century, we must invest adequately, not only for our own well-being, but for the well-being of our children and their children.

CHAPTER 9

·

·

Investing in the American People

·

·

The prime purpose of the massive investment program outlined in chapter 8 would be to rebuild America's stock of public and private capital so that productivity growth is brought back to its historic levels. Vital as physical capital is to our growth and material well-being, it is only half the story. The other half involves people. Investing in people through jobs, through education and training, and through adequate health care is equally essential to ending the silent depression.

PUBLIC POLICY AND JOBS

The torrent of antigovernment rhetoric of the last two decades caused the public to lose sight of a fundamental lesson from Keynes—public and private investment is the real key to job creation in the modern economy. Economically speaking, World War II was a massive, publicly financed investment program which finally brought the nation out of the Great Depression. True enough, the investment was in weapons of great destructive power, but the economic effects cannot be denied. Unemployment fell from over 17 percent of the civilian labor force in 1939 to 1.2 percent in 1944 at the height of the war effort.[1] The infrastructure program described in chapter 8 would not match the scale of World War II, but such investment would in time put millions of people back to work in construction and manufacturing, areas where the loss of good jobs has been most severe in recent years. Further, this is the most direct way to rebuild the nation's industrial base, because infrastructure investment involves large outlays for construction projects and a demand for heavy, specialized machinery.

What has also been neglected, if not forgotten, over the last two decades is the necessity for a full-employment policy. Among other things, the 1946 Employment Act stated that "The Congress hereby declares it is the continuing policy and responsibility of the Federal Government . . . to promote *maximum* employment, production, and purchasing power."[2] The Full Employment and Balanced Growth Act of 1978 went further, establishing goals of a 3-percent unemployment rate for all workers over the age of twenty, and a 3-percent inflation rate, both targets to be reached by 1983. Obviously, this did not happen. Among the post–World War II administrations, only those of Kennedy and Johnson (1961–68) took the 1946 Employment Act seriously; the 1978 act has simply been ignored. In effect, the nation has not had a full-employment policy since President Kennedy, in his 1962 *Economic Report,* established a 4-percent unemployment rate as a "temporary target" on the road to a full-employment economy.[3] Unemployment averaged 6.2 percent of the civilian labor force in the 1970s and 7.3 percent in the 1980s, levels significantly higher than the 4-percent rate President Kennedy established as a "temporary" full-employment target.[4]

Part of the blame for the absence of a full-employment policy since the 1960s lies with the Reagan and Bush administrations. Neither president believed in using government's power to pursue actively the goal of full employment. Blame also rests with the mainstream economists and their uncritical acceptance of

Milton Friedman's curious doctrine called the "natural rate" of unemployment, defined as a rate below which the unemployment rate could not be pushed without causing serious inflation. In theory, some such rate no doubt exists, but in practice, too many economists in the 1970s and 1980s stipulated that the natural rate lay somewhere in the 5-to-6-percent unemployment range, thus implying that there was little the government could do to bring unemployment down. This came about largely because of a misreading by mainstream economists of the causes of inflation in the 1970s. The inflation was triggered initially by Vietnam War spending, followed by the cost upheavals caused by the Arab oil embargo of 1973, which in turn led to wage demands that ran ahead of productivity gains during the rest of the decade. In economic jargon, the inflation of the 1970s was "cost-push"–based, rather than a "demand-pull" inflation caused by too much money, the view that Friedman expounded. It was the high rate of inflation in the 1970s that, in conjunction with high unemployment caused by the severity of the 1974–75 recession, gave apparent factual support to the natural-rate argument. If economists had looked more carefully at the cost side of the 1970s inflation, they might not have accepted so readily the natural-rate idea, especially since increases in the money supply do not correlate closely with price increases during the 1970s.[5]

The development of an aggressive full-employment policy that aims to bring the unemployment rate down to 3 or 4 percent is essential, but it is not sufficient to solve America's job problem. As Jane Bryant Quinn said, "The MIAs of the American economy are the workers shot down from well-paying jobs."[6] In the Age of Keynes, full employment was an appropriate policy, because most jobs were full-time and provided adequate incomes. This is no longer true. Millions of workers who have lost jobs since the late 1980s have been unable to find new full-time jobs or, when they do, have had to accept reductions in pay. What a new full-employment policy must tackle is not just the creation of jobs, but the creation of *good* jobs—jobs that carry with them an income appropriate to middle-class hopes and aspirations. This won't be easy, for policy-makers do not know much about how to replace the well-paying jobs lost in recent years in manufacturing, banking, and insurance and from the ranks of middle management in large corporations. Over the long run, of course, improving productivity is the key to adequate income for all jobs, but in the shorter term, an up-to-date full-employment policy must address the quality of jobs created as well as their quantity. This is one of the toughest tasks facing the nation.

The experience of Omaha, Nebraska, in the 1980s underscores the complexity of the problem of good jobs in today's economy. Because of its location and the quality of its telephone system, Omaha has become a national center for telemarketing, telecommunications, and computer services, calling itself the "1-800 Capital of America."[7] Between 1980 and 1991, nonfarm employment in the Omaha area grew by sixty thousand jobs; of these, twenty thousand were in high-tech telecommunications and related areas.

The rub is that, in this same period, real weekly wages fell by nearly 10 percent, more than the national decline of 7 percent.[8] Two things explain this development. The first is the loss of high-paying manufacturing jobs in Omaha—especially in meat-packing—because of bankruptcies and nonunion competition. The second is that most of the new jobs are either low-paid or part-time, beginning at around $6 an hour and offering either meager or no health and pension benefits. Annual earnings for many workers are no more than $12,000 to $15,000 a year, very close to the official 1990 poverty threshold of $13,359 for a family of four.

Two aspects of the good-jobs problem cannot be easily separated from one another. In the short run, full-employment policy must also be concerned with existing jobs that do not pay well. The U.S. Bureau of the Census study *Workers with Low Earnings: 1964 to 1990* found in 1990 that 18.0 percent of workers—nearly one-fifth of the work force—had earnings below the poverty level for a family of four. These are workers with a year-round, full-time attachment to the labor force, defined by the Census Bureau as persons who spent at least fifty weeks during the year at work, or looking for work, and if they worked less than thirty-five hours per week it was done so involuntarily.[9]

For low-paying jobs that already exist, public policy must aim at supplementing the income of the working poor. This is best done through existing policies. One way would be to raise gradually the minimum wage to a level that would lift a single person out of poverty. The second would be a gradual increase in the Earned Income Tax Credit (EITC) for married couples and families with children. Through the EITC, the government provides payments to workers whose incomes fall below a stipulated amount, thereby raising their incomes to a more adequate level. The EITC is a rudimentary form of the negative income tax invented by Milton Friedman. It works through the tax system, avoiding the stigma often attached to income received through the welfare system, including food stamps and Medicaid. Both these actions must be phased in over time, because abrupt movements upward in both the minimum wage and the EITC could cause more unemployment, defeating the objectives of these policy changes.

In the long run, the problem of improving the quality of jobs that come into existence through a full-employment policy is the thornier aspect. As repeatedly stressed, productivity gains are the ultimate source of the income that makes possible increases in real living standards. But workers must possess the necessary skills that will justify wages commensurate with increasing productivity. In the longer run, this means major attention must be given to K-through-12 education, the topic of the next section. In the shorter term, policies should be developed to implement three promising approaches. The United States provides support for college students that is often generous, but does little to aid those *not* bound for college, especially in the transition from secondary school to work. Thus, policies should be developed for apprenticeship programs, and increased on-the-job training for the non-college-bound, as is done in most other industrialized nations. Second, policies are needed that will encourage private firms to work toward upgrading the knowledge and technological skill of their employees, rather than seek profitability by closing plants in the U.S. and moving to low-wage areas in Third World countries. As *Fortune* magazine said recently, "innovative U.S. companies are starting to realize that rather than to continue to dumb-down tasks and save money by cutting wages, they'd be better off striving to hire, train, and reward a better-prepared work force. Flexible, responsible delivery of products and services, rather than mass production, is the new watchword in the global economy, and only highly skilled employees can quickly master these challenging new processes."[10] Finally, it is essential to reform health-care insurance in a way that separates it from employment. Spiraling costs for health insurance depress the take-home pay of workers, push small firms toward bankruptcy, and raise the price of products consumers buy. It is estimated that health insurance costs per worker for an American-made car are $1000 per vehicle, more than twice the cost of steel used in the car.

PUBLIC POLICY AND INVESTMENT IN HUMAN CAPITAL

Investment in what economists like to call "human capital"—in plain English, education and job training—is another crucial piece in the overall picture of investment, productivity growth, and public policy. Hardly a day passes without some reference in the press or on television to the sad state of America's schools, to the failure of American education to train workers to compete and survive in the global economy. This is not just idle chatter—the educational "crisis" is real.[11]

The late Edward Denison, a senior fellow with the Brookings Institution in Washington, D.C., was one of the nation's leading economic experts on the sources of economic growth and productivity gains. Denison's findings clothe this crisis in hard numbers. The economy grows because we use more resources (capital and labor), and because we use these resources more efficiently (productivity gains). From 1948 through 1973, Denison discovered, 63 percent of productivity increases could be accounted for by increased knowledge—education, in other words. But between 1973 and the early 1980s, productivity gains from more knowledge all but disappeared, sad but powerful evidence of the depth of the nation's problems with education.[12]

What can be done about the crisis in education? Is there a role for the federal government? If so, what is it? To say that there are no easy answers to these questions is a cliché, but nevertheless true. It is equally true that we have barely begun to find workable answers to these questions. No pretense is made here to supply such answers, but some observations are offered, and one far-reaching, radical proposal is suggested.

First, Americans cherish the deeply ingrained principle of local control of schools. Hardly anyone wants the federal government to try to change this. That would be foolish. A constructive role for the federal government is to supply financial assistance to hard-pressed local school districts, especially those in the inner cities. The excessive dependence of school districts upon local property taxes is a major reason for large money imbalances between the schools of the suburbs and the schools within cities. Federal investment in inner-city schools should be part of any federal plan for investment in the nation's cities.

Second, the public school should retain its historic role as the source of a standard education for the overwhelming majority of American children. Public primary and secondary schools played a major role in establishing the democratic values of the nation. This "common-school" tradition, which reaches back into the nineteenth century, should not be discarded lightly. Crime, drugs, and violence have eroded faith in the public schools, giving rise to demands for voucher systems, tuition tax credits, public support for private schools, and other techniques leading presumably to greater student and parental choice. Such proposals should not be rejected out of hand, but they need be approached with extreme caution. They could easily lead to a further polarization of American society, along lines of income and class, rather than improve the overall quality of education. Since nearly 90 percent of Americas's children in school attend public schools, the ultimate answer to the nation's educational crisis lies in improving the quality of *all* the nation's public schools.

Finally, the federal government has a constructive role to play in the establishment of national educational norms for all primary and secondary schools in the nation, both public and private. The closest we come to this in the United States are the Scholastic Aptitude Tests (SATs), but these are oriented primarily toward the college-bound. National standards are commonplace in practically all advanced economies. Obviously, there are important national differences in educational objectives, but the common element in all of them is, first, the establishment of educational goals or standards for students, normally met by national testing, and, second, designing a curriculum to meet these standards. To be successful, *all* students must have an equal opportunity to learn, an ideal that is far from realized in the United States. Some may fear that national standards will dilute local control of education, but this need not be the case. Any system of national standards must concentrate on the basic subjects—reading, writing, mathematics, and science—which is what polls show all parents want. There would be ample room for imaginative and innovative curriculum development at the local level. Over time, a new system of national standards could become a powerful means to challenge the entrenched power of local educational bureaucracies and administrators. It could also be used to change the nature of teacher training, requiring more subject knowledge and less pedagogy, a reform that is badly needed but will take both time and prodding from the federal government. Teachers need more power and say in the classroom, but only if they are far better trained in their specialty areas than currently is required.

Not long after the Los Angeles riots in the spring of 1992, the late Arthur Ashe, television commentator and former tennis champion, published an article in *The Washington Post* saying that a program of national service modeled on the Depression-era Civilian Conservation Corps (CCC) is needed to rescue thousands of young adults—mostly black and Hispanic—from the deadend, crime-ridden lives confronting the urban underclass in major American cities.[13] Ashe believed that through a program of national service young adults now unemployed and uneducated could be trained for useful lives in an economic system that is increasingly technological-driven and tied into a fast-moving global economy. Local communities would benefit in many ways from such a program, just as they did from the CCC in the 1930s. National leaders like President Clinton and Senator Sam Nunn of Georgia favor some version of national service.

Although national service may be an idea whose time is coming, the versions offered by the president, Senator Nunn, Arthur Ashe, and others are much too limited. True enough, the problems of crime, of poverty, and in education are heavily concentrated in the decaying cores of many of America's great cities. A program of national service for the threatened youth of the inner cities is worthwhile, but not sufficient. What the nation needs is a one- or two-year program of national service that applies to *every* person who completes high school or reaches the age of eighteen, with very few exceptions, even for those with severe physical disabilities. This would not be military service; the young men and women enrolled in the program would do many of the things that were done in the days of the CCC—conservation work, cleaning up the environment, building simple structures, helping the disabled and the elderly, and other civic tasks. Education and job training should also be a part of the program, with participants having the opportunity to earn cash credits that could be applied toward either college or vocational education after completing service.

Why such a program? Many may fear the authoritarian

character of national service, seeing in it an image of the perverted youth programs of Nazi Germany. Though there may be such dangers, they are remote. The young people will benefit enormously from the experience of being needed and working together with other young people from every race and every social and economic class, but the greatest benefits will accrue to the nation. Among the many critical economic and social needs America has today, none is so great, perhaps, as the need to restore and deepen a sense of community, an awareness that America is indeed a nation, held together, as Arthur M. Schlesinger, Jr., says, not by a common ethnic origin but by "a common adherence to ideals of democracy and human rights. . . ."[14] This is what is threatened today by the resurgence of racism, ethnic and cultural beliefs that one's own group is superior, separatist impulses, religious intolerance, and a rejection of the ideal of the "melting pot." As Theodore Roosevelt once said, "The one absolutely certain way of bringing this nation to ruin, of preventing all possibility of it continuing to be a nation at all, would be to permit it to become a tangle of squabbling nationalities, . . . each preserving its separate nationality."[15] The rights that give the United States its special claim to uniqueness—the rights embodied in the first ten amendments to the Constitution—are *individual* rights, not rights derived from membership in any particular group. This is the ultimate bond of community in America.

PUBLIC POLICY AND INVESTMENT IN THE NATION'S HEALTH

Adequate health care is a major element in the *real* standard of living of the American people. Unfortunately, there is no easy way to measure its true importance. Along with the fear of losing one's job, worry over health care and its costs is a major source of anxiety for Americans and their families. Hardly a day passes without some reference in the media to America's health-care crisis—costs out of control, persons without health insurance, reductions in health-care coverage by employers, families made bankrupt by nursing-home bills, and spiraling prices for prescription drugs.

Health-care reform is another crucial area where far-reaching measures are necessary to help end twenty years of economic stagnation—the silent depression. There is a common saying, "If it ain't broke, don't fix it." Unfortunately, America's health-care system *is* "broke" and needs fixing. This is paradoxical, for American medicine is undoubtedly the best in the world, but the nation's health-care delivery system is perhaps the worst among economically advanced nations.

Health-Care Spending in the United States

Before we look at the specifics of what is wrong, some facts are in order about health care in the United States. Figures from the Congressional Budget Office (CBO) show that in 1992 Americans spent $808.0 billion for health care, an amount equal to 13.6 percent of the GDP. On a per-person basis, Americans spent $3,149 for medical care, a figure equal to 18.2 percent of per-capita disposable income. For a family of four, medical spending was $12,596, or 31.3 percent of the average family income of $40,261 in 1992.[16] This 31.3 percent figure should not be misunderstood. It is not the amount that families spent out of their own pockets for medical care—that was only 18.6 percent of all spending for medical care—but a way of showing the overall size of the nation's medical bill on a per-family basis in comparison with family income.

In the year 2000, health-care spending is expected to equal $1,679 billion, which will absorb 18.0 percent of the nation's output. In 1965, by contrast, spending for health care took 5.9 percent of the GDP. Since 1980, health-care spending adjusted for inflation has risen at an annual rate of 11.1 percent, nearly 50 percent faster than all other kinds of spending—by government, by consumers, or by businesses. Some fear that, in another twenty years, Americans will be spending one-third of their national output for health care! In contrast to the United States, Canada and Germany get their health care for less than 9 percent of their GNP, as do Japan and Britain.

How do Americans spend their health-care dollar? And who pays for their health care? In 1992, for every $1,000 spent on health care in the United States, $384 was for hospital care, $189 for physicians, $78 for prescription drugs, $80 for nursing-home care, and $269 for all else, including dental care, chiropractors, other health-care professionals, and home nursing care. For every $1,000 spent on medical care in 1992, private insurance paid $314, individuals and their families paid $186 out of pocket, $313 was paid by the federal government, $142 by state and local governments, and the balance of $45 from other sources, including charity.[17]

If Medicare (health care for the elderly) and Medicaid (health care for the poor) are viewed as public insurance, then we get a different picture of the overall role that insurance—both private and public—plays in paying for America's medical bill. From this perspective, for every $1,000 spent on health care in 1992, private insurance paid for $314 worth of care, public insurance (Medicare and Medicaid) $320, individuals and their families $186, public agencies other than Medicare and Medicaid $135, and other sources $45. Private and public insurance together thus paid for 63.4 percent of all spending for medical care in 1990. Payment for medical services by someone other than the actual recipient of those services—the individual and the individual's family—is called a "third-party" system. In the United States in 1990, thirdparties—private insurance, government agencies, or charities—paid 81.4 percent of all health-care bills.[18]

What Is Wrong with America's Health-Care System?

Beyond the fact that Americans spend a disproportionate share of their national output on health care with less than satisfactory results, what else is wrong with the nation's health-care system?

There are three large and specific failings, and a number of other, lesser, but related failings. First, the system is excessively cumbersome and complex, top-heavy with administrative costs. Second, in spite of expenditures on health care that may reach $1 trillion per year by 1995, millions of Americans are without health insurance. Third, there has been an uncontrolled explosion of health-care costs, ruinous for many private businesses and even governments. Tucked into these major failings are some less dramatic problems, nevertheless of vital concern to both patients and providers of health care. The American College of Physicians recently listed some of the latter as excessive use of high technology, increases in spending without parallel gains in health status, the promotion of acute care at the expense of primary care, and technology-based care at the expense of primary care.[19]

One way to underscore the magnitude of the first failing listed above is to suggest that, if we had an economic law measuring the value of simplicity in human affairs, America's health-care system, on a scale of one to ten, would not even make the scale. To describe the current arrangements by which health care is delivered to the American people as a "system" is an oxymoron. As *Newsweek*'s economic columnist, Robert J. Samuelson, once said, "You can't describe our system, let alone control it. It's not private medicine. . . . Our health care system is a jumble of groups (doctors, hospitals, government agencies, health-maintenance organizations, private insurers) working under a bewildering array of regulations and pursuing different objectives. No one is in charge. . . ."[20] What we have is a patchwork, jerry-built structure consisting of more than fifteen hundred health-insurance programs, each with its own marketing scheme, compliance forms, and detailed instructions. No overall philosophy or control exists to provide direction for the nation's health care. The structure is near the breaking point.

The second major failing of the nation's health-care system is failure to provide insurance coverage for many people. In 1990, according to the Bureau of the Census, 14.0 percent of

Americans—34.7 million people—were without *any* private or government health insurance.[21] The largest number of persons without insurance are under age eighteen (8.5 million), followed by twenty-five-to-thirty-four-year-olds (8.3 million). Next in order are eighteen-to-twenty-four-year-olds (6.5 million), thirty-five-to-forty-four-year-olds (5.1 million), forty-five-to-fifty-four-year-olds (3.3 million), fifty-five-to-sixty-four-year-olds (2.7 million), and, finally over-sixty-five-year-olds (0.3 million). The proportion of Americans without health insurance has barely changed since 1979: it was 14.6 percent then and is 14.0 percent now. More serious is the fact that the percentage of employment-based private insurance plans has declined from 67.4 percent in 1979 to 65.2 percent in 1990, a 3.3 percent drop.[22]

Third, there is the continuing explosion of health-care costs, a development best understood by looking at what has happened to the price of medical care as compared with the price of other important items that enter into the cost of living (the consumer price index, or CPI). Prices for health care rose much faster than prices for every other major item that consumers buy. As *Time* once said, there are two kinds of prices in America today: regular prices and health-care prices.[23] From 1980 through 1991, prices for all consumer prices rose by 87.6 percent, but in this same period prices for medical care leaped by 162.6 percent. The price of food rose by 71.2 percent, housing by 90.6 percent, clothing by 51.6 percent, transportation by 75.6 percent, and entertainment by 80.4 percent.[24] Medicare and Medicaid spending, which are both a cause and a consequence of the explosion in costs, jumped by 231.5 percent between 1980 and 1991; in comparison, federal government spending overall rose by 148.6 percent.[25]

The explosion in costs for health care in the United States is fact. There are several "villains" to point to in this gloomy picture, although there is no real agreement on which are most responsible and what should be done about them. Before I discuss the specifics of the cost explosion in medical care, a few words are in order on the distinction between demand and costs in medical care and the interaction between them. As a rough rule of thumb, spending as described earlier reflects the demand of Americans for medical care. The rate of growth in medical spending consists of two things: how much more medical care people want, and the increased costs of providing medical care. Costs, of course, are just that—what it costs in money for the goods, the wages, salaries, and profits needed to provide medical care. It is also well to keep in mind that costs for some people are income for others, so you can't affect the one without affecting the other. This means, too, in trying to understand what has been happening with respect to medical care, one must not lose sight of both overlap and interaction between developments that increase the demand for medical care and those that increase their costs.

High on most lists of causes for soaring medical-care costs is the excessive use of high technology, plus expensive, sometimes extensive, and often unnecessary testing. Cardiac-bypass surgery is now widely used, even though less expensive medication may be equally successful in the treatment of heart disease. X-rays and magnetic resonance imagining (MRI) are used more than necessary—per-person use of X-rays is four times greater in the United States than in England. Electronic fetal monitors have replaced the ordinary stethoscope during birth for an estimated 75 percent of women in America, even though studies show there is little difference in the outcome of a pregnancy according to whether the fetus is monitored electronically or with a stethoscope.[26] Healthy persons going to a physician for a routine physical examination often get a blood count, a blood profile, and an EKG, tests that are not necessary in most instances.

Fear of malpractice suits plays a role in both the overuse of high technology and unnecessary testing. The American Medical Association estimates that "defensive medicine" adds as much as $21 billion a year to the nation's health bill. Another factor is that the market for health care differs from most other markets in that the patient, knowing very little about the appropriateness of medical treatments, must of necessity delegate the treatment decision to the doctor. Because both patient and doctor have an interest in reducing the uncertainty involved in medical care, resort to the latest of technology seems appropriate in many cases.

An excess of hospitals—hospitals are operating at about 66 percent of capacity—forces prices higher. In most cities there is also excessive duplication within hospitals of high-tech services—open-heart surgery, magnetic resonance imaging, X-ray radiation therapy, angioplasty—rather than the concentration of such services in a few regional centers. Further, when hospitals lose money on Medicaid patients, these losses are shifted to other patients and insurance companies.

There is little doubt that the growth of "third-party" payment systems—government and private insurance now pay almost 80 percent of all medical bills in America—is another piece in the health-cost puzzle. Since neither the patient nor the doctor is as directly concerned with price and cost as when most patients paid directly out of their own pockets, it is not surprising that the system is conducive not only to overcharging and waste, but to outright fraud as well. It has been estimated that fraud adds as much as $80 billion to the nation's medical bill.[27]

Waste is endemic to a system in which there are more than fifteen hundred health-insurance programs, each with its own methods of payment and record-keeping, not to mention marketing and promotion. According to the CBO, administrative costs for private insurance equal 17.1 percent of benefits paid, whereas the administrative costs for Medicare and Medicaid combined are 3.2 percent of benefits paid.[28] Record-keeping alone by health-care providers adds as much as $90 billion to overall costs.[29]

There also appears to be a close relationship between the third-party payment system and the overuse of expensive medical technologies and drugs. It is argued that improved but costly medical technology increases the demand for health insurance and with it the demand for more health care. But the pervasiveness of insurance encourages the development of cost-increasing technologies. Together, the interaction of insurance and technology help drive health-care costs upward.[30]

Finally, there is the cost of drugs, the prices for which rose faster than that of any other item or service entering into the nation's medical bill. A University of Minnesota study found that in 1991 the average wholesale prices for ten widely used drugs for the treatment of such well-known illnesses as heart disease, epilepsy, arthritis, ulcers, hypertension, and postmenopause were $68.28 per hundred tablets in the United States, but only $39.60 in Canada (in U.S. dollars).[31] Most drugs are produced by a handful of giant firms for markets in which the firms do not compete by price. Drug companies blame research costs, but this is more of an excuse than a reason. A report by the Office of Technology Assessment released in late February 1993 stated not only that the profits of firms in the pharmaceutical industry were higher by 2 to 3 percentage points than those of firms in other industries, but that pharmacaceutical companies spent on the average about $10 billion per year on advertising, $2 billion *more* than they spent on research for new drugs.[32]

The Specifics of Health-Care Reform

America's health-care system needs fundamental reform. On this 90 percent of the public is in agreement, as are the leaders of American business. Key elements in the medical profession have swung around to the view that a total restructuring of the system is necessary.[33] The next several paragraphs outline the essential ideas and principles that must undergird a restructured system, noting both agreement and disagreement with the arguments developed.

The fundamental need is a system of *universal* health insurance that provides a minimum level of basic medical care, including preventive health services and access to long-term care. Basic benefits should include hospital and physician care, diagnostic services, home health care, prescription drugs and durable medical equipment, mental-health services, and possible substance-abuse treatment. No person should be excluded because of a pre-existing medical condition.

Widespread agreement exists on the need for a universal system, even within the medical profession. A universal system would involve a single payer, which is a major means to reduce the excessive administrative costs that now characterize America's health-care situation. In the Canadian system, administrative costs are only about 25 percent as high as they are in the United States.

Can the United States afford a comprehensive system? If we seek to create an entirely new system and impose it on top of the existing structure, the answer is obviously no. In the face of federal deficits in the $300-billion range, it would be absurd to attempt to repair our broken health-care system with major increases in public spending. The problem in America is not one of insufficient spending for medical care. We are now spending more than enough to provide every citizen with adequate and decent medical care. It is a matter of how we spend the money, a question of the inefficient structure of the health-care system. At root, our problem is more political than economic. We need to find the political vision and will to rearrange existing spending patterns to provide decent medical care for all citizens.

Major disagreement exists over the method of payment, especially with respect to finding an appropriate mix of public and private finance. Plans proposed by the American Medical Association, the American College of Medicine, many members of the Congress (both Democrats and Republicans), other groups, and President Clinton favor some modification of the current mix of private, employer-based insurance and public financing. I reject this approach. What we need is a system of national health insurance, one in which all, or nearly all, of the costs would be borne by the federal government. National health insurance is *not* socialized medicine, although critics seek to portray it as such. Socialized medicine means that the government—the federal government, in the case of the United States—would own all health-care facilities, such as hospitals, clinics, and nursing homes, and be the primary, if not the sole, employer of health-care professionals. Britain has a system of socialized medicine, but there are few advocates of this for the United States.

A system of national health insurance applies the basic insurance principle of pooling and spreading risks across the largest group possible—the entire population of the United States. It is generally well known in private insurance that, when risks can be shifted from the individual to a group, the costs of insurance to any member of the group will be reduced. In a practical sense, this means that the administrative costs in a system of national health insurance will be far lower than those for the nation's present jumbled mix of private and public plans. If American administrative costs for health care could be brought to the same level as Canada's national system, they would average 4.3 percent, as against the current 17.1 percent for private insurance plans. In 1992, an estimated $32.5 billion in administrative costs could have been saved out of the nation's $808-billion medical bill if a national plan had been in effect. A system of national health insurance would not limit the freedom of choice of physician and hospital by individuals and their families, something that is not true for so-called systems of managed competition. Freedom of choice in the matter of medical care is cherished by Americans and must be preserved. There is support on this point from the experience with Medicare, the limited system of national health insurance for the over-sixty-five segment of the population. There is no evidence that persons over sixty-five are restricted in their choice of physicians or hospitals. In Canada, which has basically a system of national health insurance, freedom of consumer choice exists in medical care.

How would we pay for a system of national health insurance? Medicare offers a point of departure. It is paid for by a portion of the Social Security tax and modest fees charged persons over sixty-five enrolled in the Medicare program. Any system of national health insurance should be financed by a combination of Social Security taxes, alcohol and cigarette taxes, general tax revenues, plus a continuation of relatively modest fees for retired persons. Persons and families with incomes below the poverty line would be exempt from the health-care taxes.

Would a system of national health insurance require an increase in taxes? The answer is yes, primarily because payment for medical care would be shifted from private sources (individual out-of-pocket spending and insurance carriers) to the federal government. If the structure for paying is carefully designed, *any* increase in taxes paid should be more than offset by reduced out-of-pocket spending by individuals and their families for health care and for health-care insurance. There is a trade-off, substituting public payments for private payments in the nation's health-care system. It will require extremely wise and skilled political action to bring this about in a manner that leaves most families better off, both with respect to the availability of health care and to the way in which they pay for this care. It can be done. This nation has a $6-trillion GDP and one of the lowest average tax burdens in the industrialized world, and spends 13.6 percent of that product for health care. There is ample room to restructure health care to provide a minimum level of care for all citizens without spending more than we are now spending, either publicly or privately. To do this, though, without abrupt and unacceptable increases in taxes, a system of national health insurance would have to be phased in over a period of several years.

One extremely important advantage that a system of national health insurance has over alternative, mixed private-public systems of payment is that it will separate *completely* eligibility for health care from employment. Most of the existing proposals for health-care reform, including some coming from the medical profession and from the political leadership in Washington, advocate some version of a "pay-or-play" system, requiring that business firms—usually firms with some minimum of employees—either offer health insurance to their employees ("play") or pay additional taxes to help finance a public plan.

"Pay or play" is the wrong approach. The availability of health care should be separated totally from employment, for two sound reasons.

First, employees would no longer have the fear of losing their insurance when they changed or lost their jobs. Many Americans live in fear because they may be just a job loss away from losing their health insurance. With health care separate from employment, dependents, including children, would be protected from a loss of insurance if one spouse became divorced or widowed from the spouse whose employment was the source of insurance benefits for the family. Further, the risk of workers' losing their health-insurance benefits because an employer goes bankrupt would be eliminated. Thus, labor would enjoy increased mobility, a development that would be good for the economy.

The second set of reasons for separating health insurance from the job concerns employers. Employers would be free of the administrative burdens involved in providing health care for their employees, a cost item that is of major significance for small firms. Eliminating such costs would also have favorable effects on the employment picture, because many employers in recent years have turned to part-time or temporary employees as a way of avoiding paying health-insurance costs for their workers. Labor-management conflicts over health-care benefits would also be eliminated, clearly a positive gain.

Will a system of national health insurance be able to control recent excessive, escalating costs for medical care? One fact stands out: the health-care "crisis" has had the nation's attention for at least twenty years, but there has been almost no progress in controlling costs over the years. As one recent study of medical costs phrased it, "Neither the regulatory policies of the 1970s nor the competitive policies of the 1980s have slowed the growth of health care spending."[34] There is no guarantee that national health insurance will succeed in slowing the escalation of costs, but there are some reasons for optimism.

In the first place, the administrative arm for a system of national health insurance will be in an exceptionally strong bargaining position vis-à-vis the major suppliers of medical services—hospitals, organizations of physicians, and the pharmaceutical companies. At present, the antitrust laws do not allow health-care providers (such as hospitals or physicians) to form organizations that could engage in bargaining with the administrative agency of a national health service. If such a system came into being in the United States, there would have to be some modification of the antitrust laws to permit this practice. Fee schedules that are fair and agreeable to payers and suppliers have to be worked out through a bargaining process; there is no other way to do it in this society. Medicare does this now in a limited way for private-practice physicians, so this is not entirely new territory. The administrative agency for a national health-care system would be in a favorable position to bargain with private practice physicians and private insurance companies, which can play an important supplementary role in a national plan.

In the view of many experts, the best approach to cost containment—beyond a reasonable and mutually acceptable schedule of fees—is a combination of a per-capita payment system and an overall budget: for the total system, for parts within the system (hospitals, physicians, and other providers), and possibly by geographic areas, such as the states. In Canada and Germany, two countries that combine a unified national payment system with fee-for-service medical practice, the medical organizations do not have much control over the total amount of money being spent for medical care, but they have significant control over how the money is divided up. Overall budgets based upon a per-capita payment system have a built-in incentive for economizing on the use of medical services.

No matter how health care in the United States is reformed, one caveat cannot be ignored. There will have to be some limit on the kinds of disease, disability, and injury that are eligible for treatment under a reformed, national system. As former Governor of Colorado Richard D. Lamm has said, "Health care is a fiscal black hole that can absorb all our children's resources. We have invented more health care than we can afford to deliver to everyone. Unless we set some limits on 'high-cost / low-benefit' procedures, we will bankrupt our children."[35] This raises the ugly topic of health-care rationing, something Americans are reluctant to face. The reality, though, is that medical care is already rationed, but largely by chance, depending upon the income and other economic resources of people who get sick. The real choice is not whether to ration health care, but whether to do so in a careful and wise way, or to continue to allow it to be done in a haphazard, unplanned way.

Where do private insurance companies fit into this picture? Since they have such a strong vested interest in the present hodge-podge of private health-insurance plans, they will bitterly resist any change. Their choice, assuming the present system will be changed, is for the managed-competition option; this would leave the insurance industry with about as much power and influence as they now have for shaping health-care policy. In testimony before a House subcommittee on health, Robert Reischauer, director of the CBO, said that a specific managed-competition bill introduced into the House of Representatives (HR 5936) would not produce any long-run savings. In several years, he said, national health expenditures under managed-competition would rise to the levels they would have reached otherwise.[36] The insurance industry and the big guns of the health-care delivery system—hospitals, doctors, and drug manufacturers—have the money to battle for the *status quo* or, if change is to come, guide it to meet their interests. The long-established and highly respected citizens' lobby Common Cause says that, between 1981 and 1991, medical-industry political-action committees (insurance companies, doctors, hospitals, and drug manufacturers) spent

$60 million on congressional candidates, more than half of which went to incumbents.[37]

Assuming, however, that some form of national health insurance is adopted, is there a constructive role for private insurance? The answer is yes. Having one national system for paying the nation's bill for basic health care does not mean there is no room for additional health-care schemes offered by private insurers. This is now being done with respect to Medicare; any person who watches TV must be aware of advertising that seeks to sell supplemental health insurance to persons over sixty-five. Since a national-health-care program will establish *minimal* standards of health care, the private companies would be free to develop health-care packages that go well beyond what is available to everyone through national legislation. There is nothing unusual in this; banks, insurance companies, and investment firms are highly skilled in developing and marketing "products" that supplement public or private group arrangements for pensions, health care, or savings, including Social Security.

National insurance is clearly superior both to the present system and to proposals for "pay-or-play" and managed competition systems. Polls show that more than 60 percent of Americans support a Canadian-style system which retains the fee-for-service practice, yet has the federal government set fees and pay the overwhelming bulk of the costs. Will it happen in the United States? Harry Truman sounded the call for national health insurance nearly fifty years ago, but it has not happened yet.

CHAPTER 10

Taxes and American Civilization

axes are what we pay for civilized society," Justice Oliver Wendell Holmes, Jr., once said. Indeed, societies require taxes. There are good and bad tax systems, however, and if we rate late-twentieth-century American civilization by the quality of the nation's tax system, the nation is in deep trouble. What has happened to the federal tax system since the end of World War II is both a cause and a consequence of the silent depression. Thus, the third place where major changes are needed to move the nation back to its historic path of growth, justice, and opportunity for all Americans is tax reform—a complete overhaul of the federal tax structure.

What is wrong with the federal tax system? There are two things badly wrong, so wrong that, if they are not corrected, the nation may face a tax revolt and crisis of massive scope. The first is the growing complexity and incomprehensibility of the tax code. Second, increasingly, the federal tax code violates principles of efficiency and equity that should apply to all taxes. These wrongs are closely related, continually interacting with each other. President Carter once called the income tax "a disgrace to the human race." Although the Tax Reform Act of 1986 simplified the rate structure for federal income taxes, in other respects this act—the most comprehensive revision of the nation's tax laws since 1954—added to the complexity and incomprehensibility of the code.

No general economic law measures the economic worth of simplicity in human affairs, but if such a law existed, the federal income tax would undoubtedly have negative ratings on all counts. The basic tax code contains more than two thousand pages, consists of over fifty different "titles"—or parts—and fills more than 180 volumes. The income-tax part of the code is contained in eight volumes, which fill fourteen inches of library space, include more than five thousand pages, and weigh over twelve pounds. At one time, only about 10 percent of taxpayers sought professional help in preparing their taxes. Now it is close to 60 percent. The sheer complexity of the tax and the labor involved in completing the tax have spawned a not-so-small "cottage industry" devoted to tax preparation: H & R Block is a big business. Many lawyers make a good living from the discovery and legal exploitation of loopholes in the tax system.

"Efficiency in taxation" means that a tax interferes as little as possible with the choices people and business firms make in economic activities. The tax code departs drastically from the principle, primarily because of a long history of policy decisions by the federal government to use taxes to encourage or discourage particular types of economic behavior. Deductibility of mortgage interest by home buyers is one of the oldest examples of this, the purpose being to encourage families to own their own homes. Some observers describe using the tax code in this fashion as "social engineering," a practice that is good or bad, depending upon one's perspective. In any event, the federal tax code, especially the income-tax portion, has spawned an enormous array of exclusions, deductions, tax credits, and preferential rates with respect to taxation that change economic behavior in significant ways. Economists call the tax revenue lost to the federal government because of loopholes in the tax code "tax expenditures." Although this term is not widely known, it is appropriate, because it often has the same effect upon economic behavior as an outright gift of cash. We could, for example, encourage home ownership through a direct subsidy to the home buyer, as well as indirectly. In 1992, the revenue lost to the federal government because of "tax expenditures" benefiting both individuals and corporations was estimated at $374.9 billion, a figure equal to 65.5 percent of actual income-tax collections from individuals and corporations in 1991.[1] At last count, there were forty-four different types of tax expenditures for corporations, and seventy-three that applied to individuals.

"Equity in taxation" refers to commonly held notions about the fairness of a tax system. Economists talk about horizontal and vertical equity. "Horizontal equity" means that taxpayers in the same situation pay the same amount of taxes, "vertical equity" that persons with more income pay more taxes than persons with less income. The latter is not so simple as it may sound: there is much controversy over whether or not persons with higher incomes *should* pay a greater proportion of their incomes in taxes. An income-tax system is "progressive" if higher-income persons and families pay a larger percentage of their incomes in taxes than those with less income. If all persons and families paid the same proportion of their incomes in taxes, the system would be "proportional.." A "regressive" system is one in which persons and families with higher incomes pay a *smaller* percentage of their incomes in taxes than persons and families with lower incomes. No politician would publicly design and advocate a regressive tax, though in practice some taxes work out that way.

Critics of the federal income-tax system maintain it grossly violates both efficiency and equity principles. The main culprit is the enormous array of loopholes and tax expenditures spawned by the system. These make the system inefficient in the sense that people in equal economic situations are not treated the same. Critics also charge that changes in the tax laws in the last decade have contributed to the growth in income inequality in the United States, because these changes reduced the degree of progression in the system. The latter is generally correct. Between 1977 and 1993, according to the Ways and Means Committee of the House of Representatives, effective tax rates for all federal taxes—the proportion of income actually taxed—dropped by 21.1 percent for the top 1 percent of all taxpayers, by 10.1 percent for the top 5 percent, and by 5.6 percent for the top 10 percent. For taxpayers in all other brackets save the lowest 20 percent, the effective rate remained unchanged. For the lowest 20 percent, there was a reduction of 19.4 percent, because the Tax Reform Act of 1986 removed many low-income families from the tax rolls.[2]

It is time for a total change in how the federal government taxes American citizens. This involves three basic questions. First, which taxes are in need of total reform? Second, what should be taxed? This involves what economists call the "tax base"—the thing that is being taxed. In the income tax, for example, income is the tax base. And, third, how should the object of taxation—say, income—be taxed? This involves controversial questions about tax rates, the percentage of the base that must be paid in taxes. As far as income taxes are concerned, the key issue is whether the rate should be "graduated," which means applying higher rates to higher portions of a person's or family's income. Progression should be distinguished from graduated rates, for, as we shall see, an income-tax system can be progressive—higher-income persons pay a higher percent of their incomes in taxes—without a system of graduated rates.

Answering these three questions leads to a comprehensive plan involving near-total reform in the federal tax system, a plan characterized by far greater simplicity and fairness than now exists. With one crucial exception, the plan proposed here abandons the idea of using the tax system for "social engineering." It is better and more healthy in a democracy to do things openly and by a direct subsidy whenever there is a major economic and social role for federal government, whether it is the promotion of home ownership, private investment, exploration for minerals, stimulation of capital expenditures by state and local governments, or any of the hundreds of other activities encouraged or discouraged by tax-expenditure loopholes.

The two taxes where reform is needed most are the personal and corporate income taxes. These taxes combined now account for 51.1 percent of federal revenues. Social Security taxes account for another 41.8 percent of federal tax receipts, and are second only to the personal income tax as a source of federal revenue.[3] The reforms proposed for the personal and corporate income tax can be applied readily to Social Security taxes, although the arithmetic of reforms developed later in this chapter is limited to income taxes. Finally, a new and vital role is proposed for estate and inheritance taxes, now of minor importance in the federal tax structure.

What should be the tax base is the second question. Currently, the tax base for the personal income tax is what the Internal Revenue Service (IRS) defines as "taxable income." Taxable income is obtained by deducting from the taxpayer's total money income excluded income (like tax-free interest income from state and local bonds, or a part of Social Security retirement income) to arrive at "adjusted gross income." From this, allowable deductions (either "itemized," such as interest on a home mortgage, or a standard amount) plus personal and dependency exemptions are subtracted to arrive at the taxable-income figure. Anyone who has struggled through on his or her own to determine income and itemize deductions on IRS Form 1040 knows how utterly confusing, time-consuming, and difficult the process can be.

There is a vast difference between IRS figures on income and the measure of income, "personal income," widely used by economists. Personal income is a broad and comprehensive measure of the money income actually earned or received by persons in the economy from all sources—wages and salaries, profits from owning a business, dividends from corporations, rents from owning property, interest income from securities, and retirement income from pension plans and Social Security. It *does not* include taxes paid by employers for Social Security, but it *does* include employer contributions to private pension and medical-insurance funds. Since 1947, adjusted gross income as measured by the IRS has averaged 74.8 percent of personal income, whereas taxable income has measured but 44.4 percent of personal income.[4] Thus, the tax base for the personal income tax (taxable income) is usually less than 50 percent of the amount of income actually received by persons in the economy from all sources. The base for the income tax proposed in this book is personal income with *no exceptions or exclusions!* This is a major change, one that will affect drastically the market value of homes with mortgages, the market value of existing state and local bonds, and the income of churches and other charitable activities. Deductions for these items in the calculation of taxable income represent some of the largest of existing tax expenditures. Because of the impact of such changes on property values and incomes, they would have to be phased in gradually, as was done when the deductibility of credit-card and other kinds of consumer interest was eliminated from the personal income tax. Over time, the benefits of developing a federal tax system free of the enormous number of exemptions, exceptions, special treatment of favored kinds of income, and such complexity that the nation's tax code is incomprehensible to the average citizen, will far outweigh the transitional costs of the change.

The tax base for the corporate income tax is the gross earnings of corporations minus the costs of earning the income (primarily wages and salaries, materials purchased, interest charges on debt, and depreciation allowances for buildings and equipment, plus a broad array of tax expenditures). Tax expenditures, which totaled 46.9 percent of corporate income taxes actually paid in 1992, have drastically reduced the importance of the corporate income tax in the overall revenue picture of the federal government.[5] In 1947, the corporate income tax supplied 24.9 percent of federal tax revenue; by 1991, this figure had slipped to an estimated 7.1 percent.[6] I am proposing that the corporate income tax be wholly abolished. Corporate income not now distributed to shareholders as dividends should be allocated annually to them on an individual basis, thereby becoming a part of personal income (even though not distributed), and thus included in the broadened tax base for the personal income tax.

For Social Security and Medicare taxes, the current base for Social Security taxes is wage-and-salary income up to an amount of $55,500 annually, and for Medicare $130,200. This base covers 94.3 percent of all wage-and-salary earnings in the economy. No change is being proposed in this base, although, as stated earlier, the reforms proposed for the personal and corporate income taxes could be broadened to include Social Security. The immediate problem with Social Security taxation is in the rates, not the base, a matter that will be addressed shortly.

Federal estate and gift taxes are levied upon the transfer of property. In 1991, these taxes brought $12.2 billion into the federal treasury, or 1.1 percent of all federal income, not including proceeds from borrowing.[7] The federal government does not levy inheritance taxes, which are taxes levied upon the value of property actually inherited. What is proposed in this book is that the federal government replace the estate tax with an inheritance tax designed to reduce in a major way the inequality in the distribution of wealth in the United States. How this can be done is discussed below, in the section headed "Taxes and the Distribution of Income and Wealth."

What rate should be applied to the three different bases for taxation that lie at the heart of the reform proposals of this book? This is the third question. As the details of the reform plan discussed in the next section will show, only in the case of Social Security taxes is a specific rate being recommended. For the income tax, the actual rate will depend upon the revenue needs of the federal government in any particular year. The next section will show how tax reform will work, using the known figures for 1990. As for a federal inheritance tax, the rate is not the crucial issue.

Rather, it is to show how this tax may be used as a major means to change the distribution of wealth in the nation.

A PLAN FOR INCOME-TAX REFORM

The starting point for tax reform is an idea of great simplicity, talked about occasionally, but never examined seriously. This is a "flat"—or single-rate—tax applied to an appropriate base. When properly designed, a flat-rate tax would be simple—one's tax return could be filed on a postcard—and would be fair, because in practice a flat-rate tax can be progressive. The secret lies in including income from all sources in the tax base, and having an adequate personal exemption. The basics of such a tax are outlined here, using income and population figures from 1990. The tax plan developed here can be varied in a number of ways, but the basic principles for a flat-rate system are easily understood.

The starting point is personal income. In 1990, personal income in the United States was $4,664.2 billion (in 1990 prices). With the corporate income tax being abolished, we need to add to this figure corporate taxes paid in 1990 ($136.7 billion) and profits that corporations did not distribute as dividends to their shareholders ($69.4 billion). These additions bring the total for personal income to $4,870.3 billion.[8]

The next step is to determine the basic exemption for each person. The exemption could easily be framed in terms of a family, the individual, or both.[9] For simplicity of explanation, a basic exemption of $15,000 for each person over twenty years of age is used. The $15,000 figure is 125.5 percent greater than the 1990 poverty threshold of $6,652 for a person living alone. In this version of a flat-rate tax system, an individual living alone would not pay any tax on his or her income until it reached $15,000, but all income above that amount would be taxed at a single rate—the "flat" tax.

What is the appropriate rate? This depends upon the total of money income not subject to taxation because of the exemption, and the amount of money the federal government needs to raise through taxation. In 1990, there were 179.2 million adults in the United States over the age of twenty, and the federal government raised $596.5 billion from the personal and corporate income tax. These two numbers determine what the rate for a flat tax would have had to be in 1990 to raise the same amount of money as was raised by the combined personal and corporate income tax. The total money income exempt from taxation is $2,688.0 billion, a figure derived by multiplying 179.2 million by $15,000. If we subtract the $2,688.0 billion from the revised personal-income figure of $4,870.3 billion, we get $2,182.3 billion, which is the adjusted tax base for 1990. This compares to the actual IRS figure of $2,263.7 billion for taxable income in 1990, as reported in *SOI Bulletin,* the quarterly publication of the Internal Revenue Service, which contains the most recent detailed numbers on all federal taxes.[10] By dividing $596.5 billion (the money needed) by $2,182.3 billion (the adjusted tax base), we derive the appropriate flat tax rate of 27.3 percent. These calculations ignore the federal government's deficit, for their purpose is to calculate a flat tax rate that would raise the same amount of money that the existing personal and corporate income tax raised in 1990.

Table 10-1 shows how a flat tax rate of 27.3 percent works out in practice, applied to single individuals, for incomes ranging between $15,000 and $100,000. The basic $15,000 exemption is assumed. The effective tax rate—the percentage of total income received that is taxed—starts at 6.8 percent for an income of $20,000 and ultimately approaches a maximum effective rate of 27.3 percent.

Because of the personal exemption, 55.2 percent of income received from all sources is exempt from taxation. In contrast, under the current system, 51.6 percent of personal income is not taxed, but there is no uniformity as to which or what kind of income is taxed or not taxed. More to the point, in the flat-rate tax model shown in table 10-1, no tax was paid until an individual's

Table 10-1 *Taxes and Effective Tax Rates for Selected Incomes (in dollars and in percent)*

Income Received	Taxable Income*	Income Tax	Net Income†	Effective Tax Rate‡
$ 15,000	—	—	$15,000	—
20,000	$ 5,000	$ 1,365	18,635	6.8%
25,000	10,000	2,730	22,270	10.9
30,000	15,000	4,095	25,905	13.7
35,000	20,000	5,460	29,540	15.6
40,000	25,000	6,825	33,175	17.1
45,000	30,000	8,190	36,810	18.2
50,000	35,000	9,555	40,445	19.1
75,000	60,000	16,380	58,620	21.8
100,000	85,000	23,205	76,795	23.2

*Income received, minus the basic exemption of $15,000.
†Income received minus tax.
‡Tax divided by income received.

income reached $15,000. Under the present system, taxpayers (single and married) in 1990 with less than $15,000 in taxable income paid $13.6 billion in taxes, which was 3.1 percent of the total of $432.9 collected through the personal income tax.[11] Overall, a flat tax system, as shown in table 10-1, would be more progressive than the current system. This is because in the example incomes below $15,000 are not taxed, but taxes actually paid in 1990 were equal to 15.3 percent of reported taxable income in the under-$15,000 bracket in that year.[12]

A major point is that, with a flat-rate tax, progression can be obtained without having graduated rates, one of the most controversial and divisive features of the income tax. The degree of progression built into a flat-rate tax system depends upon the size of the personal exemption—the higher the exemption, the lower the tax burden on lower- and middle-income taxpayers. Higher exemptions require a higher tax rate, so there is a trade-off between exemptions and the tax rate.

The plan developed in table 10-1 illustrates the principles involved in taxing income under a flat-rate system—it is *not* a recommendation for a specific rate for taxing income, or a specific figure for a personal exemption. To satisfy the need for horizontal equity, exemptions for families with children, married couples without children, and individuals living alone necessarily should be different. A major virtue of a flat-rate tax system without loopholes is that all income after subtracting exemptions would be taxed at the same rate.

Another advantage of a flat-rate tax system is that the principle of the negative income tax could be readily factored into such a system as a way of reforming the welfare system and eliminating poverty. The negative income tax, invented by the leading conservative economist Milton Friedman, provides an income grant to all persons or families whose incomes fall below a designated level. As income is increased through work, the grant is reduced, reaching zero when the family or person achieves through work the designated, or "break-even," income level. The beauty of Friedman's negative-income-tax proposal is that an individual or a family is always better off economically by working than by not working. Thus, it lends itself to building incentives for people to work into plans for reforming the welfare system. The nation already has a negative income tax in rudimentary form in the Earned Income Tax Credit, so the basis exists to develop a full-fledged negative-income-tax approach to the reform of the welfare system and the elimination of poverty in conjunction with the shift to a flat-rate system for taxing all income.

One final but major point in favor of a flat-rate system. It would probably reduce significantly the tax revenue lost because of the nonfiling of returns, tax cheating through fraud and evasion, and tax avoidance through searching out the loopholes in the system. Tax avoidance is legal, but evasion is not. The

Internal Revenue System estimates that in 1992 the "tax gap" was at least $127 billion, a figure large enough to put a sizable dent in the federal deficit.[13] The IRS tax-gap concept, which applies to personal and corporate incomes taxes, but not to Social Security or excise taxes, refers to taxes that are due but not yet paid, and that will require enforcement action by the IRS for their collection. On the average, about 83 percent of individual income taxes and 85 percent of corporate income taxes are paid voluntarily—that is, without any enforcement action by the IRS.

The IRS's estimates of revenue losses through the tax gap is not the same thing as tax revenue lost because of tax cheating that can be linked directly to the so-called underground economy—legal and illegal activity that escapes the tax collector's net. The common phrase is "paying under the table." Sometimes these payments are for legal activities—cash payments to baby-sitters and other household workers—but those for drug dealing, numbers running, and prostitution support illegal activities. Although income from illegal activity is taxable—as nearly everyone knows, Al Capone's downfall came from his failure to pay income taxes on his gangland earnings—the IRS believes illegal earnings are so difficult to measure that it does not include them in its estimates of the size of the tax gap.

Nonetheless, the size of the underground economy is significant. How big is it? A recent Department of Labor study estimate based upon IRS numbers put the size of the legal underground economy at $500 billion; illegal activity added another $250 billion to this, giving a total of $750 billion.[14] This is 12.6 percent of the nation's 1992 GDP of $5,950.7 billion. If all income generated in the underground economy had been taxed and collected in 1991 at the same rate as legal income, more billions would have been added to the coffers of the U.S. Treasury. Shifting to a flat-rate tax system won't eliminate the illegal side of the underground economy, but it could reduce significantly the amount of legal economic activity taking place "off the books."[15]

SOCIAL SECURITY TAXES

It was noted earlier that *in principle* Social Security taxes could be incorporated into a flat-rate tax system. For several reasons, this is not recommended. Irrespective of its flaws, the Social Security system is indeed the crown jewel of the American welfare state, the most widely respected and supported program of the federal government. Politically, it would be both unrealistic and unwise to attempt major changes in this system along with trying to bring about major reforms in the way in which income is taxed in the United States. In recent years, there has been much discussion about Social Security and Medicare—the two largest of the so-called entitlement programs—and the need to means-test Social Security so that high-income people don't receive benefits they do not need. The answer to this problem is not to be found in means-testing, a degrading action both for welfare mothers and the well-to-do. The answer lies in including Social Security income, along with all other income, in the tax base, coupled with a taxing system that closes all loopholes. The flat-rate tax fits this bill.

Social Security tax *rates* are another matter. In early 1983, a blue-ribbon National Commission of Social Security Reform, headed by Alan Greenspan, now chairman of the Federal Reserve System, recommended that scheduled increases in the Social Security tax be accelerated. The commission was in a mild state of panic over the possibility that the surpluses in the Social Security trust funds—for pensions, disability, and medical care for persons over sixty-five—would soon be exhausted. Consequently, the Social Security tax (levied in equal parts on employees and employers) was raised from 13.4 to 15.3 percent, a 14.2-percent increase. Whereas most low-income families escape the federal income tax, this is not so for Social Security taxes, as long as anyone in the family works for wages.

The commission's fear about immediate shortages in the trust funds turned out to be largely unfounded, as Senator Daniel Patrick

Moynihan of New York, a member of the commission, recognized in late 1989. Senator Moynihan introduced a bill in the Senate on January 1, 1990, to repeal the 1983 increases and, further, to scale the Social Security tax back to a 5.1-percent rate for employees and employers. His bill failed to pass. What Senator Moynihan sought was to set Social Security taxes at a level that would maintain a balance in the trust funds roughly equal to one year's outlay.[16]

What is at issue in this matter are questions about the fundamental nature of the Social Security System. Since its founding in 1935, Social Security has essentially been a "pay-as-you-go" system in which persons currently employed pay for the retired, the disabled, survivors, and other beneficiaries of the system. After the 1983 Social Security tax increases, the Reagan administration saw an opportunity to transform Social Security into a "pay-for-yourself" system, one in which money collected in taxes from employees is paid into a fund out of which benefits would be paid to the employees at retirement, if disabled, or to their survivors.

The flaw in the "pay-for-yourself" view is that tax money flowing into the Social Security Administration in excess of benefits paid is not really accumulated in a "fund" in a manner similar to the workings of private insurance. Any yearly surplus is invested in special interest-bearing government securities, which means the funds become a part of the general revenues of the government, to be spent for any legitimate government purpose. When the Social Security Administration, which is a part of the government, presents these securities to the U.S. Treasury for redemption in order to pay Social Security benefits, where will the Treasury get the money? Taxes will have to be raised, or other spending cut. This does not mean that the Social Security trust fund is fraudulent—not in the least. But what is involved is an internal bookkeeping transaction, in which one part of the federal government—the Social Security Administration—is lending its surplus revenues to another part—the U.S. Treasury.

This makes the overall federal deficit look better, because trust-fund surpluses offset the deficit created by the overall shortfall of revenues relative to general government spending.

As Senator Moynihan suggested in 1990, the Social Security tax should be cut back to a level that would maintain a rough balance between tax receipts and outlays for Social Security benefits. The notion that Social Security can be anything but a "pay-as-you-go" system is an illusion. The sooner we discard this illusion, the better. Currently, the surpluses in the Social Security and Medicare trust funds make the government's deficit look better, but if the budget outside the trust funds—what economists call the "on-budget" accounts—ever got in balance, the surpluses in the trust funds would act as a serious deflationary drag on the economy.[17]

A wide intergenerational gap exists between the perceptions of Social Security held by today's over-sixty-five generation and by millions of baby-boomers, the first of whom won't enter into retirement until around 2010, in the twenty-first century. Today's retirees are firmly convinced that Social Security is a system of insurance in which the benefits they are receiving were paid for by Social Security taxes—euphemistically called "contributions" by the Social Security Administration—collected from them over their working lives. Reality is different. Currently, the average male retiree will receive in benefits what he paid into the system in taxes within 3–5.3 years.[18] Baby-boomers, though understanding that Social Security is necessary for elderly Americans, also believe overwhelmingly that the system may collapse and that they won't see any benefits when it comes time for them to retire.[19]

In these differing perceptions lie the seeds for a bitter conflict, one that, perhaps, can only be avoided if it is clearly understood that Social Security is a transfer system in which the working population pays for the benefits received by the retired population. The ability of those who work to pay for benefits now or in the middle of the next century does not depend upon the labels given the financial machinery through which income transfers are made. It depends upon the productiveness of the employed population, now and in the future. This is another reason why restoring productivity growth to its historic trend and ending the silent depression is crucial, not only to the well-being of American society today, but also to assure the baby-boomers that Social Security benefits will be there when they become senior citizens sometime in the next century.

TAXES AND THE DISTRIBUTION OF INCOME AND WEALTH

In comments made earlier about the need for total reform in the tax system, the point was made that, with one exception, using the tax system for "social engineering" was an idea that should be abandoned—its time has gone. It is appropriate to turn now to discussion of the exception. What is discussed and proposed here may be the most far-reaching, radical, and politically controversial idea in the entire book.

In 1992, Herbert Inhaber, a physicist, and Sidney Carroll, an economist, jointly authored a book, *How Rich Is Too Rich? Income and Wealth in America*.[20] What makes this book both original and unusual—aside from the fact that it is not every day that a physicist and an economist collaborate in writing a book on economics—is that the authors believe that there exists a scientifically grounded economic law that answers the question "How rich is too rich?" From Biblical and earlier times down to the current era, human beings have sought without much success an answer to this question. Inhaber and Carroll's answer, which they dub "the 3% solution," involves the distribution and taxation of *both* wealth and income. Although the underlying mathematics and economics are complicated, the basic thrust of their ideas is not only relatively easy to understand, but well suited for public policy. The inheritance tax, not now used by the federal government, can—and should—play a crucial role in the translation of their ideas into public policy. This section will show how this can be done.

Many people have some familiarity with the idea of a bell-shaped curve, or "normal distribution." When the distribution of a large number of measures for many things—test scores, heights, lengths, rainfall—are plotted on graph paper the resulting curve, or picture of the distribution, is shaped like a bell. The same proportion of measurements fall below the middle measurement—the high point of the bell-shaped curve—as above it. Students, for example, like to be graded "on the curve," for this means there will always be the same proportion of high and low grades.

The distribution of income and wealth is different. It is what statisticians call "skewed" toward the higher ranges of income and wealth. On graph paper it looks like a lopsided bell, with a bulge or tail to the right. For both income and wealth, the proportion of low-income or low-wealth-owning persons or families is far greater than the proportion of those at the top of the scale. In mathematical terms, a skewed distribution is called "lognormal," because, if the distribution's logarithms are used instead of the distribution itself, the plotted curve again will be "normal"—or bell-shaped. Now we encounter another interesting mathematical property. If a bell-shaped or normal curve is plotted on probability paper—a special type of graph paper—it becomes a straight line sloping upward from left to right. The steepness of the line reflects the degree of inequality present in the pattern of income distribution—the steeper the line, the greater the inequality.

Now comes the crucial part in the Inhaber-Carroll analysis. Using 1987 tax data from the IRS, they plotted on probability paper the lognormal distribution of adjusted gross income (AGI) from the lowest income bracket, of under $1,000, to the highest bracket, of over $1 million. They found that the line was straight through 97 percent of the tax returns, showing a particular pattern of income distribution as reflected in the steepness of the line up to that point. But at the 97-percent point there was a "kink": after that point, the lognormal curve becomes much steeper. This means that the distribution of income among families in the top 3 percent is much more unequal than among families in the lower 97 percent of income brackets. There are, in other words, *two* distinctly different patterns of income distribution in the United States, one for the lower 97 percent of taxpayers and another for the top 3 percent. Inhaber and Carroll argue that this appears to be a fundamental characteristic of the way the American economy is organized, because the kink *always* appears around the 97-percent point, irrespective of changing economic conditions. They thus believe they have discovered an unchanging economic "law."

What does this have to do with fairness in taxation and in the distribution of income? The distribution of income would be fairer, in the opinion of Inhaber and Carroll, if the nation had just *one*, rather than two, patterns of income distribution. In terms of tax policy, this means that, after the 97-percent point is reached in the cumulative distribution of income, steeply graduated rates for the income tax are needed to bring the pattern of income distribution for the top 3 percent into line with the pattern that prevails for the lower 97 percent. This is why they call their proposal "the 3% solution." The "too rich" are those persons and families found above the kink, in the upper 3 percent of the income-distribution scale.

How does the Inhaber-Carroll proposal mesh with the idea of a flat tax discussed earlier? Fairly easily. The flat-rate tax should prevail up to the point at which the income level covering 97 percent of taxpayers is reached. After that, steeply graduated tax rates would have to be applied to bring the distribution of income among the top 3 percent of taxpayers into line with the distribution of income below the 97-percent point.

Where do we find this "magic" 97-percent income level where the boundary of the "too rich" begins? Using 1987 tax data for AGI, Inhaber and Carroll discovered that the break in income distribution came at about the $110,000 level.[21] Above this level, the distribution of income was far more unequal than it was for all income. For example, Census Bureau numbers show that, overall, the top 5 percent of households received 18.2 percent of household income, but tax figures reveal that, in income ranges over the 97-percent level, the top 5 percent receive 30 percent of the income.[22]

To bring the distribution of income above the 97-percent level into line with the income distribution below the 97-percent level—to eliminate the "kink," in other words—this income would have to be taxed at steeply graduated rates. How steeply? Their calculations show that the effective tax rate would have to rise from 27.2 percent for incomes between $120,000 and $1 million and reaching 90 percent for incomes over $100 million.

A 90-percent effective tax rate is steep, as Inhaber and Carroll admit. But before too many tears are shed for those in the $100-million-per-year income class, Inhaber and Carroll also point out that , even with a 90-percent tax rate, persons in this income class would have had $10 million of income left. Only 590 taxpayers had an income this large in 1987. A $10-million income would have been greater than the incomes of 99.999 percent of all taxpayers![23]

On the thorny question of the distribution of income, society really faces two problems. The first is what overall distribution of income is desirable—how steep, in other words, should be the line representing the 97 percent of persons below the kink in the line. Perhaps there is no answer at all to this question, especially not in tax policy. What can be done—and has been done— through taxes and government spending is to shore up the incomes of those at the bottom. This is a main objective of the welfare state, both here and in other nations. The other problem is the one sketched out by Inhaber and Carroll—namely, what to do about the excessive, if not obscene, inequality in the distribution of income in the ranks of the upper 3 percent. Here taxes are the answer. Thus, the best way to reform the income tax is to develop a flat-rate system with generous personal exemptions for the vast majority of taxpayers, coupled with steeply graduated rates for persons and families in the upper 3 percent of the income scale.[24]

How does wealth and its taxation enter the picture? Income, it will be recalled, is a flow of money received over a period of time, wealth the quantity of economically valuable assets in possession of a person or a family at a given point in time. Aside from inheritances, gifts, or the chance winning of a lottery, wealth is accumulated by saving—not spending all of one's income.

Information on the distribution of wealth in America is scarcer than information on the distribution of income. Nevertheless, available evidence reveals that the ownership of wealth is much more heavily skewed toward the favored few at the top than is the distribution of income. Recent figures from the Federal Reserve System show the top 1 percent of the population owns 37.0 percent of the nation's financial wealth (chapter 5).

Two other points about wealth are important. First, Inhaber and Carroll find that a kink similar to the one found in the distribution of income exists for the distribution of wealth.[25] Second, anywhere from 43 to 50 percent of the number of great fortunes that exist in this country are inherited. Inheritance plays a key role in the pattern of wealth distribution in the American nation.

A close relationship exists between income and wealth. In their study, Inhaber and Carroll found that the ratio of net wealth to income steadily rises as a family's income rises—a not unexpected development, because, the higher one's income, the easier it is to save and add to one's wealth. But more is involved than this. Ownership of wealth is a source of income, so increasing wealth leads to increasing income. At some point in this ongoing cycle of interaction between income and wealth, the "magic" of compound interest enters the picture. A critical point is reached in this process at which wealth begins to accumulate faster than any one person or family can spend the income generated by the wealth, and the fortunes of a family will begin to increase at an ever faster pace. What puts an end to this process? Theoretically, there is no end; but in reality, death and the capricious transfer of wealth by the wealth-holder ends, or at least interrupts, the process. This is why Inhaber and Carroll say inheritance is a key link in the cycle of income and wealth.

What is to be done? Inhaber and Carroll offer a sound prescription. They propose in their book, *How Rich Is Too Rich?*, that we switch from the present taxation of the deceased's estate to a tax aimed at the heirs.[26] Now the federal government (as well as the states) taxes the *estate*—the value of wealth held at the time of death—and then allows the proceeds to be distributed in accordance with the wishes of the wealth-holder. Instead, Inhaber and Carroll propose first that the proceeds of an estate be distributed, and then that the *inheritance* be taxed. Each heir would be taxed on the amount he or she inherited from a given estate. For example, if an estate were worth $10 million, and there were ten heirs, then the $1 million that each heir received would be subject to the tax. In their judgment, an inheritance tax is a much more potent and effective tool for limiting the extremes that exist in the distribution of wealth, especially among the upper 3 percent of wealth-holders.

As to specifics, Inhaber and Carroll propose that an individual's lifetime inheritance be limited to $2.5 million. During a lifetime, $1 million could be inherited tax-free. A second inherited million would be taxed at 25 percent; the third at 50 percent; the fourth at 75 percent; and the remainder at 100 percent. The cumulative after-tax amount of wealth an individual could receive over a lifetime from gifts or inheritance is, thus, equal to $2.5 million. Any wealth-holder who did not want the IRS to get a penny of his or her fortune would only have to distribute his or her estate widely, in increments of $1 million each, to assure that none of the bequests were taxed. Under the Inhaber and Carroll plan, there would no longer be taxes on estates. Of course, the problem is not so simple. Wealthy individuals could still perpetuate their power and influence by funneling money facing the 100-percent tax rate into foundations, charities, or colleges and universities, especially those in the Ivy League. In this age of global liquidity and the near-instantaneous transfer of money to almost any country, clever lawyers would find ways of avoiding inheritance taxes. This, however, is no reason not to tackle head-on the problem of the excessive concentration of wealth, any more than tax avoidance by some clever or unscrupulous people is a reason to abandon efforts to tax income fairly.

The amount chosen for tax-free distribution ($1 million) is semiarbitrary, as are the tax rates on inheritances above this amount. But the principle involved is plain. The reasonable accumulation of wealth is not discouraged—$2.5 million is not a small sum to inherit—but the excessive transfer of wealth is discouraged. Americans are curiously ambivalent regarding income and wealth. Though they believe strongly that no one should get anything for nothing, especially when it comes to women on welfare, Americans largely look the other way when a relatively small number of people get large amounts of wealth and income for nothing through inheritance.

Can our attitudes toward wealth and inheritance be changed? It would take extraordinarily courageous and imaginative leadership to bring about such a change, but it could be done. In 1891, Andrew Carnegie, one of America's richest men of the nineteenth century, a man who gave away most of his wealth before his death, said, "The parent who leaves his son enormous wealth generally deadens the talents and energies of the son and tempts him to lead a less useful life."[27] Was he right? A recent study from the National Bureau of Economic Research indicates he was. Three economists, one from Princeton University, one from Syracuse University, and one from the Treasury Department, analyzed tax returns for forty-three hundred people who received inheritances in 1982 and 1983. What they found was that, the higher the inheritance, the more likely it was that a person would reduce his or her work effort.[28]

John Maynard Keynes in *The General Theory* had some wise

thoughts on the distribution of income and wealth. "For my own part," Keynes said, "I believe that there is a social and psychological justification for significant inequalities of incomes and wealth, but not for such large disparities as exist today. There are valuable human activities which require the motive of money-making and the environment of private wealth-ownership for their full fruition. Moreover, dangerous human proclivities can be canalised into comparative harmless channels by the existence of opportunities for money-making and private wealth, which, if they cannot be satisfied in this way, may find their outlet in cruelty, the reckless pursuit of personal power, and other forms of self-aggrandisement. It is better that a man should tyrannise over his bank balance than his fellow-citizens. . . . But it is not necessary for the stimulation of these activities and the satisfaction of these proclivities that the game should be played for such high stakes as at present. Much lower stakes will serve the purpose equally well, as soon as the players are accustomed to them. . . ."[29]

The bottom line is that a fundamental change in the way we tax wealth in this country is an absolutely necessary complement to reforms in the income tax designed to eliminate the excess concentration of income found above the 97-percent level. In this stratospheric range, wealth and income feed upon each other, widening the gap between the upper 3 percent and the rest of the population. The changes for both income and wealth outlined here also interact with each other; both are required for a major overhaul of the nation's tax system.

EPILOGUE

One of the more ominous consequences of the silent depression of the last two decades is the splintering of the American community into the favored fifth at the top—those who belong to John Kenneth Galbraith's "culture of contentment"—and the other four-fifths, farther down the income scale. As this book has stressed, the division clearly shows up in the income statistics. But the threat it poses to the nation's well-being goes well beyond income. Secretary of Labor Robert Reich argues it is deeply social, involving not just income but an array of activities that touch the lives of all citizens. What is happening, according to Reich, is that the "fortunate fifth" at the top are increasingly able to buy their way out of the decay, the troubles, the crime, and the worry that beset much of the rest of the population. Public schools, playgrounds, law enforcement, streets, and neighborhoods are deteriorating because local governments are increasingly strapped for funds. While this is happening, privately supported residential enclaves, recreational facilities, schools, and security forces are growing rapidly, shattering further the idea of community in America.[30]

New York's Senator Daniel Patrick Moynihan, one of the nation's most astute observers of emerging social and economic trends, warns that a profound and disastrous social crisis is under way in America, one that the nation, unwilling to confront, pretends is not happening. Behavior and events once regarded as wholly unacceptable, as deviations from civilized norms, are gradually being accepted as a normal part of life in America.[31] Crime is the most obvious example of this, but the statistical evidence for a developing social disaster includes teenage pregnancy and suicide, the breakup of families, murders by primary-age schoolchildren, guns in the schools and senseless gun violence everywhere, the rapid spread of AIDS, sexual abuse of children, the battering of women, an exploding jail population, drug abuse, and homelessness. Part of the process by which behavior once regarded as unacceptable—"deviant behavior," in academic jargon—becomes accepted as normal involves changing the words used to describe behavior. For example, "illegitimate birth" becomes "out-of-wedlock birth," and then "single parenting."

One way to reverse these unhealthy trends, to mobilize the material resources that surely will be needed to cope with the economic side of this emerging crisis, is to restore vigorous and widely shared growth to the American economy, ending the silent depression that lies behind much that has become divisive in American life since the 1970s. The main proposals developed in this book—public and private investment to restore productivity growth plus a total overhaul of the federal income-tax system and the nation's health-care structure—are radical only in the sense that they represent a major departure from the "business-as-usual" mentality of the last twenty years. They also threaten interest groups across the board that have grown comfortable with the way things are. The programs themselves are not radical. Investment, both public and private, is the time-tested way to improve and stimulate the economy. Achieving the degree of simplicity sought in both taxes and health care would yield dividends to the vast majority of citizens in time, in money, and in peace of mind worth many times the costs of getting from where we are to where we could be. Imaginative political leadership is essential, but it is equally important that Americans have the will to change. This requires that all citizens listen, look, and understand what is happening to their economy. Leadership and the will to change are the intangibles needed for ending the silent depression.

Notes

I The Unraveling of the American Dream

1. David A. Levy, "1900s: A Contained Depression," *Challenge*, July–August 1991, pp. 35–42; Wallace C. Peterson, "The Silent Depression," *Challenge*, July–August 1991, pp. 29–34.

2. John Kenneth Galbraith, *The Culture of Contentment* (Boston: Houghton Mifflin, 1992), p. 18.

3. *Economic Report of the President* (Washington, D.C.: U.S. Government Printing Office, 1991), p. 288.

4. The Truman administration offered Marshall Plan aid to the Soviet Union and the states of Eastern Europe, but it was refused. Although Japan was not included in the Marshall Plan, it received similar aid during the occupation.

5. The "West" in this context includes not only the nations of Western Europe, but the United States, Canada, Japan, Australia, and New Zealand.

6. Between 1839 and 1959 (120 years), the American economy grew at an average annual rate of 3.7 percent.

7. *Time*, September 8, 1991, pp. 54–55.

8. *Fortune*, March 8, 1993, p. 41.

9. *Current Economic Indicators*, August 1991, p. 11; December 1992, p. 11.

10. *Nation*, February 22, 1993, pp. 222, 223.

11. *Business Week*, March 23, 1992, p. 57.

12. Ibid.

13. *Fortune*, March 8, 1993, p. 43.

14. *U.S. News & World Report*, October 19, 1992, pp. 54–59.

15. *New York Times*, March 29, 1992, p. 1.

16. Frank Levy and Richard C. Michel, *The Economic Future of American Families: Income and Wealth Trends* (Washington, D.C.: Urban Institute Press, 1991), p. 87.

17. Juliet B. Schor, *The Overworked American* (New York: Basic Books, 1991), p. 29.

2 Diagnosing the Silent Depression

1. Wallace C. Peterson, *Income, Employment, and Economic Growth*, 7th ed. (New York: W. W. Norton, 1992), p. 592. A complete business cycle is usually measured from trough (low point) to peak (high point) to trough, although it can be measured from peak to trough to peak.

2. John Maynard Keynes, *The General Theory of Employment, Interest and Money* (New York: Harcourt, Brace & World, 1936).

3. The Great Depression of the 1930s contained two distinct cycles, the one running from a peak in 1929 through a trough in 1933 to a peak in 1937, and the second from the 1937 peak through a trough in 1938 and then a recovery to a new peak in 1945. The latter peak occurred at the end of World War II, which was the event that finally brought the nation out of the Great Depression.

4. Paul Krugman, *The Age of Diminished Expectations* (Cambridge, Mass.: MIT Press, 1990), p. 9.

5. In 1990, for example, there were 91.6 million people in private employment. Of this total, 74.2 million, or 81 percent, were production workers. Total employment in 1990 was 117.9 million. (Data furnished the author by the Bureau of Labor Statistics, U.S. Department of Labor.)

6. *Economic Report of the President* (Washington, D.C.: U.S. Government Printing Office), 1991, p. 336; 1992, p. 346. Wages in current dollars were deflated by the revised consumer price index, known as CPI-U-X1.

7. Bureau of the Census, Current Population Reports, ser. P-60, no. 167, *Trends in Income by Selected Characteristics: 1947 to 1988* (by Mary F. Henson), April 1990, p. 17; ser. P-60, no. 174, *Money Income of Households, Families, and Persons in the United States: 1990*, April 1991, p. 9. Updated data supplied to the author by the Bureau of the Census.

8. *Economic Report of the President*, 1992, p. 337.

9. Bureau of the Census, Current Population Reports, ser. P-60, no. 180, *Money Income of Households, Families, and Persons in the United States: 1991*, August 1992, p. B-21.

10. Over most of this century, productivity growth in the American economy has averaged close to 2.5 percent annually, including the years of the Great Depression.

11. Output per employed worker per year is computed from data in the *Economic Report of the President*, 1991, pp. 288, 324.

12. Ibid., p. 336.

13. Wallace C. Peterson, *Transfer Spending, Taxes, and the American Welfare State* (Boston: Kluwer Academic Publishers, 1991), pp. 31–55.

14. Bureau of the Census, Current Population Reports, ser. P-60, no. 174, p. 216.

15. *New York Times*, March 5, 1992, p. 1; *Wall Street Journal*, May 11, 1992, p. A12.

16. Bureau of the Census, Current Population Reports, ser. P-60, no. 174.

17. *USA Today*, July 15, 1992, p. 1; Lawrence A. Hunter, "The Never-ending Recession," *Wall Street Journal*, September 14, 1991, p. A14.

3 The Shrinking of the Middle Class

1. Donald L. Barlett and James B. Steele, *America: What Went Wrong?* (Kansas City, Mo.: Andrews and McMeel, 1992), pp. 15, 18.

2. *U.S. News & World Report*, August 18, 1986, pp. 36–41; *Time*, November 3, 1986, pp. 54–56; *Lincoln Journal* (Lincoln, Neb.), November 30, 1987, p. 14; *Washington Post*, Outlook sec., December 1, 1991, pp. C1–C2; *Newsweek*, July 1, 1985.

3. *U.S. News & World Report*, August 18, 1986, p. 36.

4. Barbara Ehrenreich, *Fear of Falling: The Inner Life of the Middle Class* (New York: Pantheon, 1989), p. 15.

5. *U.S. News & World Report*, January 27, 1992, p. 13.

6. Lawrence Lindsey, assistant professor of economics at Harvard, as quoted in *Time*, November 3, 1986, p. 54.

7. *Nation*, March 23, 1992, p. 361.

8. Robert Heilbroner, "Middle-Class Myths, Middle-Class Realities," *Atlantic Monthly*, vol. 238, no. 4 (October 1976), pp. 37–42.

9. Katherine L. Bradbury, "The Shrinking Middle Class," *New England Economic Review*, September–October, 1986, p. 43.

10. Michael W. Horrigan and Steven E. Haugen, "The Declining Middle-Class Thesis: A Sensitivity Analysis," *Monthly Labor Review*, May 1988.

11. Setting the boundaries for the middle class is not just a matter of judgment. As a practical matter, these boundaries must fit the income ranges available in the Census Bureau and Internal Revenue Service data, since these are the main sources for details of persons and families by income ranges.

12. Bradbury, "Shrinking Middle Class," p. 45.

13. Bureau of the Census, Current Population Reports, ser. P-60, no. 174, *Money Income of Households, Families, and Persons in the United States: 1990*, March 1991, p. 216, table B-13.

14. Internal Revenue Service, Statistics of Income, *SOI Bulletin*, Summer 1974, p. 14; Fall 1992, p. 142.

15. Bureau of the Census, Current Population Reports, ser. P-60, no. 177, *Trends in Relative Income: 1964 to 1989*, December 1991, pp. 1–7.

16. *Business Week*, March 23, 1992, p. 56.

17. Greg J. Duncan. Timothy M. Smeeding, and Willard Rodger, "W(h)ither the Middle Class? A Dynamic View," paper prepared for the Levy Institute Conference on Income Inequality, Bard College, June 18–20, 1991.

18. Quoted in Richard Morin, "America's Middle Class Meltdown," *Washington Post*, December 1, 1991, p. C1.

19. In the University of Michigan study, individuals living alone are counted as a "family." Thus, there are more families in the Michigan study than in Census Bureau studies.

20. Bruce Bartlett, "A Class Structure That Won't Stay Put," *Wall Street Journal*, November 20, 1991, p. A16.

21. *U.S. News & World Report*, April 22, 1991, p. 40.

22. Duncan, Smeeding, and Rodger, "W(h)ither the Middle Class?," p. 10.

23. Greg J. Duncan, Timothy M. Smeeding, and Willard Rodgers, "U.S. Middle Class Steadily Shrinking," *Lincoln Journal-Star*, August 9, 1992, p. J1.

24. Duncan, Smeeding, and Rodger, "W(h)ither the Middle Class?," pp. 5, 10.

25. *Business Week*, March 23, 1992, p. 22.

26. Duncan, Smeeding, and Rodger, "W(h)ither the Middle Class?," p. 22.

27. David M. Gordon, "The Myth of Upward Mobility," *Washington Post*, June 14, 1987, p. H3.

4　The Stressed-out American Family

1. Bureau of the Census, Current Population Reports, ser. P-60, no. 175, *Poverty in the United States: 1960*, August 1991, p. 16, table 2.

2. U.S. Congress, Joint Economic Committee, *Families on a Treadmill: Work and Income in the 1980s*, January 17, 1992.

3. Bureau of the Census, Current Population Reports, ser. P-60, no. 175, p. 20, table 4.

4. U.S. House of Representatives, Ways and Means Committee, *Green Book*, (Washington, D.C.: U.S. Government Printing Office, May 1992), p. 1287.

5. *U.S. News & World Report*, August 18, 1986, p. 42.

6. *Green Book*, 1992, p. 1410.

7. Frank Levy and Richard C. Michel, *The Economic Future of American Families: Income and Wealth Trends* (Washington, D.C.: Urban Institute Press, 1991), p. 56.

8. Ibid., p. 59.

9. *U.S. News & World Report*, August 18, 1986.

10. *Green Book*, 1992, pp. 1379, 1380, 1407.

11. Ibid., p. 1402.

12. U.S. House of Representatives, Ways and Means Committee, *Green Book*, (Washington, D.C.: U.S. Government Printing Office, May 1991), pp. 1025, 1027.

13. Bureau of the Census, Current Population Reports, ser. P-60, no. 175, p. 20, table 4. Poverty statistics begin in 1959.

14. *Green Book*, 1992, pp. 1380, 1404.

15. Ibid., pp. 1274, 1275.

16. Bureau of the Census, Current Population Reports, ser. P-60, no. 167, *Trends in Income by Selected Characteristics: 1947 to 1988* (by Mary F. Henson). Washington, D.C.: Updated data supplied to the author by the Bureau of the Census.

17. *Economic Report of the President* (Washington, D.C.: U.S. Government Printing Office, 1992), pp. 324, 325.

18. U.S. Congress, United States Senate, Committee on the Budget, *Wages of American Workers in the 1980s* (Washington, D.C.: U.S. Government Printing Office, 1988), p. 1; *Fortune*, February 24, 1992, p. 40.

19. *Sunday World Herald* (Omaha, Neb.), February 23, 1992, sec. A, p. 1.

20. Bureau of the Census, Current Population Reports, ser. P-60, no. 167.

21. Levy and Michel, *Economic Future of American Families*, p. 27. The authors point out that the good-jobs / bad-jobs controversy is primarily a story about men and their wages. For women, there was less growth in inequality, and a moderate improvement between 1973 and 1986 in their real wages and their wages relative to men.

22. *Economic Report of the President*, 1992, p. 344.

23. Levy and Michel, *Economic Future of American Families*, p. 27.

24. Ibid.

25. Ibid.

26. *Economic Report of the President*, 1992, p. 346.

27. Douglas Copeland, *Generation X: Tales for an Accelerated Culture* (New York: St. Martin's Press, 1991).

28. Bureau of the Census, Current Population Reports, ser. P-60, no. 178, *Workers with Low Earnings: 1964 to 1990*, March 1992, pp. 1, 3.

29. *Economic Report of the President*, 1992, pp. 307, 345.

30. *Business Week*, November 9, 1992, p. 22.

31. For most families with children, the head is likely to be under the age of thirty-four, but more younger families than older families today are likely to have a head with more than a high-school education. Thus, the percentage of younger families headed by someone with only a high-school education will be below the average for all families.

32. U.S. Congress, Joint Economic Committee, *Families on a Treadmill*.

33. Ibid., p. 4.

34. Ibid.

35. Ibid., p. 6.

36. Ibid.

37. Ibid., p. 6.

38. Ibid., p. 10.

39. Ibid., p. 13.

40. Ibid., p. 16.

41. Sandra L. Hanson and Theodora Ooms, "The Economic Costs and Rewards of Two-Earner, Two-Parent Families," *Journal of Marriage and the Family*, vol. 53 (August 1991), pp. 622–34.

42. U.S. Congress, Joint Economic Committee, *Families on a Treadmill*, p. 21.

43. *Time*, October 10, 1988, pp. 30–32. The ages given are as of 1988.

44. Ibid.

45. Paul C. Light, *Baby Boomers* (New York: W. W. Norton, 1988), p. 21.

46. Levy and Michel, *Economic Future of American Families*, p. 76.

47. Ibid., pp. 76, 77. Levy and Michel concentrated their research on male earnings, but they expected that family income would generally follow the same path.

48. Levy and Michel, *Economic Future of American Families*, p. 78.

5 ... And the Rich Get Richer

1. *Wall Street Journal*, April 8, 1992, p. 1. Details of Willy Theisen's birthday are from the *Omaha World Herald*, June 14, 1985.

2. Kevin Phillips, *The Politics of Rich and Poor* (New York: Random House, 1990), p. xxiii. Professor Robert Reich of the Kennedy School of Government at Harvard University coined the phrase "the fortunate fifth."

3. William Greider, *Secrets of the Temple* (New York: Simon and Schuster, 1987), p. 37.

4. Herbert Inhaber and Sidney Carroll, *How Rich Is Too Rich? Income and Wealth in America* (New York: Praeger, 1992), p. 137.

5. Ibid., p. 140.

6. Bureau of the Census, Current Population Reports, ser. P-60, no. 174, *Money Income of Households, Families, and Persons in the United States: 1990*, p. 202.

7. Data in the *Green Book* on income are supplied to the Ways and Means Committee of the House of Representatives by the Congressional Budget Office.

8. Committee on Ways and Means, U.S. House of Representatives, *Green Book* (Washington, D.C.: U.S. Government Printing Office, 1991), p. 1299.

9. Ibid.

10. *Green Book*, 1992, pp. 1529–31.

11. Bureau of the Census, Current Population Reports, ser. P-60, no. 164-RD-1, *Measuring the Effect of Benefits and Taxes on Income and Poverty: 1986*.

12. Table 5-5 summarizes the key findings.

13. Bureau of the Census, Current Population Reports, ser. P-60, no. 164-RD-1, pp. 18, 19.

14. Ibid.

15. *New York Times*, April 22, 1992, p. 1.

16. Arthur B. Kennicksell and R. Louise Woodburn, "Estimation of Household Net Worth Using Model-based and Design-based Weights: Evidence from the 1989 Survey of Consumer Finance," unpublished manuscript from Board of Governors, Federal Reserve System, Washington, D.C., April 1992, p. 24.

17. Greider, *Secrets of the Temple*, p. 706.

18. *Green Book*, 1992, pp. 1562–77.

19. Greider, *Secrets of the Temple*, p. 38.

20. *Green Book*, 1992, p. 1570.

21. Ibid., p. 1567.

22. Jan Pen, *Income Distribution* (Harmondsworth, Eng.: Penguin, 1971), p. 289.

23. *U.S. News & World Report*, November 18, 1991, pp. 34–42.

24. *Christian Science Monitor*, national ed., May 15, 1992, p. 8.

25. See Richard B. McKenzie, *The "Fortunate Fifth" Fallacy* (St. Louis: Center for the Study of American Business, Washington University, 1992).

26. Inhaber and Carroll, *How Rich Is Too Rich?*, pp. 19–37.

27. Jonathan Hughes, *American Economic History*, 3rd ed. (Glenview, Ill.: Scott, Foresman, 1990), p. 60.

28. From 1914 to 1919, consumer prices rose by 72.5 percent, annual wages by 99.7 percent, bond yields by 19.1 percent, stock yields by 14.7 percent, and stock prices for industrials by 58.4 percent (ibid., pp. 434, 436).

29. *Green Book*, 1992, p. 1564; Kennicksell and Woodburn, "Estimation of Household Net Worth."

30. Board of Governors of the Federal Reserve System, *Historical Chart Book* (Washington, D.C.: Board of Governors of the Federal Reserve System, 1978), p. 94.

31. Bureau of the Census, *Historical Statistics of the United States*, (Washington, D.C., U.S. Government Printing Office, 1975) ser. G 319-336, p. 301.

32. *Historical Chart Book*, p. 94.

33. George Gilder's *Wealth and Poverty* provided the basic intellectual rationale for the Reagan Revolution. Arthur Laffer's famous curve, allegedly drawn upon the back of a napkin in a Washington, D.C., restaurant, provided the theoretical justification for the massive tax cuts of 1981. This curve, which has no empirical foundation, showed that under certain circumstances government revenues would rise if taxes were cut. Jude Wanniski, former editorial writer for *The Wall Street Journal*, was the key publicist for the ideas of Gilder and Laffer.

34. Wallace C. Peterson, *Transfer Spending, Taxes, and the American Welfare State* (Boston: Kluwer Academic Publishers, 1991), pp. 1–30.

35. Ibid., pp. 89 ff.

36. Ibid., p. 25.

37. Bureau of the Census, Current Population Reports, ser. P-60, no. 1768, *Workers with Low Earnings: 1964 to 1990*, p. 2.

38. United States Senate, *Wages of American Workers in the 1980s* (Washington, D.C.: U.S. Government Printing Office, 1988), p. x.

39. Robert Samuelson, "The American Job Machine," *Newsweek*, February 23, 1987, p. 57.

40. Graef S. Crystal, *In Search of Excess* (New York: W. W. Norton, 1991), pp. 27–28.

41. See Robert B. Reich, *The Work of Nations* (New York: Alfred A. Knopf, 1991), esp. chap. 14, pp. 171–84. See also Lester Thurow, *Head to Head* (New York: William Morrow, 1992), esp. chap. 5, pp. 153–205.

42. *Economic Report of the President* (Washington, D.C.: U.S. Government Printing Office, 1992), p. 332.

43. Bureau of the Census, Current Population Reports, ser. P-60, no. 175, *Poverty in the United States,* pp. 15–20.

44. *Historical Statistics of the United States,* op. cit. ser. 319–336, p. 301.

45. Charles Murray, "Of a Conservative (Created) Caste," *Harper's,* October 1991, pp. 17, 18.

6 . . . While Life at the Bottom Goes On

1. Toni Wood, "Urban Nomads," *Kansas City Star,* May 24–26, 1992 (3-pt. ser.).

2. The Children's Defense Fund, reported in *Kansas City Star,* May 24, 1992.

3. Michael Harrington, *The Other America: Poverty in America* (New York: Macmillian, 1962).

4. Michael Harrington, *The New American Poverty* (New York: Penguin, 1984), p. 20.

5. Ibid., p. 8.

6. Bureau of the Census, Current Population Reports, ser. P-60, no. 175, *Poverty in the United States: 1990,* p. 194. Adjustments are made in the threshold to reflect family size. For example, in 1990 the poverty level for a single person was $6,652, and for a family of eight, $25,268. (Committee on Ways and Means, U.S. House of Representatives, *Green Book* [Washington, D.C.: U.S. Government Printing Office, 1992], p. 1272.)

7. Ibid., p. 16.

8. Robert Reno, "Youngest Suffer Most," *Lincoln Star,* December 21, 1992, p. 8.

9. *Green Book,* 1992, p. 1289.

10. Ibid., p. 1290.

11. Harrington, *New American Poverty,* p. 26.

12. Bureau of the Census, Current Population Reports, ser. P-60, no. 175, p. 16.

13. *Green Book,* 1992, p. 1080. Only 3.1 percent of children living in single-parent families lived in families headed by the father in 1990. This is up from 1.1 percent in 1960.

14. Bureau of the Census, Current Population Reports, ser. P-60, no. 175, pp. 20 ff.

15. *Green Book,* 1992, p. 935.

16. Bureau of the Census, Current Population Reports, ser. P-60, no. 174, *Money Income of Households, Families, and Persons in the United States: 1990,* p. 207, table B-7.

17. *Green Book,* 1992, p. 1074.

18. Ibid., pp. 645, 1080, 1191; *Social Security Bulletin, Annual Statistical Supplement,* 1991, p. 108.

19. *Green Book,* 1992, pp. 1073–77.

20. Ibid.

21. Ibid.

22. Mary Jo Bane and David T. Ellwood, "One Fifth of the Nation's Children: Why Are They Poor?," *Science,* vol. 245 (September 1989), p. 1050; *Green Book,* 1992, p. 1158.

23. Bane and Ellwood, "One Fifth," p. 1053.

24. *Green Book,* 1992, pp. 1156, 1157.

25. Bureau of the Census, Current Population Reports, ser. P-60, no. 175, pp. 99, 103; David T. Ellwood, *Poor Support* (New York: Basic Books, 1988) p. 145.

26. Bane and Ellwood, "One Fifth," p. 1052.

27. *Green Book,* 1992, pp. 1082, 1083.

28. Bureau of the Census, Current Population Reports, ser. P-60, no. 175, p. 73.

29. *Green Book,* 1992, p. 1176.

30. Ibid., pp. 1578–83.

31. *U.S. News & World Report,* January 11, 1988, p. 19.

32. Bureau of the Census, Current Population Reports, ser. P-60, no. 175, p. 8; *Economic Report of the President* (Washington, D.C.: U.S. Government Printing Office, 1992), p. 341.

33. Bureau of the Census, Current Population Reports, ser. P-60, no. 175, p. 8.

34. *Green Book,* 1992, p. 1280.

35. Bureau of the Census, Current Population Reports, ser. P-60, no. 178, *Workers with Low Earnings: 1964 to 1990.*

36. Ibid., pp. 2, 3. The $6.10 is rounded to the nearest cent.

37. Ibid., p. 3; *Economic Indicators* (Washington, D.C.: U.S. Government Printing Office, May 1992), pp. 11, 12.

38. John E. Schwarz and Thomas Volgy, *The Forgotten Americans* (New York: W. W. Norton, 1992).

39. Ibid., pp. 37, 39, 73.

40. Ibid., p. 71.

41. These examples are from Bruce W. Klein and Philip L. Rones, "A Profile of the Working Poor," *Monthly Labor Review,* October 1989, p. 4.

42. *U.S. News & World Report,* January 11, 1988, p. 21.

43. Bureau of the Census, Current Population Reports, ser. P-60, no. 167, *Trends in Income by Selected Characteristics: 1947 to 1988* (by Mary F. Henson), p. 14, table 9.

44. *Newsweek,* April 6, 1992, pp. 20–23.

45. "Violence in America: A Public Health Emergency," *Journal of the American Medical Association,* June 10, 1992, pp. 3075–76.

46. Bureau of the Census, Current Population Reports, ser. P-60, no. 175, p. 191.

47. Ibid., p. 151.

48. Jack Miles, "Blacks vs. Browns," *Atlantic*, October 1992.

49. Bureau of the Census, Current Population Reports, ser. P-60, no. 175, p. 151.

50. *Newsweek*, April 6, 1992, p. 20.

51. Ken Auletta, *The Underclass* (New York: Random House, 1982), p. xiii.

52. Ibid., p. xvi.

53. William Julius Wilson, *The Truly Disadvantaged: The Inner City, the Underclass, and Public Policy* (Chicago: University of Chicago Press, 1987).

54. Ibid., p. 2.

55. Ibid., p. 142.

56. *Economic Report of the President* (Washington, D.C.: U.S. Government Printing Office, 1992), p. 341.

57. Roger Wilkins, "Employment Would Solve So Much," *Kansas City Star*, May 24, 1992.

58. Wood, "Urban Nomads," p. A-11.

59. Ibid.

60. Harrington, *New American Poverty*, p. 100.

61. *Green Book*, 1992, p. 1184.

62. Ibid., p. 1188.

7 Getting from There to Here

1. *Economic Report of the President* (Washington, D.C.: U.S. Government Printing Office, 1991), pp. 289, 322. Output is measured in 1982 prices because numbers are not yet available back to 1947 measuring output in later prices.

2. Paul Krugman, *The Age of Diminished Expectations* (Cambridge, Mass.: MIT Press, 1990), p. 14.

3. *Economic Report of the President*, 1991, p. 287.

4. Ann Markusen and Joel Yudken, *Dismantling the Cold War Economy* (New York: Basic Books, 1992), p. 35.

5. *Economic Report of the President*, 1991, p. 287.

6. Markusen and Yudken, *Dismantling*, p. 51.

7. Ibid., p. 33.

8. Ibid., p. 59.

9. Seymour Melman, *Profits Without Production* (New York: Alfred A. Knopf, 1983), p. 200.

10. Mary Kaldor, *The Baroque Arsenal* (New York: Hill and Wang, 1981), pp. 55, 20–22.

11. "Defenseless Against Cutbacks," *Business Week*, January 14, 1991, p. 14.

12. Markusen and Yudken, *Dismantling*, pp. 69 ff.

13. Ibid., pp. 75–78.

14. David Alan Aschauer, *Public Investment and Private Sector Growth* (Washington, D.C.: Economic Policy Institute, 1990), pp. 3, 16.

15. Ibid., pp. 8, 9.

16. David Alan Aschauer, *Back of the G-7 Pack: Public Investment and Productivity Growth in the Group of Seven* (Chicago: Federal Reserve Bank of Chicago, 1989), p. 8.

17. Ibid., p. 15.

18. Alcia H. Munnell, "Is There a Shortfall in Public Capital Investment? An Overview," *New England Economic Review*, May–June 1991, pp. 23–35.

19. Ibid., p. 14.

20. U.S. Department of Commerce, *Survey of Current Business*, January 1992, pp. 130, 137; *Economic Report of the President*, 1991, pp. 321, 322.

21. *Economic Report of the President* (Washington, D.C.: U.S. Government Printing Office, 1992), pp. 301, 302, 394, 411.

22. Aschauer, *Back of the G-7 Pack*, p. 19.

23. The investment tax credit was started in the Kennedy administration, dropped in the 1970s, and then revived by the Reagan administration. It allows a business to deduct from its federal tax liability a percentage of its expenditures for investment in new capital.

24. *Economic Report of the President*, 1992, pp. 230, 397, 400.

25. David L. Barlett and James B. Steele, *America: What Went Wrong?* (Kansas City, Mo.: Andrews and McMeel, 1992), p. 32.

26. *Economic Report of the President*, 1992, p. 298.

27. "The Global Economy: Who Gets Hurt," *Business Week*, August 10, 1992, p. 48.

28. *Economic Report of the President*, 1992, p. 344.

29. Secretary of Labor Robert B. Reich, in his book *The World of Work* (New York: Alfred A. Knopf, 1991), argues that, under the impact of globalization, the American work force is split three ways. In one category are the professions and jobs that have something to do with the information revolution, meaning people who work with money, words, and oral and visual symbols. They are college-educated and skilled, and have great mobility and high incomes, because they compete successfully in the world economy. Next there are workers engaged in routine production tasks, not just in manufacturing, but in the trades and the world of banking and finance. Workers in this category are generally low-skilled, and usually paid on an hourly basis. Their wages tend to be low, because they have to compete with low-wage workers across the globe. Finally, there are the routine personal service jobs, which also don't require a high degree of skill. They don't compete directly with workers in the international economy, but they do compete with workers in the second category, so, indirectly, international wage levels affect their incomes. Reich estimates that only about 20 percent of the labor force is in the high-income category able to compete effectively in the global economy.

30. *Economic Report of the President*, 1991, p. 299.

31. Ibid., pp. 348, 357.

32. U.S. Department of Commerce, *Survey of Current Business*, January 1992, p. 122.

33. Stephen S. Cohen and John Zysman, *Manufacturing Matters: The Myth of the Post-Industrial Economy* (New York: Basic Books, 1987), p. 63.

34. Ibid., p. 70.

35. Ibid., p. 75.

36. Colin Clark, *The Conditions of Economic Progress* (London: Macmillan, 1940).

37. Committee on the Budget, United States Senate, *Wages of American Workers in the 1980s* (Washington, D.C.: U.S. Government Printing Office, 1988), p. x.

38. Cohen and Zysman, *Manufacturing Matters*.

39. *Economic Report of the President, 1992*, p. 406.

40. Cohen and Zysman, *Manufacturing Matters*, p. 14.

41. Ibid., p. 18.

42. Ibid., p. 19.

43. Laura D'Andrea Tyson, William T. Dickens, and John Zysman, eds., *The Dynamics of Trade and Employment* (Cambridge, Mass.: Ballinger Publishing Company, 1988), p. 7.

44. Cohen and Zysman, *Manufacturing Matters*, pp. 21, 22.

8 Investing in America

1. *Time*, February 1, 1993, p. 52.

2. Lawrence A. Hunter, "The Never-ending Recession," *Wall Street Journal*, September 14, 1991, p. A14.

3. Felix Rohatyn, *New York Review of Books*, June 25, 1992, p. 26.

4. Governor Bill Clinton, *Putting People First: A National Economic Strategy for America* (Washington, D.C.: Clinton Campaign Headquarters, 1992).

5. *Current Economic Indicators*, January 1993, p. 33. Population for 1993 is estimated.

6. David Alan Aschauer, *Public Investment and Private Sector Growth* (Washington, D.C.: Economic Policy Institute, 1990), pp. 9, 17.

7. U.S. Department of Commerce, *Survey of Current Business*, January 1992, p. 130.

8. *Budget of the United States Government: Fiscal Year 1993* (Washington, D.C.: U.S. Government Printing Office, 1992), pp. 237–52; additional data supplied author by the Congressional Budget Office; *Economic Report of the President* (Washington, D.C.: U.S. Government Printing Office, 1992), p. 299; *Economic Indicators*, January 1993, p. 33. Fiscal-year data for annual military spending are converted to a national-income-accounts basis.

9. *Budget of the United States Government: Fiscal Year 1994* (Washington, D.C.: U.S. Government Printing Office, 1993), Appendix-7.

10. *Economic Report of the President*, 1991, pp. 287, 290; 1992, pp. 299, 302; *Budget of the United States Government: Fiscal Year 1994*, op. cit.

11. Congressional Budget Office, *Reducing the Deficit: Spending and Revenue*

Options, February (Washington, D.C.: U.S. Government Printing Office, 1992), pp. 11, 13.

12. David Evans, *Chicago Tribune*, February 19, 1993, sec. 1, p. 19.

13. The White House, "Defense Reinvestment and Conversion," March 13, 1993.

14. *Current Economic Indicators*, January 1993, p. 34.

15. In order for this to happen, the 1990 budget agreement will have to be changed, because it requires Pentagon savings to go into deficit reduction.

16. U.S. House of Representatives, Hearings, Committee on Public Works and Transportation, *How to Solve the Nation's Infrastructure Problem*, p. xii (italics added).

17. Richard P. Nathan, "Needed: A Marshall Plan for Ourselves," paper presented at a conference on the infrastructure, Jerome Levy Economic Institute, Bard College, New York, June 1992.

18. For more details on constructing a capital budget, see Pat Choate and Susan Walter, *America in Ruins: The Decaying Infrastructure* (Durham, N.C.: Duke Press Paperbacks, 1983), pp. 68–77.

19. Robert Eisner, *How Real Is the Federal Deficit?* (New York: Free Press, 1986), pp. 176 ff.

20. State and local governments have had surpluses continuously since 1960. Since federal grant-in-aids contribute significantly to these surpluses, the offset is justified.

21. *Current Economic Indicators*, December 1992, pp. 1, 2, 32, 34; *Economic Report of the President*, 1992, p. 389.

22. *Current Economic Indicators*, January 1993, p. 33.

23. St. Louis Federal Reserve Bank, "Why the Federal Deficit Has Increased So Much Since 1989," *National Economic Trends*, December 1992, p. 1.

24. Okun's Law was originally stated the other way around—how much unemployment would change with each percentage-point change in real GNP. Okun developed his Law before the government began to use GDP, rather than GNP. It can be applied to GDP.

25. The deficit concept used in these calculations is that employed in the National Income and Product Accounts—the overall deficit minus deposit-insurance transactions. The projections are based upon CBO Base Line Projections, which are made on the basis of tax and spending policies in effect at the time the projections are made. Taxes as a percent of the GDP are derived from CBO projections.

26. U.S. House of Representatives, Committee on Ways and Means, *Overview of the Federal Tax System* (Washington, D.C.: U.S. Government Printing Office, 1991), pp. 133, 141.

27. Jane Holtz Kay, "Paved with Good Intentions?," *Nation*, August 3–10, 1992, p. 132.

28. Public Law 102-240, 102nd Cong., December 18, 1991, *Intermodal Surface Transportation Efficiency Act of 1991*.

29. Alan Durning, *How Much Is Enough?* (New York: W. W. Norton, 1992), pp. 79, 85.

30. *Report of the Secretary of Transportation to the United States Congress* (Washington, D.C.: U.S. Government Printing Office, September 1991), p. 14.

31. U.S. Department of Transportation, *Heavy Vehicle Cost Responsibility Study* (Washington, D.C.: U.S. Government Printing Office, 1988), p. V-7.

32. *Report of the Secretary of Transportation*, pp. 58, 95.

33. State highway engineers believe large trailer-trucks underpay even more than is reflected in the 81-percent figure.

34. This will vary from state to state, by size and type of car, as well as by the real cost of gasoline.

35. For the full story of the development of the aerospace giants and their close ties to the military, see Wayne Biddle, *Barons of the Sky* (New York: Simon and Schuster, 1991).

36. *Report of the Secretary of Transportation*, pp. 101, 109.

37. Joseph Vranich, *Supertrains* (New York: St. Martin's Press, 1991), p. 277.

38. Richard M. Weintraub, "Overloaded Airlines Spin Out of Control," *Washington Post, National Weekly Edition*, February 1–7, 1993, p. 19.

39. Major groups that are developing a coalition to this end are the National Trust for Historic Preservation, Friends of the Earth, Scenic America, the American Neighborhood Planning Association, and the Campaign for New Transportation Priorities.

40. Statement to the author by the intermodal traffic manager for the Union Pacific Railroad.

41. Don Phillips, *Washington Post*, February 4, 1993, p. A3.

42. *Business Week*, August 24, 1992, p. 16.

43. *Economic Report of the President*, 1992, p. 375.

44. Memo supplied the author by Mr. Warren G. Brockmeier, Oak Park, Ill.

45. *Time*, March 1, 1993.

9 Investing in the American People

1. Jonathan Hughes, *American Economic History* (Glenville, Ill.: Scott, Foresman / Little, Brown, 1990), p. 478; *Economic Report of the President* (Washington, D.C.: U.S. Government Printing Office, 1962), p. 232.

2. Public Law 304, 79th Cong., *Employment Act of 1946* (italics added).

3. *Economic Report of the President*, 1962, p. 8.

4. *Economic Report of the President* (Washington, D.C.: U.S. Government Printing Office, 1992), p. 340.

5. Ibid., pp. 365, 373. Prices went down from 1970 through 1973, while the money supply was increasing. Prices rose in 1973 and 1974, but the money supply was falling. In 1975 and 1976, prices fell but the money supply rose.

6. Jane Bryant Quinn, "The Good-Job Market: RIP," *Newsweek*, November 30, 1992, p. 64.

7. Frank Swoboda, "In Omaha, the Other Shoe Drops on Job Creation," *Washington Post National Weekly Edition*, November 2–8, 1992, p. 20.

8. Ibid.; *Economic Report of the President*, 1992, p. 346.

9. Bureau of the Census, Current Population Reports, ser. P-60, no. 178, *Workers with Low Earnings: 1964 to 1990*, p. 3.

10. Brian O'Reilly, "The Job Drought," *Fortune*, August 24, 1992, p. 66.

11. *Business Week*, August 14, 1992, p. 85.

12. Edward F. Denison, *Trends in American Economic Growth, 1929–1982* (Washington, D.C.: Brookings Institution, 1985), p. 112.

13. Reprinted in *Omaha World Herald*, May 11, 1992, p. 17.

14. Arthur M. Schlesinger, Jr., *The Disuniting of America* (Whittle Direct Books, 1991), p. 67.

15. Quoted in ibid.

16. *Projections of National Health Expenditures* (Washington, D.C.: Congressional Budget Office, October 1992), p. ix.

17. Ibid., pp. ix, 40.

18. Ibid.

19. American College of Physicians, "Universal Health Insurance for American Health Care," *Annals of Internal Medicine*, September 1992.

20. *Newsweek*, October 2, 1989, p. 52.

21. Bureau of the Census, Current Population Reports, ser. P-60, no. 176-RD, *Measuring the Effect of Benefits and Taxes on Income and Poverty*, p. 10.

22. Committee on Ways and Means, U.S. House of Representatives, *Green Book* (Washington, D.C.: U.S. Government Printing Office, 1992), p. 319.

23. *Time*, November 25, 1991, p. 34.

24. *Economic Report of the President*, 1992, p. 361.

25. *Current Economic Indicators*, January 1993, p. 32.

26. William Booth, "Warning Blips of a Haywire Health System," *Washington Post National Weekly Edition*, November 25–December 1, 1991, p. 10.

27. "Health Care Fraud," *U.S. News & World Report*, February 24, 1992, p. 34.

28. *Projections of National Health Expenditures*, p. 41.

29. Janice Castro, "Condition: Critical," *Time*, November 25, 1991, p. 42.

30. *Projections of National Health Expenditures*, p. 11.

31. *Wall Street Journal*, February 16, 1993, p. A6.

32. *Los Angeles Times* wire-service story reported in *Omaha World Herald*, February 25, 1993, p. 1.

33. Early in 1989, *The New England Journal of Medicine* gave editorial support to the idea of universal health insurance. The issue in which this editorial appeared also contained two articles outlining physician-supported plans for such a system. See *New England Journal of Medicine*, January 12, 1989.

34. Stephen F. Jencks and George J. Schieber, "Containing U.S. Health

Care Costs: What Bullet to Bite?," *Health Care Financing Review*, 1991 ann. Suppl., p. 1.

35. Richard D. Lamm, "Medical Miracles, Dollar Disasters," *Los Angeles Times* wire service, *Lincoln Journal*, February 25, 1993, p. 8.

36. Statement of Robert D. Reischauer, director, Congressional Budget Office, Subcommittee on Health, Committee on Ways and Means, U.S. House of Representatives, February 2, 1993, p. 18.

37. *Common Cause News*, October 16, 1991, p. 1.

10 Taxes and American Civilization

1. U.S. House of Representatives, Committee on Ways and Means, *Overview of the Federal Tax System* (Washington, D.C.: U.S. Government Printing Office, 1991), p. 266; *Economic Report of the President*, (Washington, D.C.: U.S. Government Printing Office, 1992), p. 391.

2. U.S. House of Representatives, Committee on Ways and Means, *Green Book* (Washington, D.C.: U.S. Government Printing Office, 1992), p. 1510.

3. *Economic Report of the President*, 1992, p. 391.

4. Calculated from Department of the Treasury, Internal Revenue Service, *SOI Bulletin*, Fall 1992, pp. 144, 147.

5. *Overview of the Federal Tax System*, p. 266; *Economic Report of the President*, 1992, p. 391.

6. *Economic Report of the President*, 1962, p. 276; 1992, p. 391.

7. *Overview of the Federal Tax System*, p. 84; *Economic Report of the President*, 1992, p. 391.

8. *Current Economic Indicators*, January 1993, pp. 6, 8.

9. A system of children's allowances, as exist in most industrial nations, could be used as well as an exemption for children.

10. *SOI Bulletin*, Fall 1992, p. 147.

11. Ibid., p. 142.

12. Ibid.

13. Department of the Treasury, Internal Revenue Service, *Income Tax Compliance Research* (Washington, D.C.: Department of the Treasury, April 1990), p. 2.

14. Karen Pennar and Christopher Farrell, "Notes from the Underground Economy," *Business week*, February 15, 1993, p. 98.

15. A slightly different version of a flat tax has been proposed by Robert E. Hall, professor of economics at Stanford and fellow of the Hoover Institution, and Alvin Rabushka, also a fellow at the Hoover Institution. The Hall-Rabushka plan has two parts, a flat-rate tax on business income and a flat-rate tax on the earnings of individuals. See Robert E. Hall and Alvin Rabushka, *The Flat Tax* (Stanford, Calif.: Hoover Institution Press, 1985).

16. Office of Senator Daniel Patrick Moynihan, "Statement," January 23, 1990.

17. See Wallace C. Peterson. *Transfer Spending, Taxes, and the American Welfare State* (Boston: Kluwer Academic Publishers, 1991), pp. 133–70.

18. *Green Book,* 1992, p. 1266.

19. Paul C. Light, *Baby Boomers* (New York: W. W. Norton, 1988), p. 199.

20. Herbert Inhaber and Sidney Carroll, *How Rich Is Too Rich? Income and Wealth in America* (New York: Praeger, 1992).

21. Ibid., p. 212.

22. Bureau of the Census, Current Population Reports, ser. P-60, no. 174, *Money Income of Households, Families, and Persons in the United States: 1990,* p. 216; Internal Revenue Service, *Individual Income Tax Returns 1987* (Washington, D.C.: U.S. Government Printing Office, 1990), p. 23.

23. Inhaber and Carroll, *How Rich Is Too Rich?,* p. 226.

24. By coincidence, the rate calculated by Inhaber and Carrol for incomes in the $120,000-to-$1-million bracket (27.2 percent) almost coincides with the flat rate proposed as an example in this chapter (27.3 percent). In an actual system, the rate for the first bracket in the upper-3-percent range would be close to whatever overall flat rate was chosen for the system.

25. Inhaber and Carroll, *How Rich Is Too Rich?,* pp. 86, 194, 202.

26. Ibid., p. 194.

27. *Business Week,* September 7, 1992, p. 20.

28. Ibid.

29. John Maynard Keynes, *The General Theory of Employment, Interest and Money* (New York: Harcourt, Brace & World, 1936), p. 374.

30. Robert Reich, *The Work of Nations* (New York: Alfred A. Knopf, 1991), p. 274.

31. Daniel Patrick Moynihan, "Defining Deviancy Down," *American Scholar,* Winter 1993, pp. 17–30.

Index

295